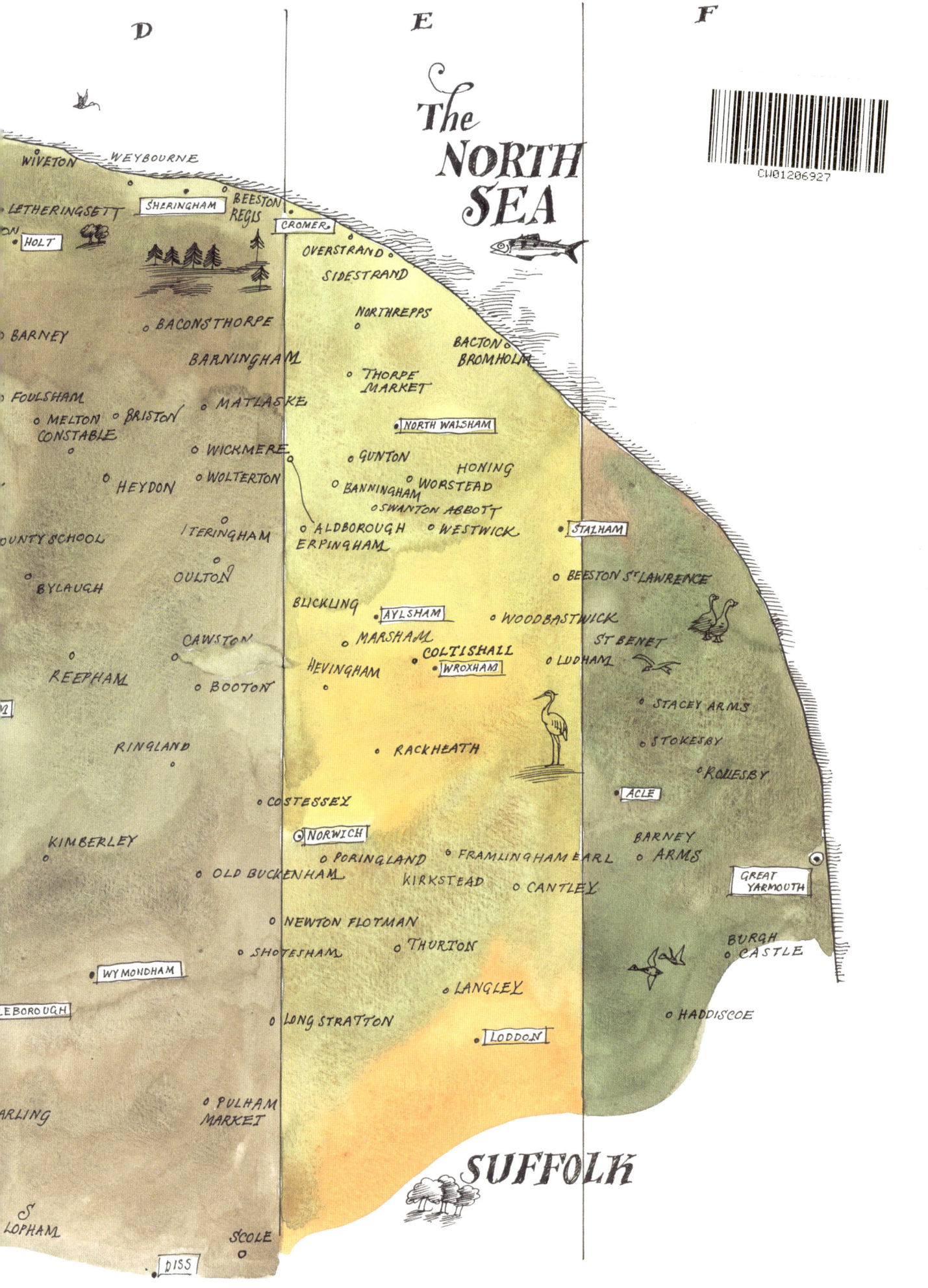

BUILDING NORFOLK

BUILDING NORFOLK

MATTHEW RICE

F

FRANCES LINCOLN LIMITED
PUBLISHERS

For Lil

Frances Lincoln Ltd
4 Torriano Mews
Torriano Avenue
London NW5 2RZ
www.franceslincoln.com

Building Norfolk
Copyright © Frances Lincoln 2008
Text copyright © Matthew Rice 2008
Illustrations copyright © Matthew Rice 2008
First Frances Lincoln edition: 2008

Matthew Rice has asserted his right to be identified as the author of this work in accordance with the Copyright, Designs and Patents Act 1988 (UK).

All rights reserved. No part of this publication may be reproduced, stored in a retrieval system or transmitted in any form, or by any means, electronic, mechanical, photocopying, recording or otherwise, without either permission in writing from the publisher or a licence permitting restricted copying. In the United Kingdom such licences are issued by the Copyright Licensing Agency, Saffron House, 6–10 Kirby Street, London EC1N 8TS.

A catalogue record for this book is available from the British Library.

ISBN 978-0-7112-2901-3

Printed and bound in China

1 3 5 7 9 8 6 4 2

CONTENTS

Acknowledgements ... 6
Preface ... 7
Introduction ... 8

PART ONE: OLD BUILDINGS ... 12
1 Vernacular building ... 14
2 Disappearing buildings ... 20
3 Cottages ... 24
4 Village houses ... 32
5 Farmhouses and small manor houses ... 44
6 Manor houses ... 54
7 Norfolk's Country houses ... 66
8 Estate buildings ... 80
9 Barns and farm buildings ... 98
10 Almshouses ... 108
11 Inns ... 112
12 Parsonages ... 120
13 Churches ... 124
14 Going Dutch ... 140
15 Transport ... 146
16 Two towns: Great Yarmouth and King's Lynn ... 152
17 Cromer - Norfolk on holiday ... 160

PART TWO: NEW BUILDING ... 164
18 Designing new buildings ... 166
19 Planning ... 170
20 New building types ... 172
21 Conclusion: What happens next? ... 184

Appendix: Details and Materials ... 192
Further reading ... 198
Index ... 199

ACKNOWLEDGEMENTS

Producing these illustrations has been a total pleasure and has involved driving around the county, or more accurately being driven by my friend and teacher Alastair Langlands, reversing, stopping, parking rather closer to the house in question than the owner has thought necessary, and drawing. All the pictures in this book were drawn in front of the subject. Not using photographs is not just a natural Luddite's bloody-mindedness; it is a recognition that the need to emphasise, exclude and exaggerate is paramount if each illustration is to do its work. Specifically, it allows me to leave out dreary modern extensions, inappropriate fenestration and other ravages of time. Where this has happened I have not invented a previous condition of the building, but have left the area concerned neutral though not, I hope, intrusive.

Alastair is the first of my acknowledgements for as well as driving a car that was endlessly reported to the police for loitering, he fulfilled the vital role of author and illustrator's assistant. This involved pacing out the rough dimensions of buildings, politely but firmly pointing out that however pretty a drawing might be it should look like the building in front of us when it did not, bravely knocking on countless front doors to ask questions, and buying chips for lunch. It was with him that I discussed the details of every building, a process gripping to us but of undescribable boredom to almost anybody else.

Second is Dr Edward Impey, Director of Research and Standards at English Heritage. He received calls for help at all times of the day or night made in the certain knowledge that he could provide the answers to a baffling range of questions, often in colourful language. His patience and extraordinary expertise have filled in some of the countless gaps in my knowledge with more information than I could possibly hope to use. Canon Jeremy Haselock, Vice Dean of Norwich Cathedral, did the same for the sections on churches and parsonages. Tom Williamson of the School of East Anglian Studies at UEA and Stephen Heywood of Norfolk County Council also kindly took calls for help. Most important of all are those who gave both access to and information about the buildings in this book, amongst whom number: Lord and Lady Leicester, Lord Raynham, Robert Miller, Andrew Holt, Geoffrey and Bill Cubitt, Gavin Paterson, Andrew Falcon, Nicholas Hills, Charles Morris, John Selby, Desmond MacCarthy, Benjy Bulwer-Long, Thomas Courtauld, Charlotte Carter, Kit Martin, Phil Hendry, Mike Macnamara, Philip Makepeace, Ian Johnston, Tony Hurn, Jonathan Walpole, Malcolm Fisher, Chris Young, Benjy Cabbell Manners, Roger Gawn, Louis De Soissons, Charlie Temple Richards, Simon Finch, Val Guinness, Mike Falcon, Brian Sabberton, and Harry Buscal. My father, Peter Rice, has very kindly produced about six of the drawings, but I don't think that any reader will be able to spot them (a small prize may be awarded).

My kind and wise agent, Caroline Dawnay, not only helped conceive the book but found John Nicoll, who has published it.

Brilliant, kind and patient Becky Clarke designed this book with terrific skill and charm which everybody should be pleased about as I would have made it an awful muddle.

Finally, I am deeply grateful for the constant care and coffee supplied by Maxine Allen, and most importantly of all to Emma Bridgewater, without whose patience and, almost, complete forbearance this book could definitely not have appeared.

PREFACE

There could be few projects more enjoyable than researching this book. Writing the text has forced me to find out facts where before I only had opinions and to change a lot of those too. There seems not to be a book that covers the subject. Pevsner's two-volume survey of the county is, of course, the definitive text, but even in the thicker second edition (edited by Bill Wilson) there is great emphasis put on church and polite architecture. Smaller buildings, the cottages, minor farmhouses and barns that are such a significant element in the built environment, do rather slip through the net. I have paid special attention to these lesser buildings as they seem to me to be particularly important. This book is not an exhaustive survey; rather it is an attempt to indicate the extent and nature of the county's buildings and to explain the conditions that influenced their construction. There are so many examples just as good as those that I have chosen and more keep coming to light, so my choices need to be seen for what they are: a completely personal selection.

A lot of the buildings illustrated are visible from the road, but some are hidden in the middle of woods or in private estates and so not available for public view. I have tried to ask the owners if they mind their houses' inclusion, but this has not always been possible. So if you find your house included, I trust you will not feel intruded upon. When a house or detail has been used to illustrate an undesirable trait, it is, in fact, always a combination of several buildings so no offence need be taken

I have used imperial measurements throughout as I am 45. The metric equivalents that are in brackets are approximations. The only time they need any more accuracy than this is in the section on brick sizes where diagrams with all dimensions are included

INTRODUCTION

Norfolk has the best preserved built environment in England. It is undeveloped, sparsely populated and contains few large towns and only one city. It also has an extraordinary number of beautiful buildings.

Norfolk is isolated by its geography. It is stuck out on its own, two sides bounded by the North Sea, a third by the fens which until recently were a malarial wetland and virtually uninhabited; only its southern boundary with Suffolk links the county to the rest of England.

Although Norwich was England's second city from the eleventh century, this ceased to be the case when the emerging British Empire across the Atlantic led to the development of the west-facing ports of Bristol and Liverpool. This was further exacerbated in the early eighteenth century, when the power-hungry incipient Industrial Revolution drew the textile industry west to the fast-flowing rivers of Lancashire and West Yorkshire and left Norwich shorn of national economic and political influence.

However, twice in England's history Norfolk was of great significance. Throughout the Hundred Years' War (1337–1453) its nearest neighbour – France – was the enemy. The vital wool trade that financed the country moved to the Hanseatic ports in the Netherlands and north Germany. The east coast ports of King's Lynn, Yarmouth, Wells and the now defunct Glaven ports of Blakeney, Wiveton and Cley rose to great prosperity, giving rise to the huge outburst of medieval church enlargement in the fourteenth century. This change of emphasis led to increased links with Flemish merchants and builders and to Norfolk being the part of England in which brick building first became re-established.

Norfolk's predominantly light soils suit arable farming better than any others in the country, and 300 years later this caused it to become the cradle of the Agricultural Revolution. Thomas Coke of Holkham and 'Turnip' Townsend of Raynham were the leading lights in the move towards industrialising British agriculture that fed the country until the colonies began their export of cheaper products. The selective breeding of sheep and cattle, the first agricultural shows – Coke's famous 'Shearings' at Holkham – and the development of mechanised arable farming and three-crop rotation all happened in the county. This led to unprecedented building of farmhouses, barns and steadings as landowners, led by Coke, vied with each other to attract more forward-thinking and industrious tenants to their estates.

At the same time as Norfolk was developing improved farming, the North of England was cradling the Industrial Revolution. Fast on the tail of Arkwright's spinning jenny was Stevenson's Rocket. In 1830 the first railway line from Liverpool to Manchester was built, followed in 1837 by the line linking the capital with the newly industrialised town of Birmingham. In the next twenty years this network of railways quickly raced across the country, not only making it possible for passengers to get from one city to another in times not so different to those of today, but also enabling huge quantities of freight to be moved from one part of the country to another in a way previously unseen.

Norfolk was not in the vanguard of railway development. Although Norwich and Yarmouth were both served by rail in the 1840s, it was not until the 1860s (Hunstanton), 1870s (Cromer and Sheringham) or even 1880s (Melton Constable) that the county's hinterlands were connected to the outside world. This had great significance for the built environment in Norfolk, as it meant that builders were reliant on local materials alone for far longer than their counterparts in other parts of the country.

Melton Constable was an insignificant estate village attached to the nearby eponymous seat of the Hastings family when in 1885 it found itself at the convergence of the LNER and the Midland and Great Northern Joint Railway lines. It became known as the Crewe-of-the-East and was suddenly engulfed in shunting yards, goods' sheds and railway offices, and a grid of tidy dark red terraces sprung up complete with working men's clubs, shops, school and Baptist chapel. All these were built, for the first time in Norfolk, in materials brought in from outside the county, and they looked exactly like their cousins in Cheshire, turning their back on the medieval church, only survivor of pre-railway Melton Constable. It is significant that this is the only example in the whole county of a town with an industrial appearance, and that as the area was sunk in economic and agricultural depression by the end of the nineteenth century, there was little further development until the 1970s.

Until the late arrival of the railways, all except the largest of houses were vernacular buildings. This means that they were made by builders local to the site using materials and techniques particular to that area, sometimes to a very small area: only one or two villages. A vernacular building is by definition an unselfconscious one designed not by an architect but by the builder and owner together.

The choice of materials in a true vernacular building is severely limited and is decided by what is most easily available. This total reliance on local materials and building styles came to an end when

KIMBERLEY · S · NORFOLK

BINHAM · N · NORFOLK

mass-produced materials — bricks from the Midlands and factory-made windows and doors — became available with the advent of the rail age. Until then bricks were normally dug, made and fired on or as near to the building site as possible. Quarrying for flint (or more unusually other freestones) was also correspondingly local, as were chalk pits yielding the materials for lime mortar used throughout the county.

Norfolk was only ever a moderately well-wooded county, and from Saxon times this has been a continuously diminishing resource. The heavier clay soils in the south of the county were the most heavily wooded. Indeed, they remain so today, and this supply of building materials makes for the heavier density of timber-framed building from Norwich southwards. Likewise, there has never been a quarry capable of providing good-quality building stone in the county, and where it is used, almost entirely in ecclesiastical buildings, it has come from Barnack and the other limestone quarries of Northamptonshire or by sea from Normandy. This was transported by boat via the river Nene and thence via the coast and Norfolk's modest river system, ending its journey by cart or pack-horse. This gives a clear illustration of why local materials were vital and their use all but unavoidable in the pre-industrial age.

Most significantly, the underlying geology of the county — chalks, clays and sands that cross in diagonal bands — set the conditions for a series of local styles to develop based on the building materials available. Flint, chalk and ragstone can be found in the north, the west and Brecklands, brick in the centre and the east, and brick and some timber in the more wooded heavy clays of the south. These regional variations are often significant, and a recognition of their importance is vital if the character of a village is to be retained.

Low property prices in the 1980s attracted Londoners, but recently there has been a more significant arrival. This time purchasers with deeper pockets have moved to Norfolk with the expectation of spending significantly larger sums than ever before on their houses and their restoration, often as second homes. They have been brought to the county not only by the relative cheapness of houses but also by its unspoilt environment, quality of life, low traffic noise, dark skies and emptiness.

Norfolk is changing more than at any time in the last 100 years. New houses are being built along the coast as the north coast's popularity continues to grow, and these are more likely to be significantly larger houses than before. The trains from Norwich have become more frequent, and although the county is outside the commuter belt, a rise in the number of weekly boarders — families where the husband works in London and returns to his wife and children at the weekend — has increased pressure on larger houses. The agricultural worker, mainstay of the nineteenth- and early twentieth-century village, has been reduced to 10 per cent of his earlier numbers as farming becomes more and more mechanised, throwing open the question of whether to convert redundant farm buildings for residential use. While Norfolk is not earmarked for massive expansion under the government's questionable plans, there is still continuing development, particularly alongside the towns of North Walsham, Fakenham and Downham Market.

If Norfolk is to retain the qualities that have made it so attractive to incomers in recent years, great attention needs to be paid to preserving and improving its built environment, observing the particular local peculiarities and details — the materials and their use and specific building practices — that characterise each part of the county. All of these need to be taken into account in new building and when working on existing buildings.

BUILDING NORFOLK

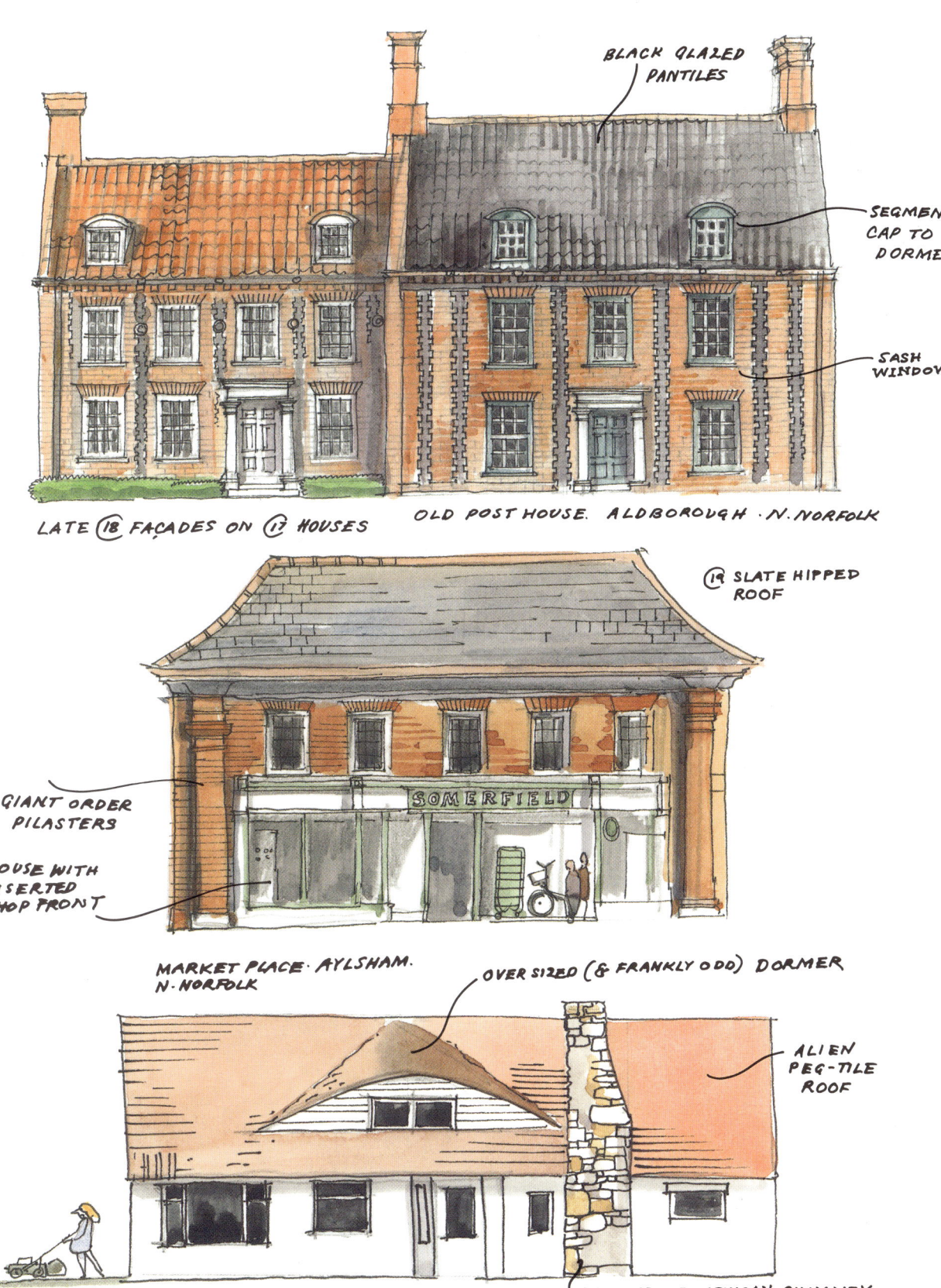

PART ONE
OLD BUILDINGS

1. VERNACULAR BUILDING

As noted in the introduction, most of the houses, cottages, shops and farm buildings built in Norfolk until the end of the nineteenth century could be called *vernacular*: erected by builders local to the site using materials and techniques sometimes particular to a very small area of one or two villages. A vernacular building is an unselfconscious one designed by the builder and owner.

When an architect becomes involved, the building can still be said to be *in* the vernacular but not *of* the vernacular, as a series of decisions have been made in the conscious knowledge of that tradition but from outside it. At its most extreme this appears as the early twentieth-century neo-vernacular style, the last flowering of the Arts and Crafts movement initiated by William Morris in the 1850s. This can be seen in the two buildings of Edwin Lutyens, at Trimingham and The Pleasance, or in the butterfly-shaped houses of Voewood or Kelling Hall near Holt.

The choice of materials in a true vernacular building is the product of what is most easily available, hence the use of beach flint (pebbles of various sizes) in Cley and Morston contrasting with the broken field flints of the villages further inland. Even this is a massive simplification. Flint is, in fact, a very varied stone and can be used in a number of ways. Pebbles can be as small as 2 inches (5. cm) in diameter, although this is usually on relatively high status buildings, or as large as giants of 9 or 10 inches (23 or 25. cm) long in agricultural buildings or garden walls. Flints can also be *knapped*. Knapped flints are stones that have been worked. Flint is a form of silica and exceptionally hard; it is also easily fractured, as any flint-country child knows, but not in the regular way of easily riven stones like slate. The stone can shear off at any angle, and so forming any kind of flat surface is an extremely skilled job. It was a significant industry, particularly around Thetford. Flints were mined in bulk at Grimes Graves, an archaeological site dating from the Neolithic age where over 200 pits were dug through the sandy Breckland soil to the flint-bearing chalk below. More recently, Brandon remained a centre of the flint industry until its demise in the 1950s. Flint also varies in colour: that of North Norfolk weathers to a blue or bright silver, and as you travel south-west it becomes first yellow and ochrous and finally at Thetford nearly black, but always with what R. F. Brunskill calls a white rind.

Worked flint can be irregular or roughly or even perfectly squared. Most extraordinary of all and very particular to Norfolk and Suffolk is flushwork. This is the use of flint, knapped flat, as a marquetry-like infill to shaped stone panels, often in the form of letters or simplified symbolic or heraldic devices. It is called flushwork because the flint and surrounding stone are flush with one another. The contrast between the silky sheen of the oyster-grey flint and the matt cream limestone is both highly sophisticated and utterly specific to the area and thus vernacular. The earliest flushwork is on the Ethelburga gate at Norwich Cathedral, and it continued until the Reformation brought church building to a standstill. There are particularly good examples at the great Perpendicular churches of Worstead and Tunstead and in the marshland cathedrals of the Walpoles and Terringtons. Flint is also used to create a pure flat surface, the stones square and fitted together in the manner of more easily worked stones, although usually in pieces less than 6 inches (15. cm) in any direction. The movement of light on the ensuing pearly surface has a very lively effect.

A limitation of flint as a building material is its irregular shape and small size. This means that it relies on the mortar employed for strength. Sometimes this can be extraordinarily successful, as in the massive Roman walls of Burgh Castle, but in most cases a more easily worked stone is needed to bind in the rubble at the corners. Interestingly, the cottage orné-type porch on a house at Burnham Norton has used flint structurally and turned several corners in the process.

Flint is an archetypical local material literally lying around in the fields around every village and requires little or no transport which was of great importance .Before the Industrial Revolution Britain had poor communications. There was the most basic and frequently seasonally disrupted road system, the only alternative being the coast or inland waterways. Getting bulky materials around was prohibitively expensive, relying on boats where rivers remained navigable, then being unloaded onto pack-horses or carts for the final part of their journey.

Bricks were also a locally produced material. You can find proof of site-specific brick making in the number of small woods and copses bearing the name brick kilns, clay pit or other brick-making-related names. Most estates or farms have one such wood, and indeed they had many such pits and kilns over the centuries. Not all pits were building related. Marl pits, which often occur in the middle of a field, are a by-product of marling, the practice of spreading highly alkaline clay on the fields to increase fertility.

The wholesale reintroduction to Britain of building in brick happened here due to its proximity to the Netherlands, where brick making and building skills were already well established. There had been a large amount of brick building during the period of Roman occupation, but this technology had been abandoned when the last Roman garrisons returned to mainland Europe in the fifth century. There are a few scattered thirteenth- and fourteenth-century examples, perhaps the earliest visible being in the ruins of Beeston Priory on the north coast between Cromer and Sheringham. By the sixteenth century brick was fully established as the county's key material, its colour and quality varying according to the clays locally available. Some of the loveliest brick buildings in the country are found in the small manor houses and farmhouses of the early sixteenth century. This farm at Metton, part of the National Trust's Felbrigg estate near Cromer, has well-preserved and highly decorative moulded and cut-brick detailing on the gable end, door-case and window surrounds, which transforms this farmhouse from workaday to outstanding. Perhaps the most elaborate piece of brickwork is the double chimney stack at the gable end, typical of the period.

ENTIRE PEDIMENT COMPOSED OF TILES & PART BRICKS BUT NO MOULDED OR PURPOSE MADE COMPONENTS

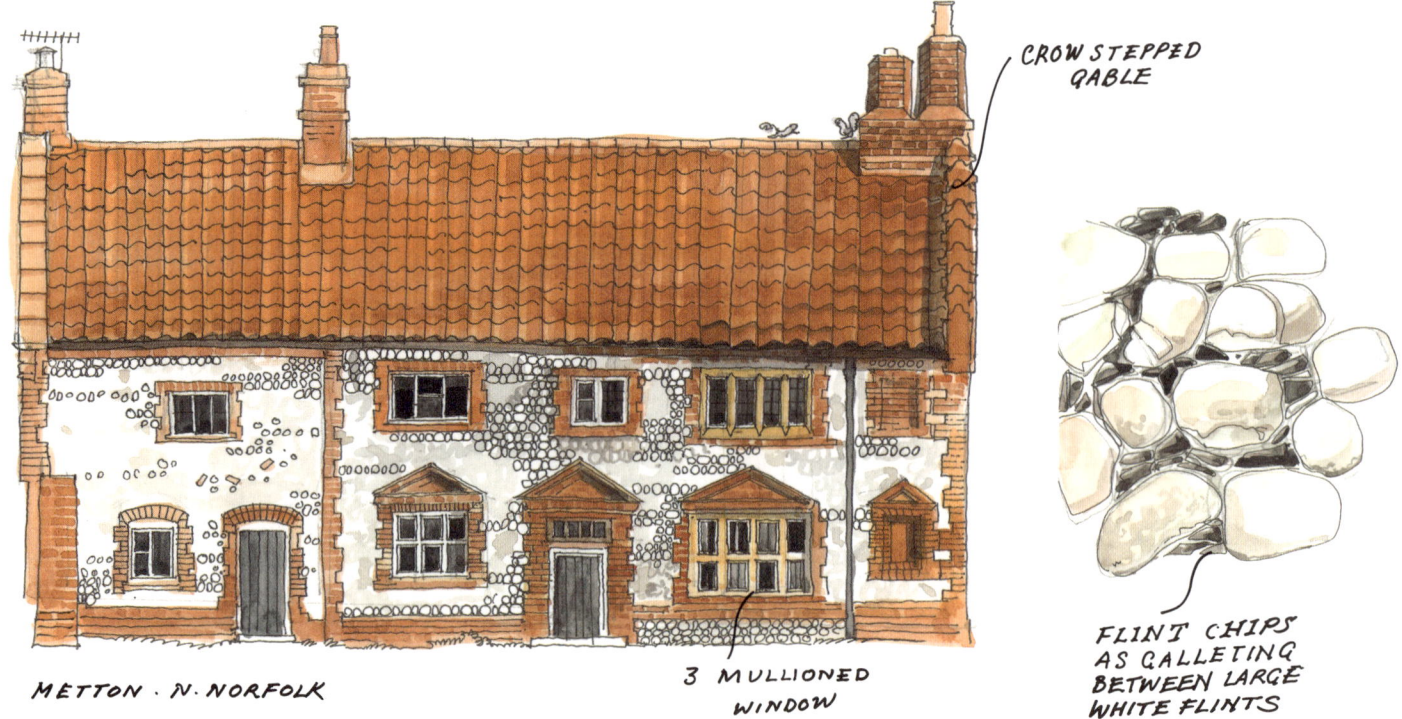

The concentration of decoration on the chimney is perhaps due to the understandable excitement at having a chimney at all. Before the fifteenth century houses of this size had a central hearth with corresponding hole in roof and a fairly smoky environment in all but the most rigorously windy days. Even quite modest houses often have either hexagonal or octagonal chimneys, sometimes with terracotta detailing and star-shaped tops grouped impressively together.

Larger houses in the county have some of the most important brickwork in Britain. East Barsham is the fanciest of all, a baroque fantasy of twisting many-faceted corbels, windows and chimneys that defies belief. Its neighbour Great Snoring is less well known but also has yards of decorative terracotta and extraordinary polygonally shafted turrets. Oxborough, another property of the National Trust, is a giant among the brick buildings with its elaborate roofscape of massed chimneys.

In smaller houses brick is often combined with the less expensive and readily available local stone: chalk, flint and, in the west, carrstone, which is a cretaceous sandstone. It is rather gritty, and because of the varying amounts of iron oxide it contains, it can be any colour from coffee brown through deep ochre to ginger. There is also a grey version visible in various buildings in Hillington, for example on the gable end of the Ffolkes Arms Inn. This is in itself quite telling, as the public front of the building is built of a nearly chocolate brown carrstone, indicating that the more unusual grey was perceived as lower status. Carrstone is used both coursed — that is, laid regularly in rows — and as random rubble and particularly appealingly as slips. These are small rectangular pieces of the stone laid very close together, with the mortar almost invisible as it is very recessed. When used in quantity the soft stone looks like thick chocolate brown fur.

The pointing between stone is sometimes galleted. Gallets — thin flint chippings, a by-product of the knapping process — are pressed into the wet mortar. Chalk lump and carrstone are also frequently galleted with either carrstone or flint or tiny flint pebbles. There is a singular example at Fring where almost every known stone in Norfolk is employed in the same (quite small) wall. This is sometimes done in random directions, but equally well it can also be applied in a more directional way so that the sharp and shiny flint chips again give the impression of being the fur of a wild animal. Baconsthorpe Castle has some very fine galleting using larger chips nearly 1 inch (2.5 cm) long. Three houses in Overstrand and Sidestrand have striking front elevations that are all gallet and no larger stones; this takes the fur effect to an extreme and makes the houses arresting even from the road.

The pointing of flint is also very varied; some is so deep that almost none of the flints are visible, although as the decades pass the pointing recedes and the pebbles or rough broken flints are revealed. Others like Stone House in Aylsham have pebbles of such regular size that they must always have been at least 50 per cent exposed. Rough flintwork on church walls was never intended to be seen and would always have been rendered and whitewashed. This was not only for aesthetic reasons – as previously stated, the mortar was significant in providing strength to a wall and so recessed pointing would have produced structural weakness. Only highly worked flint was designed to be visible, and this was often on the porch or clerestory as at Wickmere.

A bed of chalk runs parallel to the flint belt that stretches from Dorset north-eastwards to West Norfolk, and there it makes its appearance as the dominant building material. Sometimes it is regularly coursed in rectangular blocks, and sometimes it appears as more irregularly coursed rubble; it is frequently limewashed and often galleted with flint or pebbles. In old buildings it is never used completely randomly, and current builders who are prone to employing it in crazy-paving fashion as a facing to a wall would do well to observe this. The softness of the material and its consequent structural weakness mean that all edges and all door and window openings have to be faced with brick. This is the case with all the Norfolk freestone, and this contrast is a defining characteristic of many small farmhouses and cottages in the county.

Very small distances in this part of the county can produce buildings of dramatically different appearance, changing with the underlying strata, in bands often only a mile or two wide, that dominate the incidence of materials. As you drive from Fakenham to King's Lynn, the progression from flint to chalk to carrstone is a very clear illustration of how poor transport and the difficulty and expense of moving heavy stone mean that one village's vernacular may be very different from the next.

The east of the county is dominated by the Broads. This is a network of man-made lakes, frequently but not invariably linked by the rivers Thurne, Ant and Bure and further south bounded by the Yare. They are fringed by the Norfolk reeds, whose use as thatch characterises the roofs and thus the buildings of this area. There is still a vestigial reed-cutting industry in Norfolk, although increasingly less expensive Eastern European material is used. At Ranworth, the 200-acre (80.-hectare) reedbeds are regularly harvested, and although the reed is now cut by a mechanical mower the corrugated tin sheds full of bundled rushes look like an archive photograph from the 1930s. The soils in the Broads are clay with no easily available stone, and so unadulterated brick is the principal building material.

Further south in the Brecks there is a preponderance of knapped flint, often rather dark and sometimes glossy black. There is a rather strange modern take on this traditional technique easily seen on the Barclays Bank on the High Street in Brandon just over the border in Suffolk. Here preformed concrete panels of knapped flint have been let into the walls of an otherwise utterly featureless modernist shopfront. In a strange way, although here the manner of use is entirely unvernacular, the material is so characteristic of this part of south-west Norfolk that it does reinforce the message that Barclays is *the* Norfolk bank. Barclays was formed by the amalgamation of the banks of great local Quaker families – the Gurneys, Birbecks, Barclays and Buxtons – in the 1920s.

BUILDING NORFOLK

BUILDING NORFOLK

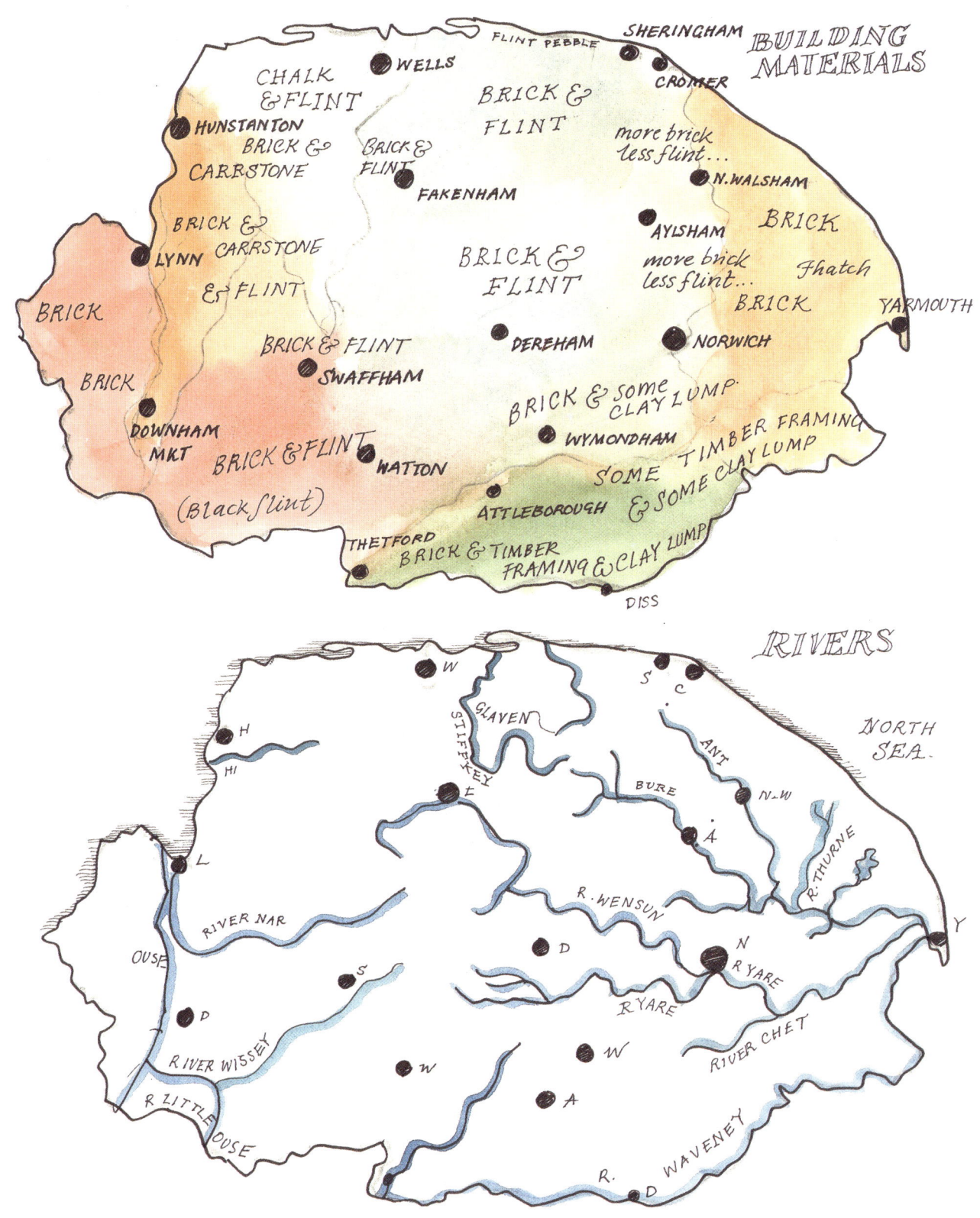

2. DISAPPEARING BUILDINGS

In the plains of India the roads are scattered with villages — thriving agricultural communities with granaries, houses, animal accommodation and small Hindu shrines. Salvaged cow or buffalo pats stacked in geometrically tidy piles await use as fuel. From the low mud houses in the morning emerge strings of implausibly spotless schoolchildren with the uniforms and demeanour of 1950s Britain. Elegant mothers in cocktail-frock saris wave them goodbye as the children straggle to school along Kipling's great trunk road. Their houses are built of dried clay or low-fired bricks and timber with lime mortar and roofed with wood and straw, reed or cane thatch. Some even have architectural elements: a carefully modelled door-case with swirling scrolled pediment or decorated cornice. But these buildings are utterly biodegradable. If they are not constantly maintained, re-rendered in daub and re-thatched, they quickly crumble away when subjected to the extreme weather conditions of the monsoon. And this does happen, as fading ex-settlements are clearly visible amongst the sugar cane and wheat, and evidenced by odd pieces of newer building materials employed, these are relatively recent.

Most of Norfolk's rural buildings were once as perishable as those of the Punjab and, until the late seventeenth century, vulnerable to the equally unforgiving English weather, to ill-repair and, in towns in particular, to fire.

Aldborough in North Norfolk is a village of 150 houses, many of them around a green that has been the site of a horse and hiring fair (now fun fair) since its charter was granted by Henry III in 1300. There should be evidence of continuous and relatively prosperous settlement. However, of the fifty buildings around the green today, only twenty date from 1900 or before and only five from before 1800. Where is medieval Aldborough? Or the sixteenth- or seventeenth-century village? A map of 1830 shows seventy-two houses around the green. Is it safe to assume that many of these were poorly built cottages of below-average materials — clay lump, local brick and thatch — and that they have proved no more durable than the Indian villages? It is not as if they were replaced with bigger and better buildings, as there are no large buildings in this profoundly 'open' village: that is, one not subjected to the influence and proprietorship of one or two major landowners. Old Aldborough has gone.

This is equally so in the countryside. Until the 1980s an isolated rural cottage that became redundant was frequently bulldozed and the site ploughed over, as farm-labourer numbers decreased and there was no perceived need for the house. This was very easily done. Many cottages were crudely built, and such timbers as they contained would be stripped and the rubble used as foundations for a nearby concrete sugar beet pad or new barn.

Indeed, in large farm estates this is often still the case, where rental income will not give a satisfactory return on the investment that restoration will require and where sale is felt inappropriate. This latter solution might be due to a perception of the ensuing change of ownership compromising the integrity and privacy of the estate as a whole. A large estate relies on total ownership, like a 'closed' village, for the retension of its character. Alternatively, many houses may still be maintained as controlled ruins pending a change in that situation or the arrival of further funds for their maintenance.

Perhaps the vernacular stock of Norfolk should be called the surviving stock and the building styles the surviving vernacular, what we see now of nineteenth-century and earlier buildings representing those that have survived the ravages of time after the loss of all the disappeared cottages and farmhouses, barns and sheds that made up the fabric of the built environment. For the most part these were not greatly valued as they fell into disrepair.

This is particularly the case for urban slums. The interwar years saw a move to improve working-class housing, one of many reactions to the age-ending social cataclysm of the First World War. Just as poor quality rural cottages were demolished to be replaced by the first council-owned social housing, so in Norwich and King's Lynn large areas of medieval or later slum houses were demolished. The yards of Lynn, many hundreds of small cottages built around long courtyards between the main streets of the town, were lost at this time. While they may have seemed undesirable and indeed been unhygienic and cramped, they would now be viewed as deeply desirable. Their replacements, land-wasting suburbia and more recently socially alienating estates of flats, have not necessarily stood the test of time, and the yard plan might have proved a more agreeable place to live today.

All this destruction occurred despite a long history of a visual appreciation of the picturesque. The seventeenth- and eighteenth-century antiquarianism that led to the nineteenth-century romanticism of Pugin's Gothic Revival and on to William Morris and the Arts and Crafts movement continuously stressed the value of irregularity, the work of the human hand as opposed to the machine, and the distressing hand of nature that together make up the 'picturesque'. In the eighteenth century the rural hovel and tumbledown church tower were the desired focus of the landscape painting of the Norwich School artists, such as John Crome, John Sell Cotman and the Stannard brothers. In the parks of great houses, follies were erected in the styles of previous ages, some as hermitages requiring the attendance or even residence of a picturesque and slightly frightening hermit to philosophise or soothsay from within its Gothic depths, alarming the ladies on their post-prandial trip into the 'Wilderness'.

CASTLE ACRE PRIORY   PRIORS HOUSE   PORCH

BUILDING NORFOLK

BARN @ BEXWELL nr. DOWNHAM MKT. WAS C15 GATEHOUSE

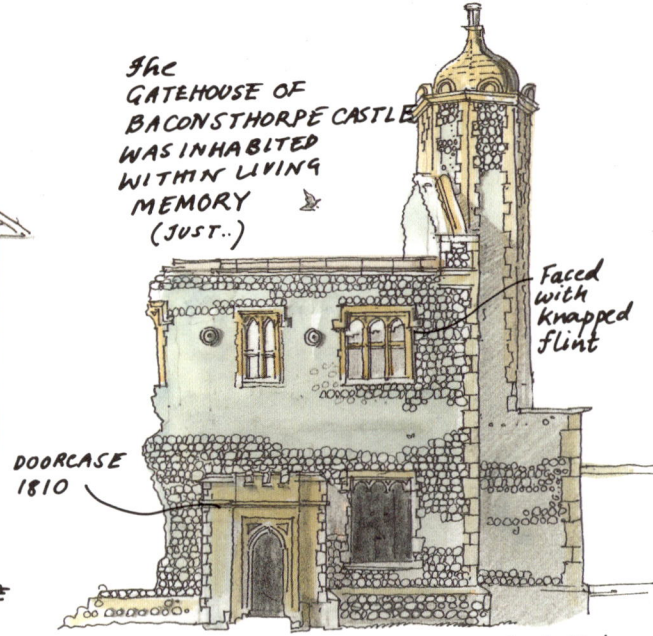

The GATEHOUSE OF BACONSTHORPE CASTLE WAS INHABITED WITHIN LIVING MEMORY (JUST..)

Faced with knapped flint

DOORCASE 1810

BACONSTHORPE CASTLE 1450-1486 but this OUTER GATEHOUSE 1551

CASTLE ACRE LATE C14 - PERHAPS ALMONERS CHAPEL now re-used as cottage

A WINDMILL HAS GROWN OUT OF THE RUINED GATEHOUSE of ST BENETS PRIORY C14 (the Mill is C18)

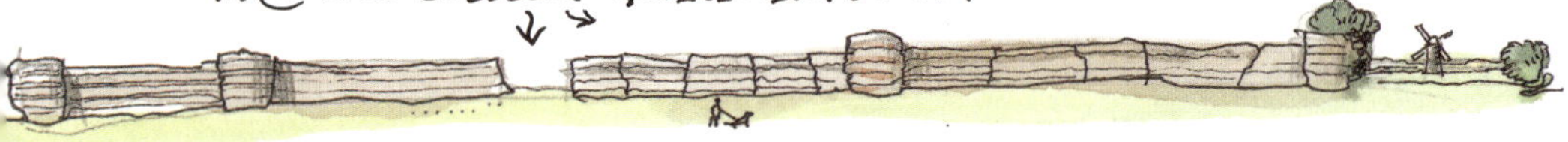

in C3 was called GARIANNONUM

WALLS of the ROMAN CAMP AT BURGH CASTLE C3 AD (This is REALLY Suffolk but not a boundary recognized by its builders....

LARGE TILE SHAPED BRICKS 18"

LIME MORTAR

UNDESIRABLES SCRAP IN THE GATEHOUSE of the WHITE FRIARS HOUSE C14

BUILDING NORFOLK

The nineteenth century saw the further development of historicism: that is, a self-conscious harking back to a previous, non-classical age in architecture. The Tudorbethan half-timbered fantasy of The Orchards in Aylsham is an early example from the surprisingly early date of 1847. Legislation has followed this interest in old buildings; the 1888 Ancient Monuments Act concerned buildings of archaeological importance but excluded those in private ownership. SPAB, the Society for the Protection of Ancient Buildings, was founded in 1877. This organisation works to identify, through its 'buildings at risk' register, those properties needing a saviour, and continues to fund research into restoration methods. It also runs a programme educating and training the craftsmen whose skills, essential to this work, are in short supply.

Later laws have continued the process of protecting the built environment, sometimes to the detriment of local development, but even now old buildings often of architectural or historical significance are lost or condemned as unsalvageable. Old ivy-wreathed church ruins like Sco Ruston continue to crumble. And while the huge abbey of Castle Acre is safe in the care of English Heritage, the once great priory of Broomholm, whose fragment of the Holy Rood made it a medieval pilgrimage site of such significance that King Henry III found time for three visits, now moulders uncared for and heaped high with sugar beet in a farmyard on the bleak east coast.

REMAINS OF THE CHAPTER HOUSE

BROOMHOLM PRIORY BACTON (E. NORFOLK)

CHEMICALS THAT DARE NOT SPEAK THEIR NAME

GOTHIC TRACERY IN THE SUGAR BEET

3. COTTAGES

Rural poverty has always been as rife as urban poverty, rural slum conditions every bit as sordid as those in the filthy alleys of Dickens's London or the jerry-built back-to-back terraces of the industrial towns of the North. But the impoverished life of the farm worker in the nineteenth century has always seemed less desperate, bathed in the warm glow of Flora Thompson's *Lark Rise to Candleford* and set against the backdrop of the country cottage.

In reality the lives of the rural poor were every bit as grimy and meagre as their city-dwelling counterparts, and from the eighteenth century onwards there was a realisation that their conditions were just not good enough. In his *Hints to Gentlemen of Landed Property* (1775) Nathaniel Kent writes:

The shattered hovels which half the poor of this kingdom are obliged to put up with is truly affecting to a heart fraught with humanity. Those who condescend to visit these miserable tenements can testify that neither health nor decency can be present.

Sixty years later William Cobbett in his *Rural Rides* describes what he saw: 'Houses made of mud and straw, bits of glass or of cast off windows.' The hovels of which he writes were not the neat brick and flint cottages that are now such desirable homes, but for the most part owner-built shelters made of wood, clay, rushes and other cheaply and locally available materials. These buildings have gone, either replaced with more solid structures or lost entirely, their sites ploughed over and reincorporated into a field: they were built without foundations after all and with few components that would have survived a winter without continuous maintenance. They are the houses of Constable's or Cotman's paintings, perceived by their middle-class clients as picturesque in their partial dilapidation and as the visual focus of a view or landscape. Through these works they have become familiar to us as symbols of rural life, but they have all but disappeared in Norfolk.

Only in South Norfolk with its heavy clay land and ready supply of timber has this type of building survived. Not the hovels but buildings of intermediate size, improved and added to but retaining the characteristics of pre-improved farming England. Everywhere else, the desire to increase agricultural output led to the great rural rebuilding of the eighteenth and nineteenth centuries, and as barns and farm buildings were being built to fulfil the new orthodoxies, so cottages were gradually being improved as well. Kent suggests that better houses should be built but warns of extravagance:

'All that is requisite is a warm, comfortable plain room for the poor inhabitants to eat their morsel in, an oven to bake their bread, a little receptacle for their small beer and provisions and two wholesome lodging apartments, one for the man and wife, another for the children. It would perhaps be more decent if the boys and girls could be separated, but [here the warm-hearted paternalist's vision is tempered with pragmatism] this would make the building too expensive.'

Independently owned non-estate cottages in villages or towns were simultaneously improved or more usually demolished and rebuilt, often reusing the older building's materials. These remain the most genuinely vernacular buildings, showing a greater unselfconsciousness than their larger neighbours. This is not to say that smaller cottages are all without grace, but few have architectural pretensions. Where this is the case, there is usually an estate connection that leads back to the eighteenth- and nineteenth-century pattern books of model cottages.

Perhaps the earliest of these is the double row of white painted semi-detached cottages at New Houghton. This highly planned and regular grouping replaces an older settlement in the park that now surrounds the Hall. This no doubt represents a significant improvement in living standards for their inhabitants, although there were heavy occupancy levels throughout the nineteenth centuries that would be unthinkable by standards of today. Drawings in the 1824 survey of Houghton show the type of house that they would have replaced: roofs and walls patched, gables crumbling and roof ridges swaying alarmingly. The new house plans showing pairs of cottages with wash houses behind are indicative of an improved paternalistic concern for the well-being of estate workers twinned, of course, with a desire to show to the outside world an orderly and graceful village.

The cottage as decorative symbol, as self-consciously rural and as what John Summerson calls 'primarily a component in an improved picturesque landscape but secondarily as an architectural toy with an intrinsic interest of its own', became increasingly popular towards the late eighteenth and early nineteenth centuries, and is most famously represented by the highly decorated model village of Blaise Hamlet near Bristol. This collection of cottage fantasies, which varied in architectural style from aggrandised hovel through Tudor cottage to Italianate, was hugely influential and gave an early counterbalance to the classical as inspiration. Most rural was its use of the tree trunk as a column. This is a key device in the cottage orné and is visible in many instances in Norfolk, both in cottages and in rustic lodges like those of Barningham Hall.

In the countryside proper it is the improved cottage that has survived. Some were built during the late eighteenth-century agricultural and economic boom, but more during the 'high farming' years of 1840–75. These are the well-built brick or brick and flint/stone two-storey cottages — either individual, paired or in short terraces — that punctuate rural Norfolk. Although they were not built by their inhabitants and often drew their plans and even elevations from pattern books, they still retain something of the vernacular — not least because through most of this period, when the greater part of the county was beyond the reach of the railway system, the materials employed in their building were local. Bricks were from a locally dug clay pit and hand made and fired in a wood fired kiln. There was an irregularity of colour in the bricks. This depended of the closeness of each brick and more spefically each face of the brick to the source of heat. This also produced burnt headers, these are the grey or black ends of bricks used in eighteenth century brickwork.; pantiles were similarly local as was thatch (wheat straw or reed), and the component wooden parts — windows, doors, bargeboards and dormers — were all made by local craftsmen often in the village. This changed when the railways afforded cheap transport of building materials, and from the end of the nineteenth century harsh red bricks from the Midlands, Welsh slate and machine-made architectural components tended to dilute the local characteristics of buildings.

This industrialisation of building is most clearly seen in the terraced cottages of Melton Constable, whose hectic red brick, slate and mass-produced windows and doors could be in any Midlands or northern town. It is almost entirely built after 1870, and it is this early 'anywhere' housing that makes it a less decorative village. It is interesting to note that although this is a well-situated and thriving village with good connections to Holt, Norwich and Fakenham and first-rate local shops, its house prices are 10–15 per cent lower than their equivalents in a village or small town with better preserved architectural credentials like neighbouring Foulsham or Aylsham. This is very important as it is this statistic that gives economic underpinning to the aesthetic imperative to preserve the built environment.

Old cottages were particularly susceptible to demolition from the 1950s to the 1980s. There was no enthusiasm for preserving houses for which there seemed neither need nor market and no return on investment available from renting them after expensive restoration. Usually sale was not perceived as an option when the property was in the middle of a farm or estate; sale would have compromised the integrity, security and privacy of the overall estate by introducing an independent house owner in an otherwise landowner/tenant-based community. This is often still the case, and there are even now many isolated cottages, far from services but central to landholdings, that remain empty today. Hundreds, perhaps thousands, of dwellings were demolished or allowed to fall into disrepair during this period; estates sold thousands more at knock-down prices, blind then to Mrs Thatcher's unforeseeable economic miracle and the digital revolution that would completely change this side of the rural economy.

From the 1980s, there arose the widespread possibility of working from home, a desire to live outside the big cities and, most significantly of all, such an increase in personal wealth that the market for second homes – either for weekend or holiday use or as investments – grew to encompass a far greater proportion of the ever expanding middle classes. The profile of the cottage was changed, isolated cottages far away from any place of work suddenly became desirably remote, and the phenomenon of the ghost village began. Houses empty all week and only populated by weekend visitors, owned at a distance and priced beyond the pocket of those inhabitants who had been born there, became common. This, combined with a continuing influx of retired people, significantly reduced the proportion of children in many rural villages, leading to the closure of more village schools. All this represents another change to the architectural fabric of the village as the former school itself is subject to conversion to one or more homes.

These may be changes of use, but are they necessarily changes for the worse? There are advantages to these new residents: they have chosen to live here, and they need not be any less community minded than their farm-worker predecessors. Indeed, more significantly, they are able to spend amounts previously unthinkable on these cottages. This can be a mixed blessing as neglect is so often a preserver, and improvements can frequently compromise the vernacular integrity of a building. A builder with a love of tradition-and-the-old-ways can cause the damage of a hurricane and tidy away the accretions of 200 years in a blitzkrieg of what he intends as a restoration. Perhaps most importantly in terms of the village built environment as a whole is the planning policy of confining new development to a village envelope and concentrating building on infill sites in former gardens and yards. This can so change the context of older cottages as to make them almost unrecognisable even before they themselves undergo improvement.

Later in this book I am going to write more about new cottages, what form they are currently taking, and how they can best take their place in the village street, square or green – and particularly about the importance of some kind of architect being involved in their design in a post-vernacular age.

BUILDING NORFOLK

C16, C18, C19 & C20 buildings in THETFORD — Jettied 1st Floor — ERSTWHILE PUB

NEWTON FLOTMAN

INDIAN HUT with ARCHITECTURAL PRETENSIONS

Cottage in GREAT BIRCHAM from the HOUGHTON HALL SURVEY of 1800

GABLE·END OF INCORPORATED EARLIER BUILDING

C20th ORIEL WINDOW

TIMBER & CLAY LUMP COTTAGE

BUILDING NORFOLK

COMPLEX DECORATIVE BARGEBOARD

S. NORFOLK · V. CHARACTERISTIC GABLE PROFILE C18?

Nr LODDON

COB

THATCHED COTTAGE Nr WYMONDHAM

COTTAGE IN COSTESSEY SHOWING MUCH USE OF BRICK DETAILING FROM COSTESSEY BRICKWORKS.

COSTESSEY

SHARED CHIMNEY STACK

LATE C19 "IMPROVED" COTTAGES · BRICK & COURSED FLINT · BINHAM · N. NORFOLK

28

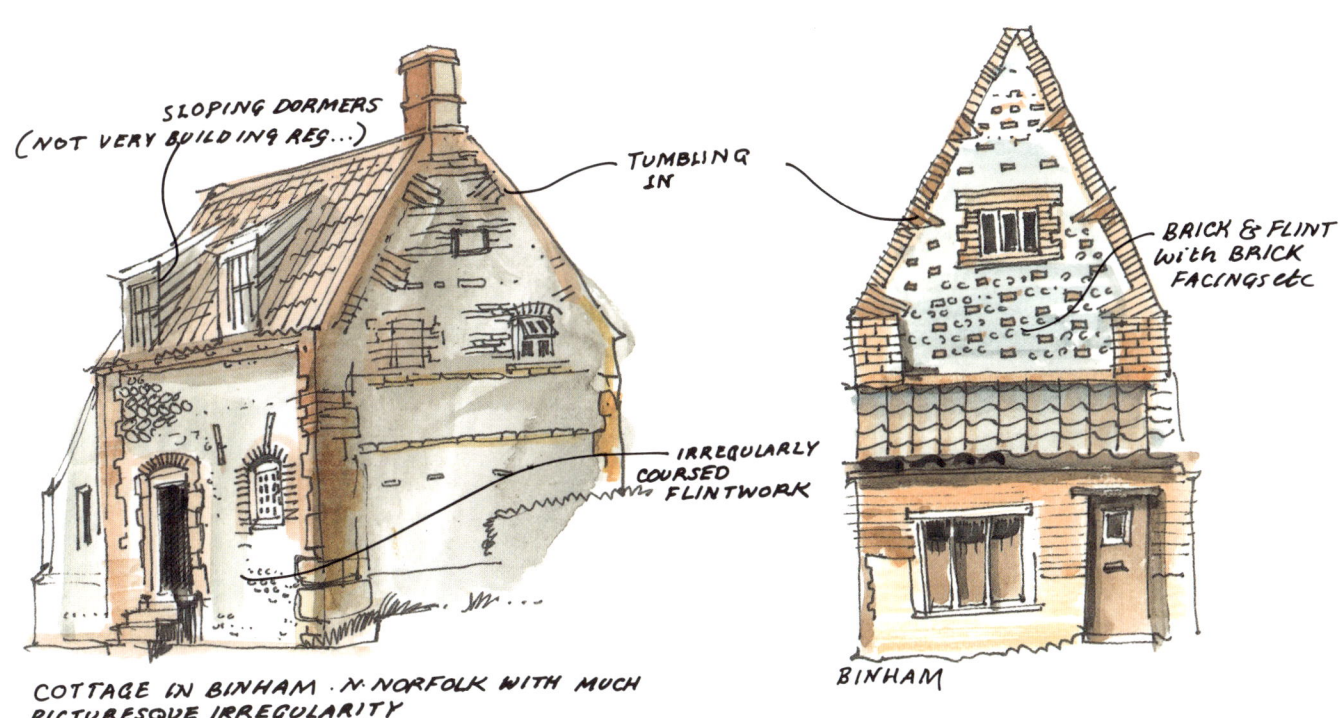

BUILDING NORFOLK

THIS IS AN INCREDIBLY SIMPLE 17 or 18 SINGLE STOREY COTTAGE - PERHAPS IT ONCE HAD DORMERS IN THE ROOF (like the cottage bottom right →)

IT IS BUILT OF CLAY LUMP BUT ON (MORE EXPENSIVE) BRICK FOOTINGS. This prevents damp from getting in from below. The ROOF protects the TOP. WITHOUT THIS PROTECTION the VULNERABLE WALLS WOULD QUICKLY DETERIORATE like that of the INDIAN HUT on Page 26.

THATCH IS MORE PREVALENT in the SOUTH OF The County often with Clay Lump or TIMBER CONSTRUCTION

THIS REFLECTS The UNDERLYING HEAVY CLAY SOILS.

— Nᵛ LOPHAM

BUILDING NORFOLK

S. NORFOK

SINGLE STOREY EAST NORFOLK COTTAGE
ON LOW-STATUS BUILDINGS PANTILES USUALLY REPLACE THATCH IN THE C18 or C19

HOODED DORMERS

4. VILLAGE HOUSES

Although Norfolk is a sparsely populated county it does have dense settlement patterns and this has been the same since Saxon times. There are, of course, open areas — ex-heathland in the north-west, for example — where historically the land was not good enough to support a viable agricultural population, or parts of Breckland with similar sandy soils. The parishes of Norfolk are geographically smaller in the south and east of the county, in direct contrast to those in the great estates that dominate the north and west up to the fens.

Villages have sometimes migrated either towards common grazing and water or in a few cases away from pestilence. After the appearance of the Black Death in Norfolk in 1349, the rate of abandonment doubled from seven in the previous fifty years to fifteen in the period 1350–1400. Very few of these settlements were abandoned at that time for this reason alone, and a combination of other contributory factors led to their movement or abandonment. There was a general depopulation in the thirteenth and fourteenth centuries. Some areas that had perhaps originally been oversettled in Saxon times proved to be unviable; from the fourteenth century onwards a gradual shift from peasant arable farming to enclosed sheep grazing ensured a reduction in rural populations in many western areas. The village of Egmere, for example, is reduced to two farms and a church; only earthworks remain of what in pre-enclosure times was the thriving village. There was considerable incentive for landlords to encourage the contraction of a village under their control. Expensive-to-maintain buildings housed expensive-to-support potential paupers who would become the proprietors' financial burden. This created 'closed' villages, their boundaries controlled by the landlord, containing only as many residents as were required to work the land. This kind of control was not possible in cases where two or more landlords held a village, thus creating a more flexible and more scattered 'open' village.

This reduction did not occur in the clay soils of the south and east where small-scale dairying and stock rearing remained stable. Ready availability of common land which could be enclosed to form small farms helped prolong the life of villages in these areas. The emergence of market towns in an area often had a depressing effect on their former village neighbours. A natural drift into an area of greater economic activity often emptied outlying villages. This was very much the case in the villages surrounding King's Lynn, and later in the sixteenth and seventeenth centuries the powerful weaving town of Worstead, famous for its eponymous strong woollen cloth, began to lose out to its growing rival, North Walsham. These two towns were too close for both to survive, and Worstead atrophied and shrank. Interestingly, only fifteen years ago, older inhabitants still referred to it as a town some 200 years after it could really be described as one.

While some landlords squeezed out and cajoled others to leave their homes with judicious demolitions and intentional lack of maintainance, others simply cleared villages wholesale. This was usually in the name of improvement of a newly created parkland landscape, as at Houghton in the 1720s or Wolterton ten years later. Residents of these demolished villages were rehoused at a place more convenient to the landowner. West Wretham was moved wholesale to East Wretham and Raynham to South Raynham. How popular this high-handed behaviour made 'Turnip' Townsend with his tenants is not recorded nor yet how much coercion was required, but as at Houghton there is no doubt that the pill was sweetened by the improved nature of the new houses.

While there have always been outlying cottages, from the seventeenth century onwards there has been a drift of rural populations into nucleated villages either along a street or (less usually) around a green. The long street format with plots at right angles to the thoroughfare has survived from its medieval or even Saxon origins, although the houses occupying these plots may have been rebuilt. In common with most early vernacular building, the majority of medieval or indeed pre-eighteenth-century houses are lost. Aldborough appears to have no pre-eighteenth-century houses on the green. Of course, it is possible that some façades conceal older buildings: on removal of a wall at the back of one mid-eighteenth-century house, an oak mullioned window frame of the seventeenth century emerged from the rubble. However, it remains the case that most of the village is nineteenth century or later. It seems likely that earlier buildings were replaced or simply destroyed in common with so much rural housing in the county.

While villages are comprised of all other housing types found in rural and town Norfolk, there are certain models that are typically of the village. These include the pub, of course, which is covered in its own section, and the village shop, although this function was fulfilled by many buildings, as what was a house becomes a shop and vice versa, leaving architectural evidence along the way. Then there is the village house: larger than a cottage but not a farmhouse, perhaps a successful craftsman's or tradesman's home with the most modest but nevertheless clearly stated architectural pretensions. The Old Post office in Aldborough is of nearly perfect doll's house proportions, with giant order pilasters and burnt headers in its very tidy Flemish-bond brickwork, a fine plat band delineating the storeys, dormers in a glazed pantile roof, and a small, low-walled garden in front, this has none of the workaday rigours of a farmhouse of similar size and yet is clearly a vernacular building with absolutely no urban sophistication.

OLD POST HOUSE · ALDBOROUGH · N · NORFOLK

BUILDING NORFOLK

CORBEL TABLE

CROWSTEP GABLE

KNEELER

FARMHOUSE IN BINHAM

PANTILES CAME TO NORFOLK IN THE EARLY C17 & WERE PREVALENT BY THE END OF THE CENTURY. (they were imported at first from the Netherlands) On LOW STATUS buildings of Pre C17 construction they replace THATCH on HIGHER STATUS Pegtile or LEAD. NARBOROUGH HALL MAY NOT HAVE BEEN ALONE IN BEING ROOFED WITH COLLYWESTON SLATE, A LIMESTONE FROM NORTHAMPTON.

HIPPED ROOF

WALPOLE ST PETER

CROSS MULLIONED WINDOW

BUILDING NORFOLK

WORSTEAD

EARLY 18

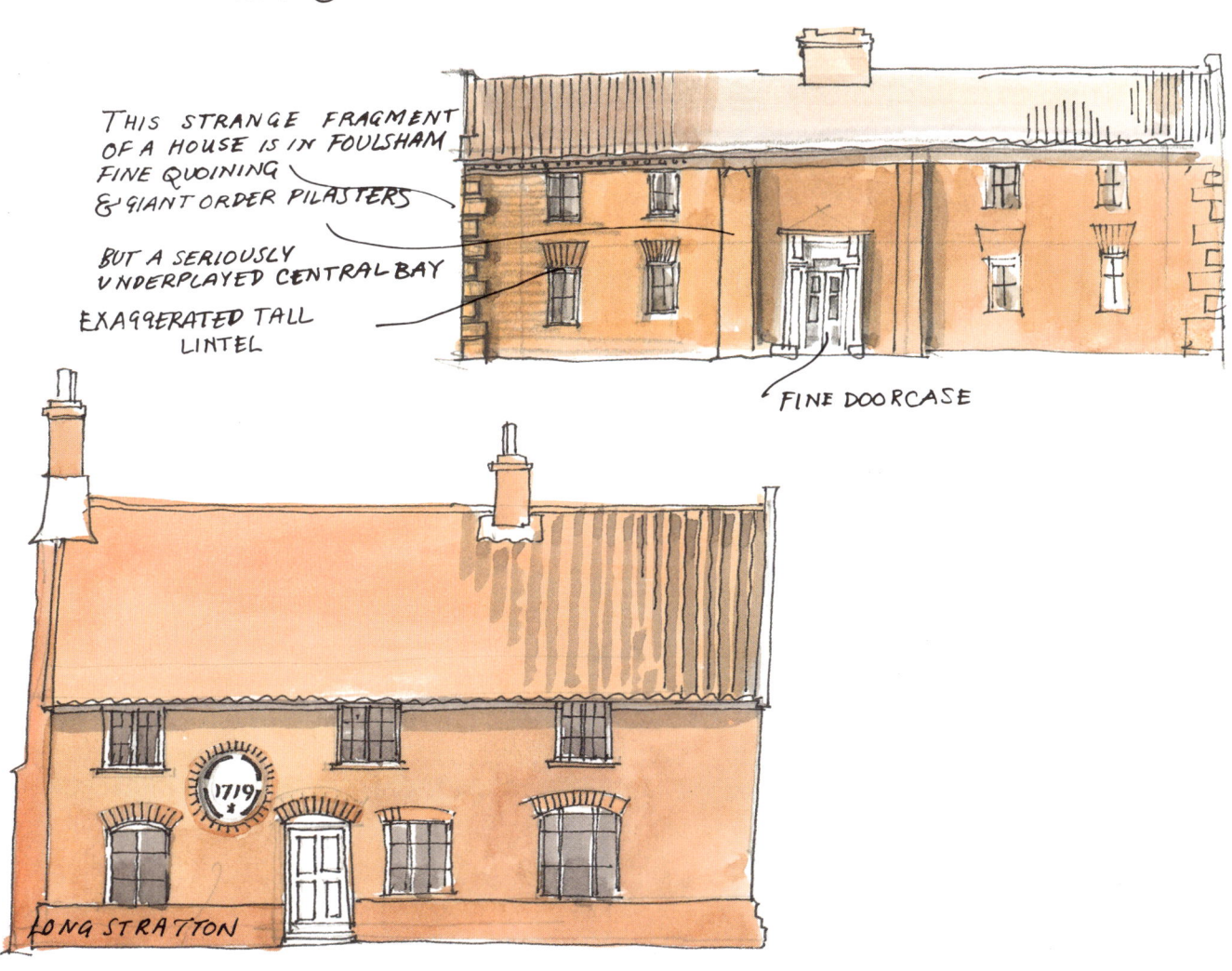

SHAPED GABLE

PLAT BAND

This strange fragment of a house is in Foulsham
Fine quoining & giant order pilasters
But a seriously underplayed central bay
Exaggerated tall lintel

FINE DOORCASE

LONG STRATTON — 1719

35

BUILDING NORFOLK

TWO ELEGANT VILLAGE HOUSES IN DENVER

SHALLOW PEDIMENT

TALL FIRST FLOOR WINDOWS

SHAPED GABLE

DISS · S · NORFOLK

BUILDING NORFOLK

RIDGE

DETAIL

BOARD TO SHED RAINWATER

HOUSE · OLD BUCKENHAM

BRICK PLINTH

SHAPED GABLE

TIMBER FRAMED & RENDERED PUB IN LOPHAM

CORNICE WITH MODILLIONS

37

BUILDING NORFOLK

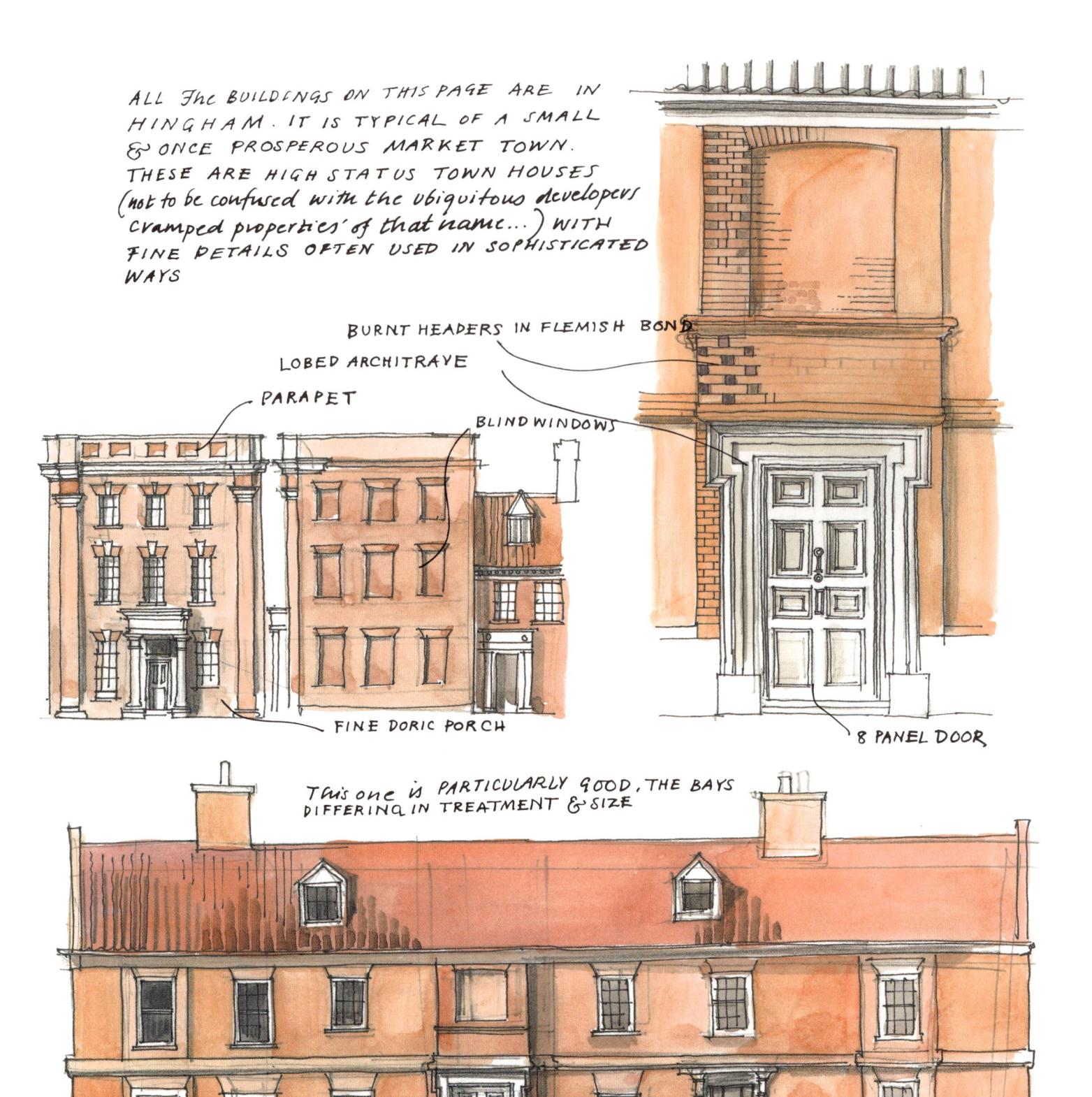

All the buildings on this page are in Hingham. It is typical of a small & once prosperous market town. These are high status town houses (not to be confused with the ubiquitous developers 'cramped properties' of that name...) with fine details often used in sophisticated ways

- BURNT HEADERS IN FLEMISH BOND
- LOBED ARCHITRAVE
- PARAPET
- BLIND WINDOWS
- FINE DORIC PORCH
- 8 PANEL DOOR

This one is particularly good, the bays differing in treatment & size

BUILDING NORFOLK

OAKLEY HOUSE · SWAFFHAM IN STEPHEN FRY'S TELEVISION TOWN HOUSE NOW PART OF IMMORTALISED AS OFFICES OF KINGDOM SOLICITORS SERIES OF that name. ALSO A VERY FINE C18 SWAFFHAM COLLEGE

- RESTLESS KEYSTONE
- QUOINING
- URN

A PROSPEROUS MERCHANT'S HOUSE

CENTRAL THREE BAYS PROJECTING

DEREHAM · (BARCLAYS BANK) 1740

- DIOCLETIAN WINDOW
- BULL'S EYE

ANOTHER SPLENDID MID C18 HOUSE IN UN-MODISH E·DEREHAM

- BULL'S EYE WINDOW
- RUSTICATED GIANT ORDER PILASTERS

HINGHAM

BUILDING NORFOLK

DOLPHIN INN
DISS.

WYMONDHAM
MARKET CROSS 1617
(N. WALSHAM HAS ONE
SIMILAR OF 1600)

FIGURE OF CERES

SWAFFHAM
MARKET CROSS 1783
BUILT BY EARL OF
ORFORD

DOWNHAM MKT
CAST IRON CLOCK TOWER 1878

MANSARD ROOF
TUMBLING IN
DOWNHAM MKT

ASSEMBLY ROOMS · SWAFFHAM

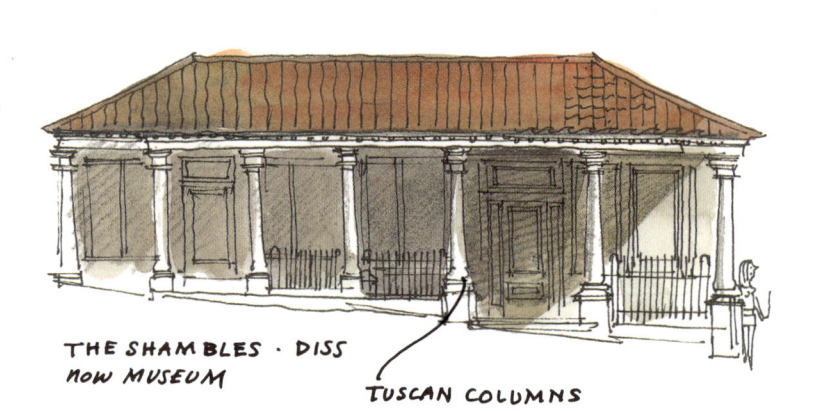

THE SHAMBLES · DISS
NOW MUSEUM
TUSCAN COLUMNS

DISS 1855 (CONCISE)

NORWICH 18 FAÇADE ON 17 HOUSE

40

BUILDING NORFOLK

TIMBER FRAMED SHOPS & PUBS IN DISS. DISS IS WELL PRESERVED as it did not suffer DESTRUCTIVE TOWN FIRES of the sort that LEVELLED HOLT or FOULSHAM in the C18 so... more MEDIEVAL & C16/C17 BUILDINGS REMAIN

JETTIED UPPER STOREY

INSERTED SHOPFRONT in C18 HOUSE (better than a new shop..)

C19 ELABORATION & GRANDEUR · DISS

WYMONDHAM

NASTY CEMENT PANTILES

INAPPROPRIATE FENESTRATION + CHEAP SOFTWOOD PLANKING

MODERN SHOPS in WYMONDHAM

41

GEOMETRIC

COMPLEX GEOMETRIC WOODWORK

ST NICHOLAS ST DISS

EDWARDIAN NEO-VERNACULAR at LUDHAM VILLAGE HALL · BROADLAND

IRON

UNSURPRISINGLY THIS IS THE SIDE DOOR OF A FORMER BOTCHERS IN WYMONDHAM (....
....THE ANIMALS ENTRANCE..)

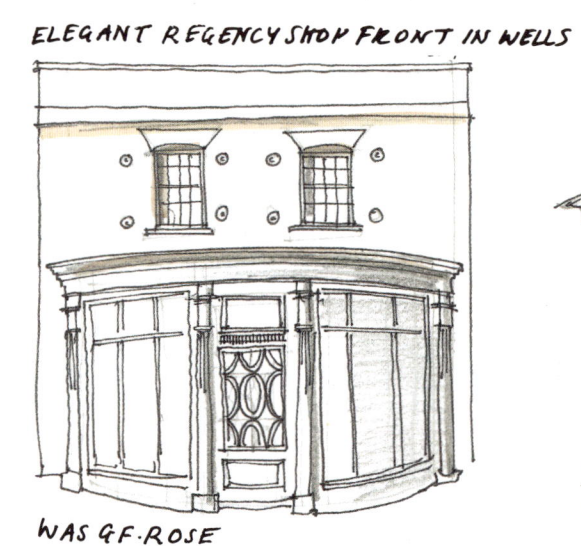

ELEGANT REGENCY SHOP FRONT IN WELLS

BUILT 1850
WELLS

WAS G.F. ROSE

FINE IONIC COLUMNS
THIS SHOP USES THE SITE INCREDIBLY WELL
i.e. MOST SHOW at most visible place on the corner

BUILDING NORFOLK

S. CREAKE SCHOOL 1850? PLAIN GOTHIC REVIVAL

HALL AT MARSHAM

SCULTHORPE SCHOOL NR FAKENHAM

NATIONAL SCHOOL ERECTED TO THE GLORY OF GOD AND WELFARE OF MAN 1840

USE OF VERNACULAR MATERIALS (LOCAL BRICK & FLINT) BUT DESIGNED BY AN ARCHITECT SO *not* a VERNACULAR BUILDING

THORNHAM SCHOOL 1858. IN THE 1962 PEVSNER IT IS DESCRIBED.... "A Nightmare of asymmetrical gothic display." Surely rather FIERCE?

IT IS NOW CONVERTED TO RESIDENTIAL USE AND SPLENDIDLY DYNAMIC & FULL OF ENTRANCING DETAIL · IT HAS A GOOD MODERN EXTENSION BEHIND

1930S VERNACULAR HOLT POST OFFICE PLAIN & ERUDITE

5. FARM HOUSES AND SMALL MANOR HOUSES

An agricultural county will be rich in farmhouses, and this is particularly the case in a region for which farming was a thriving and vibrant industry rather than a last resort for want of other occupation. Large arable farms required equally large and architecturally distinguished farmhouses to reflect the growing importance and rising status of their tenants or owners, and Norfolk is particularly rich in these. At the very top end of the market are the farmhouses at Holkham.

Thomas Coke, the great agricultural improver, was well aware of the importance of attracting the right type of farmer to be his tenant on the large arable farms that he was establishing on his vast Holkham estate. He was searching for forward-thinking entrepreneurs who had capital and, most importantly, the inclination to work within the new orthodoxy of improved farming. This involved crop rotation, marling, liming and the use of newly improved breeds of farm animal such as the longer and larger shorthorn cattle and the ever larger Leicester sheep, whose manure was a vital component in the plan to increase fertility and hence productivity of the light North Norfolk soils. Coke was derided for the palatial accommodation he was willing to provide for his tenants. His short-sighted neighbours deplored these inappropriately grand farmhouses that were dangerously close in size to their own manors and considerably more modern and convenient. One can only imagine that their wives, fed up with damp kitchen corridors, dark drawing rooms and leaking roofs, felt jolly aggrieved and made their views abundantly clear. Thomas Rowlandson, the acerbic mid-eighteenth-century cartoonist whose field of inspiration was principally political, poked fun as well by portraying overweight and overdressed farmers' wives holding court in their 'improved' drawing rooms lavishly furnished in the latest fashions and equipped with square pianos that their rosy cheeked daughters were perceived as being quite unable to play.

Coke was doubly vindicated. Holkham remained at the vanguard of the Agrarian Revolution, much admired and imitated across Europe and America, and significantly the estate was left with a hugely valuable stock of desirable small country houses now much in demand. Holkham was not the only estate with this approach. Nearby Walsingham has several similarly impressive farmhouses, as do Gunton and most of Norfolk's great estates.

Smaller and indeed earlier farmhouses also occur throughout the county, and in these too a reflection of agriculture's success in the eighteenth century and again in the nineteenth is visible. Laurel Farm in Banningham is not a large house, but it has considerable architectural presence: the product of shameless showing off by its eighteenth-century owner. Brick quoins, a generous plat band and an absurdly grand segmental pediment over the modest door are testaments to its builder's clear desire to prove that he had arrived. Beck Farm in Hindolveston is similarly gentrified with a heavy dentilated cornice, tall hipped roof, fine brickwork with burnt headers in its Flemish bond, a plat band and good rubbed brick lintels. The lintels have been particularly sensitively restored and are something of an exemplar for this kind of work.

As enclosure of the open fields from the sixteenth century onwards changed the landscape and rural communities, so smaller manors became incorporated in larger holdings. As a by-product of this change, their manor houses were downgraded into large farmhouses often styled Manor Farm (although, of course, some so named were farmhouses *to* the manor). Church Farmhouse in Poringland is one such building with its pedimented window, jettied porch and fine gallery window. The Norfolk builder's ease with brick is shown again and again, as is the imaginative and very varied use of flint and other freestones. The farmhouse in Ludham in the Broads has particularly brilliant swagger flintwork squared and knapped as well as any church work, producing a surface so flush that the whole façade shimmers in the sun.

Earlier farmhouses and small manors often have fine chimney stacks, and this being Norfolk they are of elaborate brickwork, often hexagonal or octagonal with much decoration. This is a reflection of the move from medieval central hearth fireplaces to Tudor and later chimneys. This very substantial bit of progress was well worth celebrating — it must after all have made a significant difference to life indoors — and became the focus for architectural ostentation, as did the pediment over the increasingly glazed windows in an early nod to the Renaissance that was in full flow across the North Sea.

One of the best buildings in Norfolk is Aylsham Old Hall. It was built as the dower house for nearby Blickling in 1686 and is the perfect late seventeenth-century house. As a dower house it is neither manor nor farmhouse, but has found itself in this section for reasons of size and effect. I have shown it next to its near twin, The Limes, built in 1692 in Coltishall, ten miles south-east of Aylsham. They are eerily similar in plan and elevation: seven bays, the first and last two projecting with nearly identical segmentally pedimented door-cases, heavy cornices (that of Aylsham is dentilated), and an elaborate and heavy plat band marking the change of storey. Are they the work of the same builder? It seems very likely, although he would be disappointed to find The Limes partially obscured by the wings of a later courtyard. (I have drawn them in ghostly form so as not to obscure the elevation and the similarities.)

The idea of emulation of one house by the builder of another, or indeed the recognisable style of a particular builder, comes up again and again looking around Norfolk. Sometimes this must just be simple expedience, using one set of drawings twice. The very impressive Saffron House in Catton built in 2007 is a nearly exact copy of another by the same developer in Beccles. Is there any reason why this should not have been the case 300 years ago? It certainly seems that one shaped gable follows another and that door-cases of closely related design chase each other along a street: surely a case of keeping up with the eighteenth-century Joneses.

STEEP PITCHED THATCH ON FARM AT STRACEY ARMS · HALVERGATE S. NORFOLK

BUILDING NORFOLK

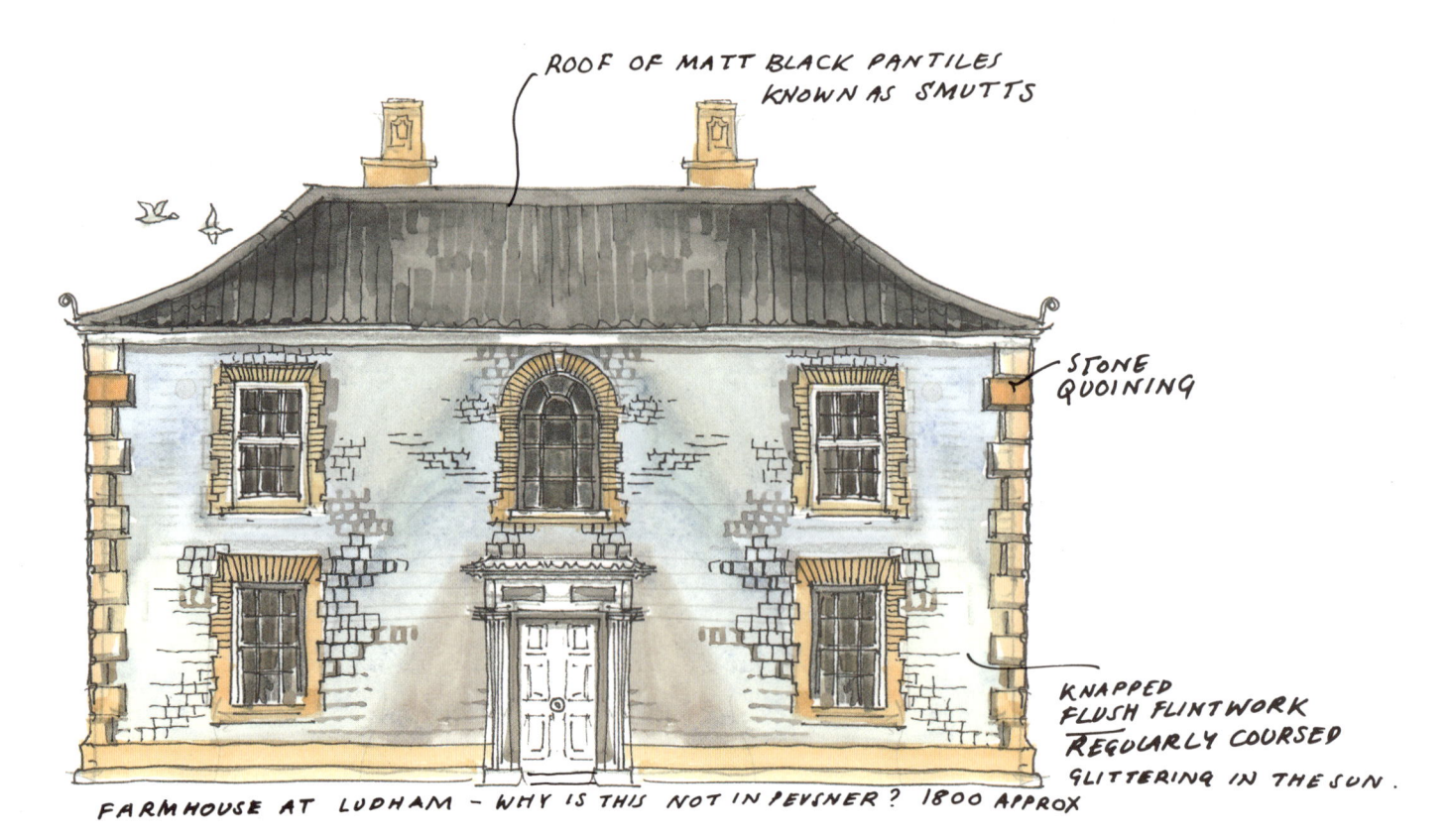

ROOF OF MATT BLACK PANTILES KNOWN AS SMUTTS

STONE QUOINING

KNAPPED FLUSH FLINTWORK REGULARLY COURSED GLITTERING IN THE SUN.

FARMHOUSE AT LUDHAM - WHY IS THIS NOT IN PEVSNER? 1800 APPROX

EXTENSION 1837

CLASPING PILASTER

PLATBAND

SEGMENTAL PEDIMENT

COLENSO COTTAGE · MARSHAM C1700 (PEV)
↑ was this named for the Battle of Colenso in BOER WAR? PERHAPS A SON KILLED?

46

BUILDING NORFOLK

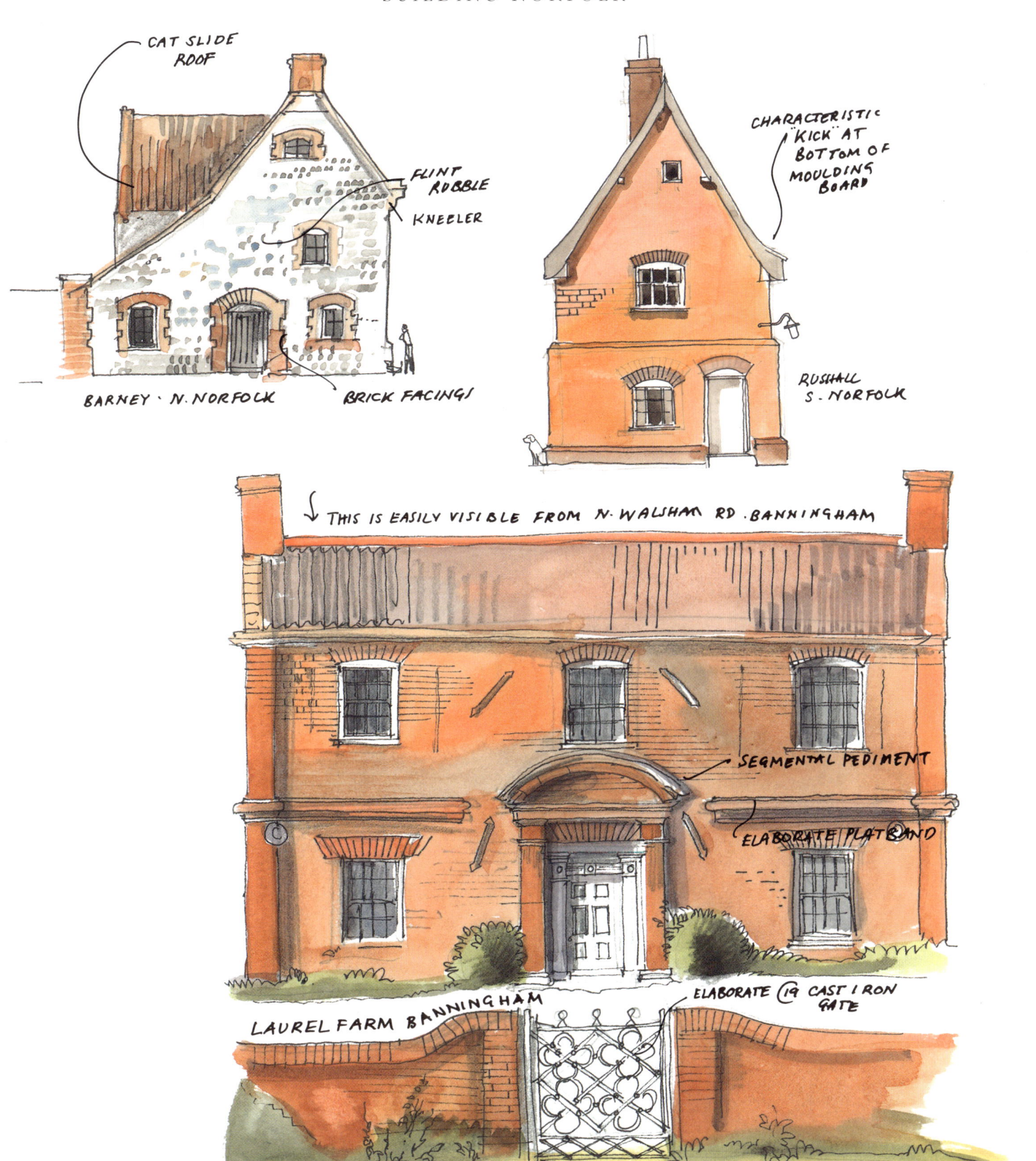

CAT SLIDE ROOF

FLINT RUBBLE

KNEELER

BARNEY · N. NORFOLK   BRICK FACINGS

CHARACTERISTIC "KICK" AT BOTTOM OF MOULDING BOARD

RUSHALL S. NORFOLK

↓ THIS IS EASILY VISIBLE FROM N. WALSHAM RD. BANNINGHAM

SEGMENTAL PEDIMENT

ELABORATE PLATBAND

LAUREL FARM BANNINGHAM   ELABORATE C19 CAST IRON GATE

IS THIS THE PERFECT SMALL FARMHOUSE?   EARLY C18

47

BUILDING NORFOLK

THURTON HALL (PRE 1664)

STEPPED OR CROW STEPPED GABLE

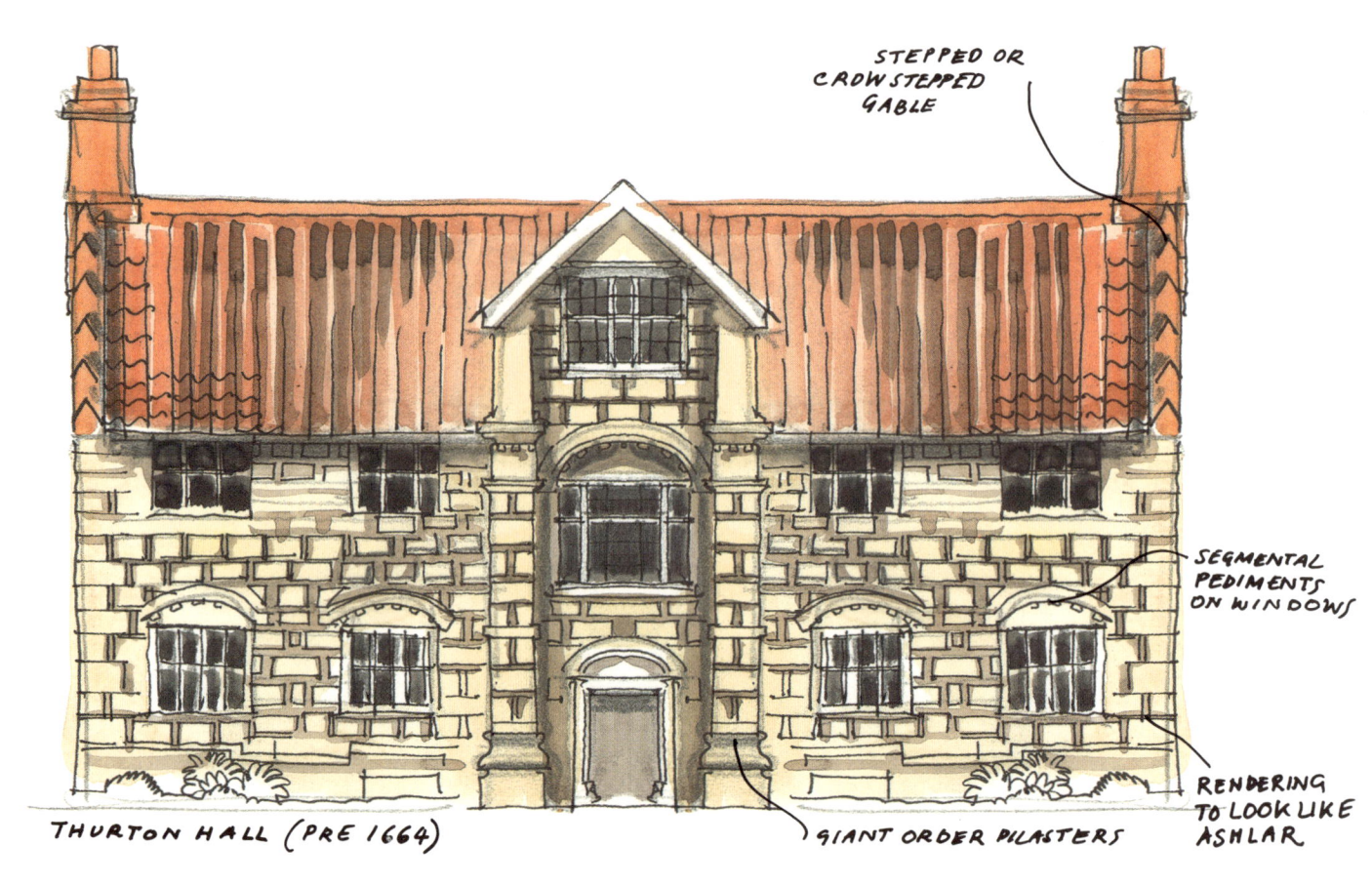

SEGMENTAL PEDIMENTS ON WINDOWS

RENDERING TO LOOK LIKE ASHLAR

GIANT ORDER PILASTERS

| PARLOUR | HALL | SERVICES |

DOOR

LOBBY OR BAFFLE ENTRY TYPE MUCH USED IN S. NORFOLK

| PARLOUR | HALL | SERVICES |

DOOR

EARLY CROSS PASSAGE-TYPE HOUSE. These are not specific houses, just TYPES

48

BUILDING NORFOLK

POLYGONAL CHIMNEY STACK

PEGTILE ROOF i.e. not PANTILE

PEDIMENTED WINDOW

FARMHOUSE/MANOR HOUSE PORINGLAND. HALL WITH ONE CROSSWING
EARLY C16

HALL

MULTIPLE POLYGONAL CHIMNEYSTACK

WHITE HORSE FARM HOUSE EARLY C17

49

BUILDING NORFOLK

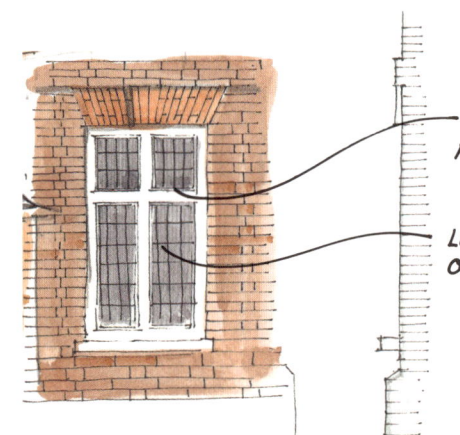

- BLACK GLAZED PANTILES
- HIPPED ROOF
- MODILLION
- FINE CORNICE
- TWO LIGHT CASEMENTS
- PRE-SASH MULLION & TRANSOM WINDOW
- LEADED QUARRIES ONE CASEMENT OPENS
- HIPPED ROOF
- FINE CORNICE

BECK FARM · HINDOLVESTON · N. NORFOLK
EARLY 18

50

BUILDING NORFOLK

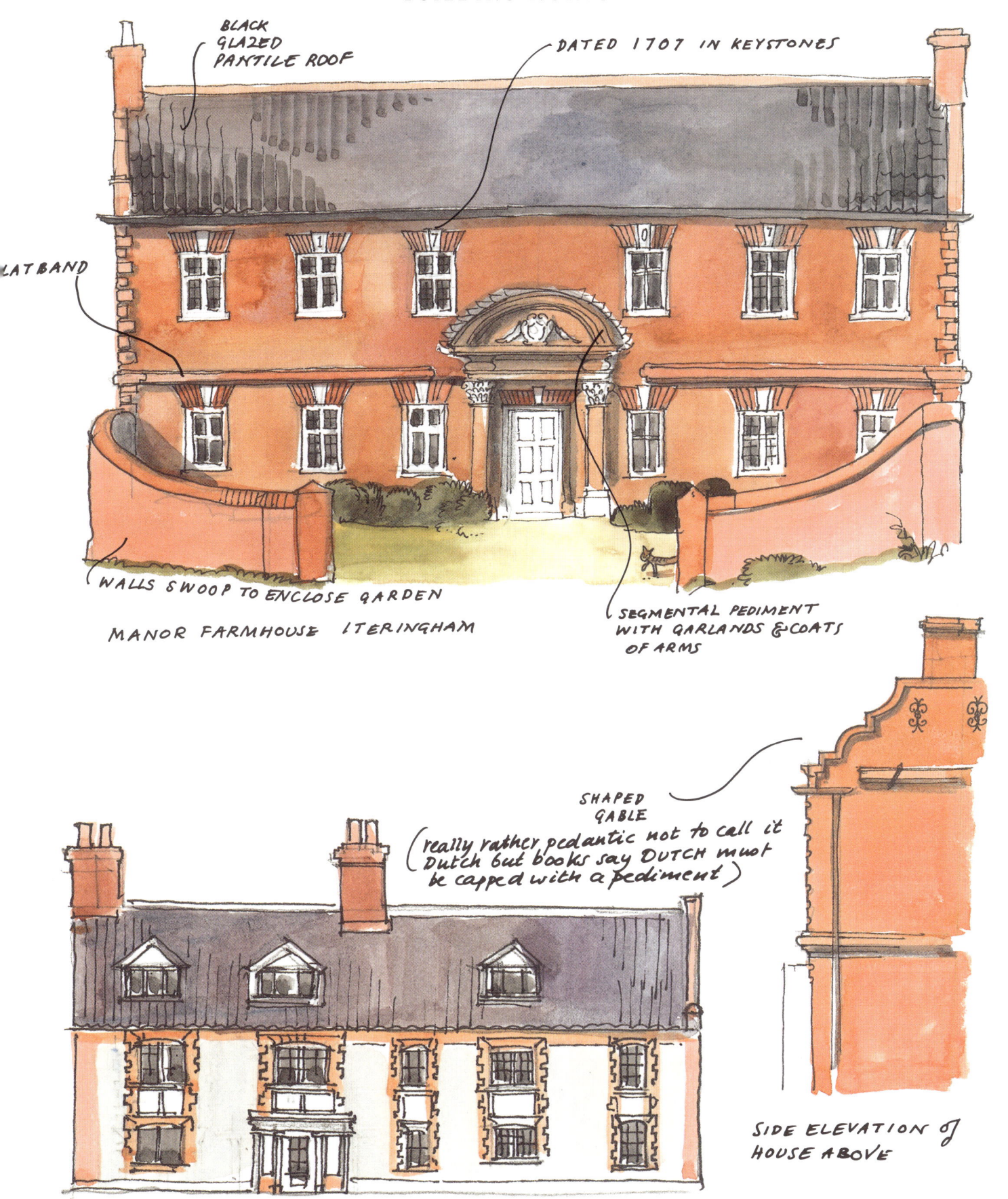

- BLACK GLAZED PANTILE ROOF
- DATED 1707 IN KEYSTONES
- FLATBAND
- WALLS SWOOP TO ENCLOSE GARDEN
- SEGMENTAL PEDIMENT WITH GARLANDS & COATS OF ARMS

MANOR FARMHOUSE ITERINGHAM

SHAPED GABLE
(really rather pedantic not to call it Dutch but books say DUTCH must be capped with a pediment)

SIDE ELEVATION OF HOUSE ABOVE

51

BUILDING NORFOLK

HIPPED ROOF WAS ONCE STEEPER AS IN THE LIMES BELOW

AYLSHAM OLD HALL 1686

SASH WINDOWS REPLACE EARLIER CROSS-CASEMENTS

PLATBAND

ARE THESE BY THE SAME BUILDER or IS THE LIMES BUILT IN EMULATION of the SLIGHTLY FINE AYLSHAM OLD HALL?

THE LIMES · COLTISHALL 1692

QUOINS

LATER SERVICE WINGS OBSCURE END BAYS

BUILDING NORFOLK

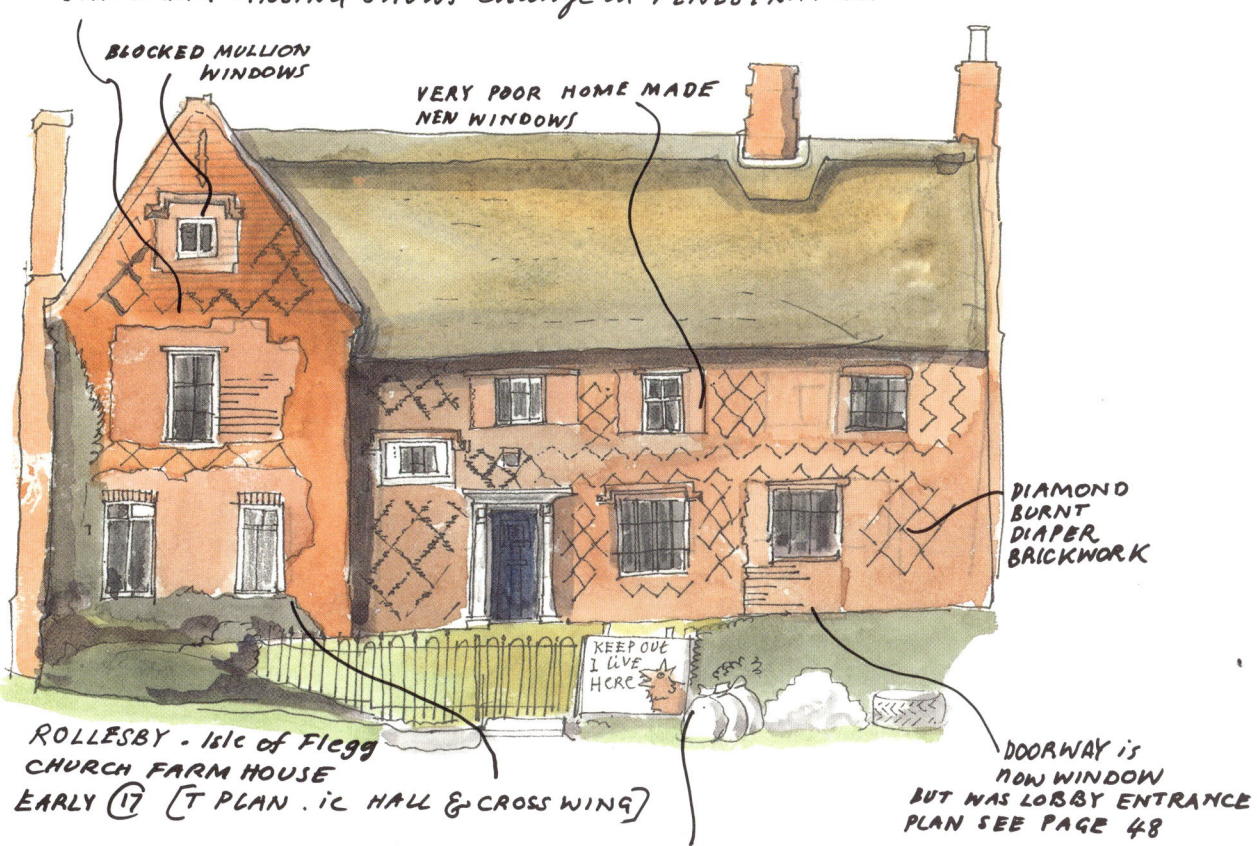

DIAPERING MISSING SHOWS CHANGE IN FENESTRATION

BLOCKED MULLION WINDOWS

VERY POOR HOME MADE NEW WINDOWS

DIAMOND BURNT DIAPER BRICKWORK

ROLLESBY · Isle of Flegg
CHURCH FARM HOUSE
EARLY 17 [T PLAN · ie HALL & CROSS WING]

WELCOMING SIGN...

(sign reads: KEEP OUT I LIVE HERE)

DOORWAY IS NOW WINDOW BUT WAS LOBBY ENTRANCE PLAN SEE PAGE 48

THIS IS AN UNUSUAL EXAMPLE OF A FINE & HIGH STATUS BUILDING IN FRIGHTFUL REPAIR · THE BARNS also early are in Danger...

STEPPED OV CROWSTEPPED GABLE

MALTHOUSE FARMHOUSE
EARLY 17

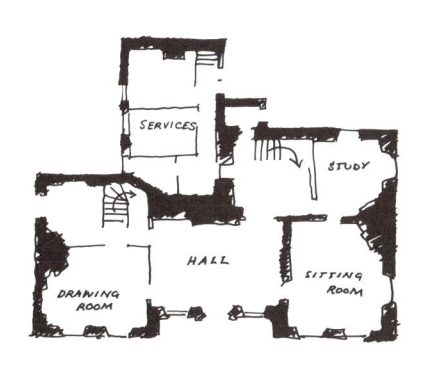

TUMBLING IN

Floor plan labels: SERVICES, STUDY, HALL, DRAWING ROOM, SITTING ROOM

LATE 17

53

6. MANOR HOUSES

The manor is a series of rights over a landholding. It is not necessarily coextensive with a parish; indeed many parishes contain two or more manors which can overlap parish boundaries, while some manors can contain part or all of two parishes. Wickmere, for example, contains the manor of Wickmere and another called Lady Cates. These are no longer visible or functional entities, although at nearby Wolterton Lord Walpole, whose forebear demolished the last manor house in the 1740s, remains lord of the manor and until recently also owned those lands. Most medieval manors were held as part of a portfolio of such entities combined to form one estate. This might cross county or even regional boundaries, and until the break with France often included properties across the Channel.

The owners of these estates were sometimes secular and sometimes religious houses, the latter often receiving manors as gifts or bequests and the former acquiring them as marriage settlements or as general consolidations of holdings. Manors were the social unit into which the country was divided, perhaps the relic of the late Roman estate system. In the medieval manor landowners, freeholders, villeins and serfs lived alongside one another – the last three classes working in part for themselves and in part for the lord.

The land was divided into extensive open fields and common. The fields were divided into strips held between the inhabitants, the lord (demesne), and the parish church and its priest (glebe); the common had controlled common rights to grazing, firewood collection, gorse cutting and pannage (the right to loose foraging swine in the autumn). Although some lords' land was comprised of strips in the open fields, it became more and more usual for the demesne to be held in a block around the manor house. This estate was managed by a bailiff and a reeve. At the centre was the manor house: courthouse, headquarters of the lord, and sometimes his home or temporary home if his time was divided between many properties, which was usual. In a period when furnishings were minimal and in the case of textiles and eating equipment highly portable, this was less restless than it might sound and allowed the lord to hold courts, collect rents, fines and dues, and consume the product of his lands as he proceeded from one manor to another.

However, not all manorial proprietors were so peripatetic, and as England settled (particularly after the accession of Henry VII in 1485), so the fabric of the house itself began to improve and the type of house that we currently think of as a manor house began to emerge. Until this time some of these buildings were of poor construction in relation to their status, and in terms of materials were closely aligned with their neighbouring and subject farmhouses and cottages. But larger and grander manors began to be built: fifteenth-century Oxburgh Hall is a good example. From this time some manor houses moved to higher ground, having previously been situated in low-lying areas of the village. When Kimberley Hall was built in 1712, it was in an elevated position and replaced the earlier fifteenth-century manor, remains of which can be found in woods below the existing house. Many early houses remain on low sites; Oxnead, later home of the Pastons, is virtually on the banks of the river Bure, Baconsthorpe Castle of 1450 and North Barningham built in the sixteenth century are low down, while the nearby Barningham Hall of 1612 was on a slight prominence. Was this an indication of a desire for a view? Were the earlier houses nearer to water to facilitate the filling of moats, tricky on a hill? Villages were often nucleated around a manor as part of the initial settlement process; they may also have been situated close to a water course for reasons of both water supply and communication. Rivers that now seem to be no more than streams were once navigable: the Nar at Castle Acre is tiny today but in medieval times could keep afloat the barges needed to transport the building stone for the abbey and castle.

Later the link with the village grew weaker, particularly after enclosure, the practice of taking land out of common cultivation and placing it under the direct control of the landlord. From the fourteenth to the sixteenth centuries this was often a response to the dropping population of rural England following outbreaks of the plague and to the increasing value of wool for export. As populations grew, it became increasingly unpopular. The unrest crystallised in a series of protests — famously in Norfolk by Kett's Rebellion in 1549, an expression of a desire to return to the old ways and bound for failure. Enclosure continued from the early seventeenth century, this time backed up by Acts of Parliament, the Enclosure Acts. Landlords no longer wanted to produce more wool but rather sought to capitalise on the improvements in agriculture. With these changes came the manor's move away from the old village and towards the splendid isolation of the country house.

Wiveton Hall mid C17 but Jacobean style 1652

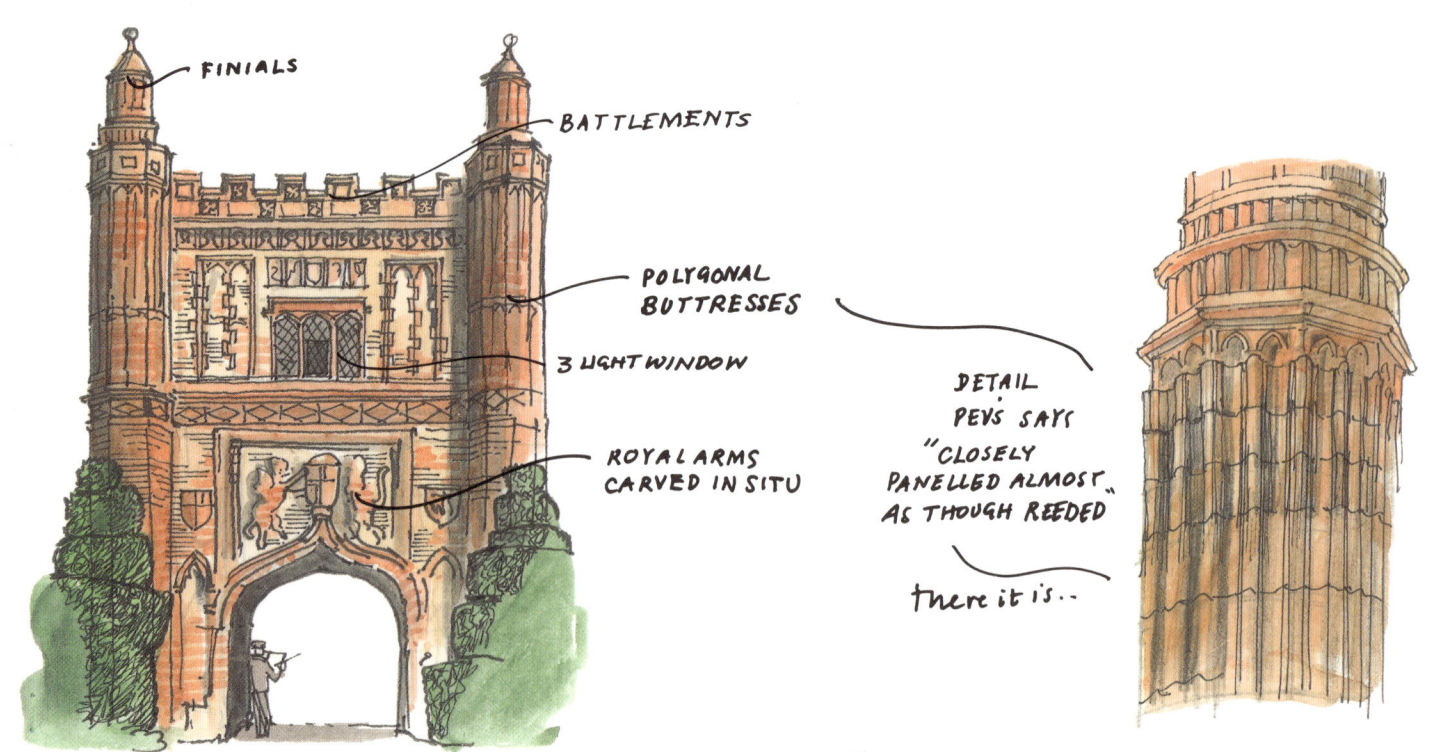

BUILDING NORFOLK

- FINIALS
- BATTLEMENTS
- POLYGONAL BUTTRESSES
- 3 LIGHT WINDOW
- ROYAL ARMS CARVED IN SITU

GATEHOUSE. AFTER 1527

DETAIL. PEVS SAYS "CLOSELY PANELLED ALMOST AS THOUGH REEDED"

there it is..

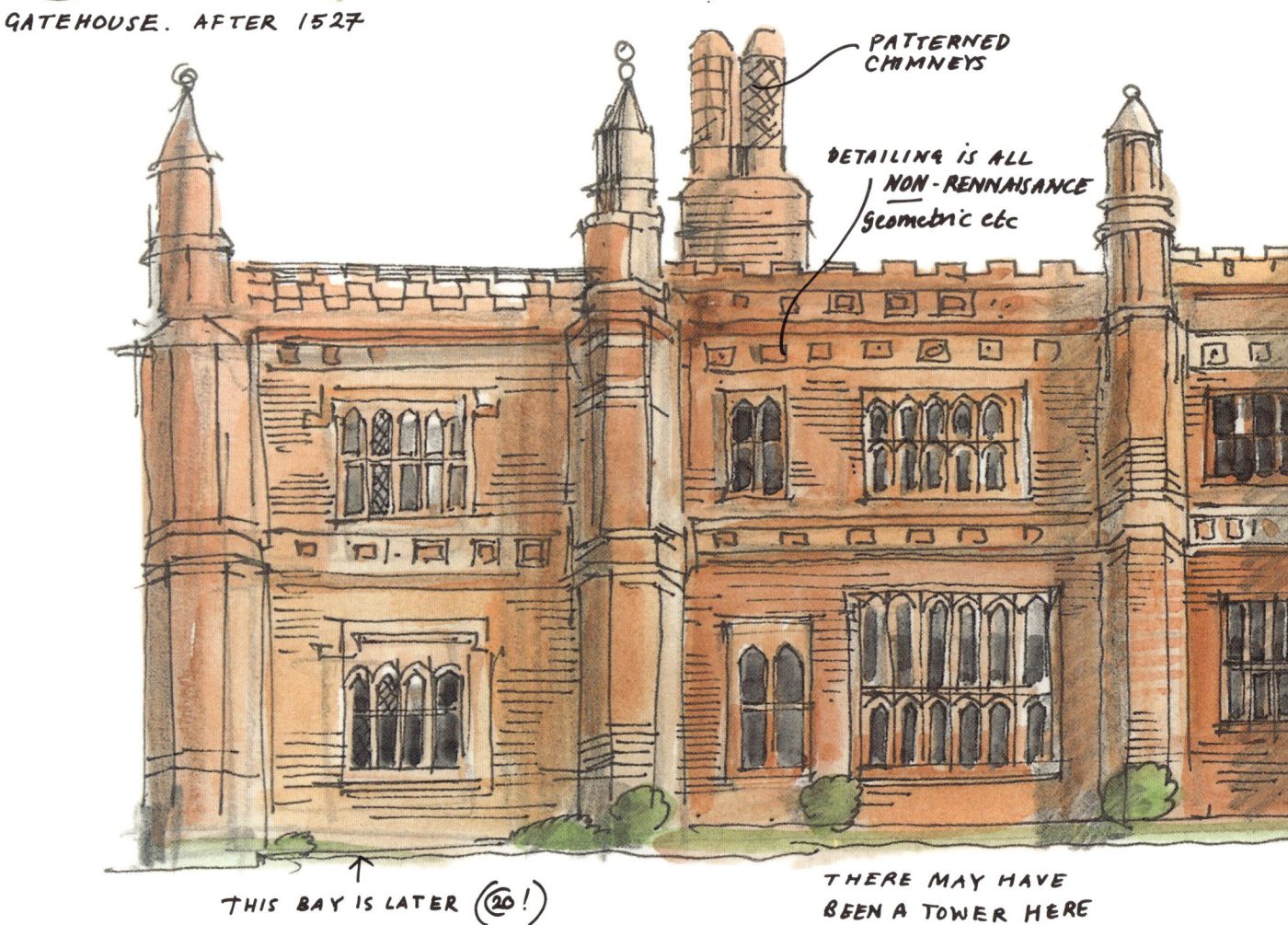

- PATTERNED CHIMNEYS
- DETAILING IS ALL NON-RENNAISANCE geometric etc

THIS BAY IS LATER (20!)

THERE MAY HAVE BEEN A TOWER HERE AS WELL

56

E. BARSHAM. 1520/30
ONE of BRITAINS BEST BRICK BUILDINGS WITH EVERY KIND of FANCY BRICKWORK & TERRACOTTA PANELS. GLORIOUS ASYMMETRY.

IT HAS BEEN MUCH RESTORED BUT SENSITIVELY

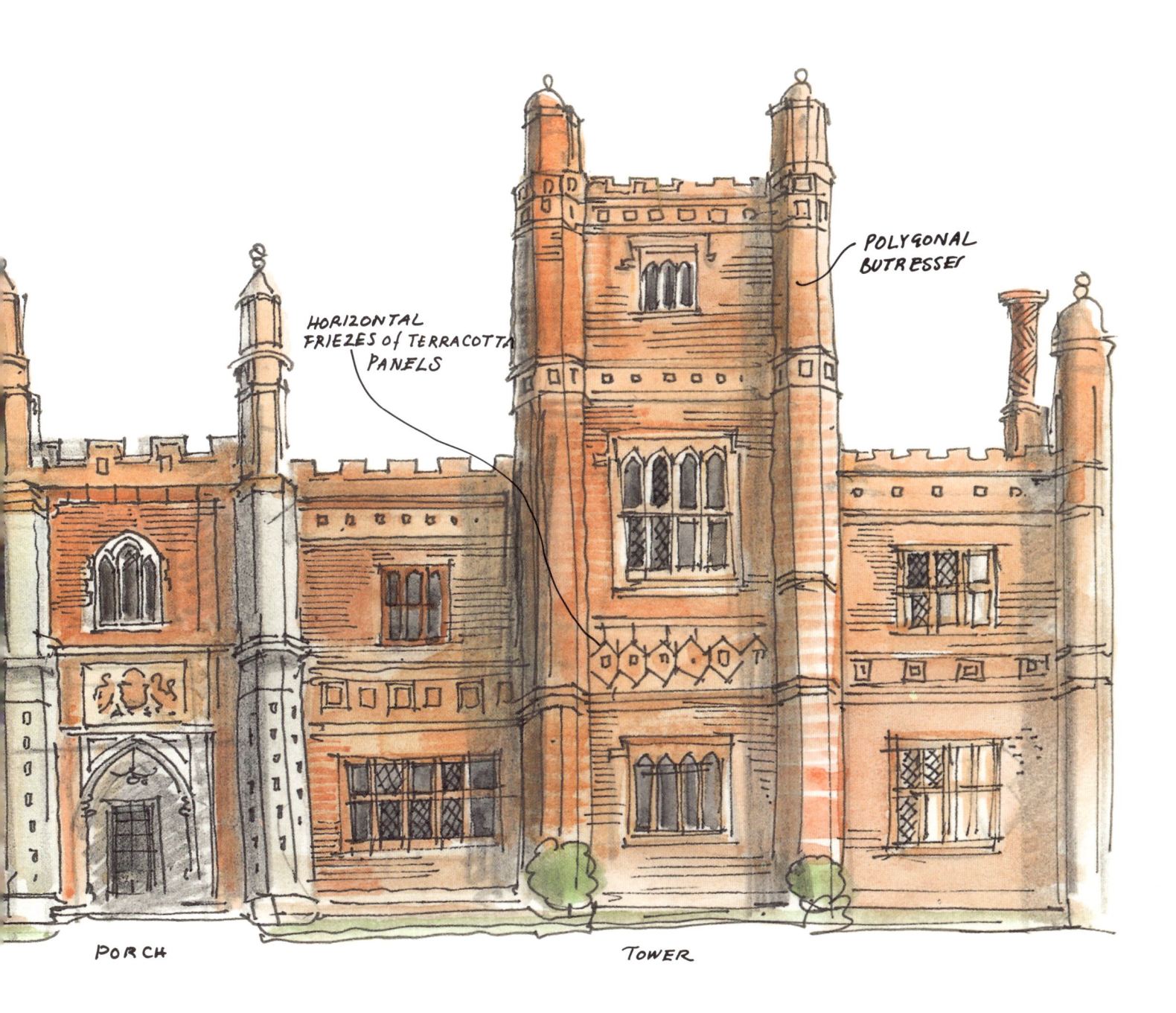

HORIZONTAL FRIEZES of TERRACOTTA PANELS

POLYGONAL BUTRESSES

PORCH

TOWER

BUILDING NORFOLK

This is Remarkable — an 11 bay façade

AYLSHAM
THE MANOR HOUSE (11(!) BAYS)

BOUGHT 1611
by BISHOP JEGON
after Palace at LUDHAM BURNT DOWN

WOODEN CROSS-CASEMENTS (WINDOWS/DOORCASE)
BRICKWORK TUDOR
CORNICE (17)
2 STOREY PORCH

SHAPED GABLE

SWANTON ABBOTT · OLD MANOR FARMHOUSE

BUILDING NORFOLK

SPARROWES HOUSE WINDOW as in IPSWICH

STALHAM HALL 1670.
BEST EXAMPLE of ARTISAN MANNERISM IN NORFOLK ie Transitional mid C17 style where builders produced work of Dutch Influence using Classical detail but in an unsophisticated way

THIS WINDOW TYPE WAS ADOPTED by THE ARCHITECT NORMAN SHAW in the late C19 so is INFLUENTIAL beyond E. ANGLIA

STEPPED GABLES

DETAIL OF PILASTERS

DOUBLE PILASTERS

59

BRICK DETAILING RENDERED OVER

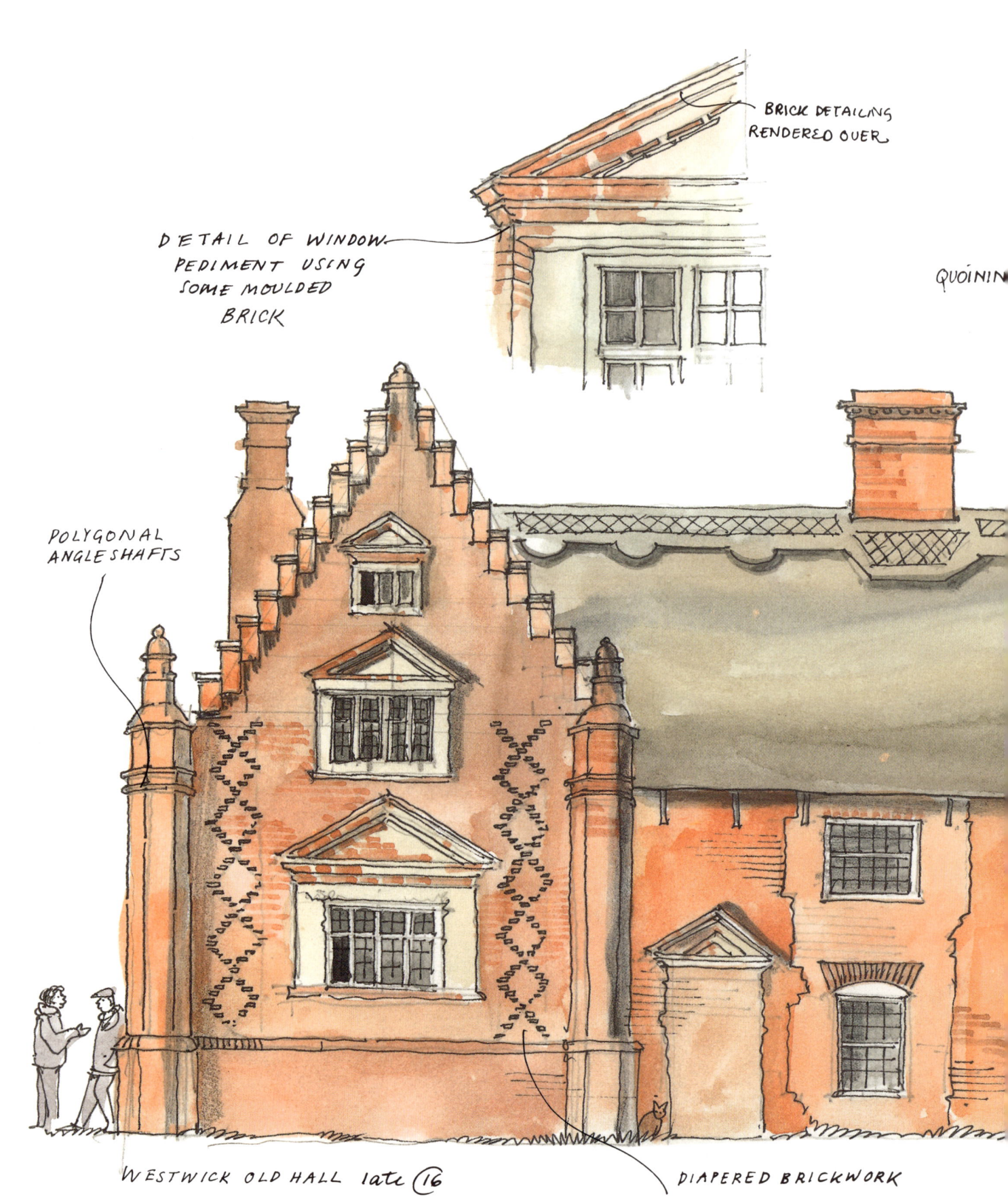

DETAIL OF WINDOW PEDIMENT USING SOME MOULDED BRICK

QUOININ

POLYGONAL ANGLE SHAFTS

WESTWICK OLD HALL late 16

DIAPERED BRICKWORK

BUILDING NORFOLK

STAIRCASE TURRET

HIPPED ROOF

1700 EXTENSION

THE MANOR HOUSE · WORSTEAD · EARLY 16 · PLATBAND — 1700

THIS WAS THE DOORWAY (LEADING TO HALL PASSAGE)

THIS HOUSE CAUGHT THE EYE OF THE ARCHITECT CHARLES RENNIE MACKINTOSH WHEN ON AN EAST ANGLIAN DRAWING TRIP. A CAREFUL & BEAUTIFUL DRAWING EXISTS.

HEIGHT REDUCED HENCE LOW WINDOW

was symmetrical but this wing is gone.

61

BUILDING NORFOLK

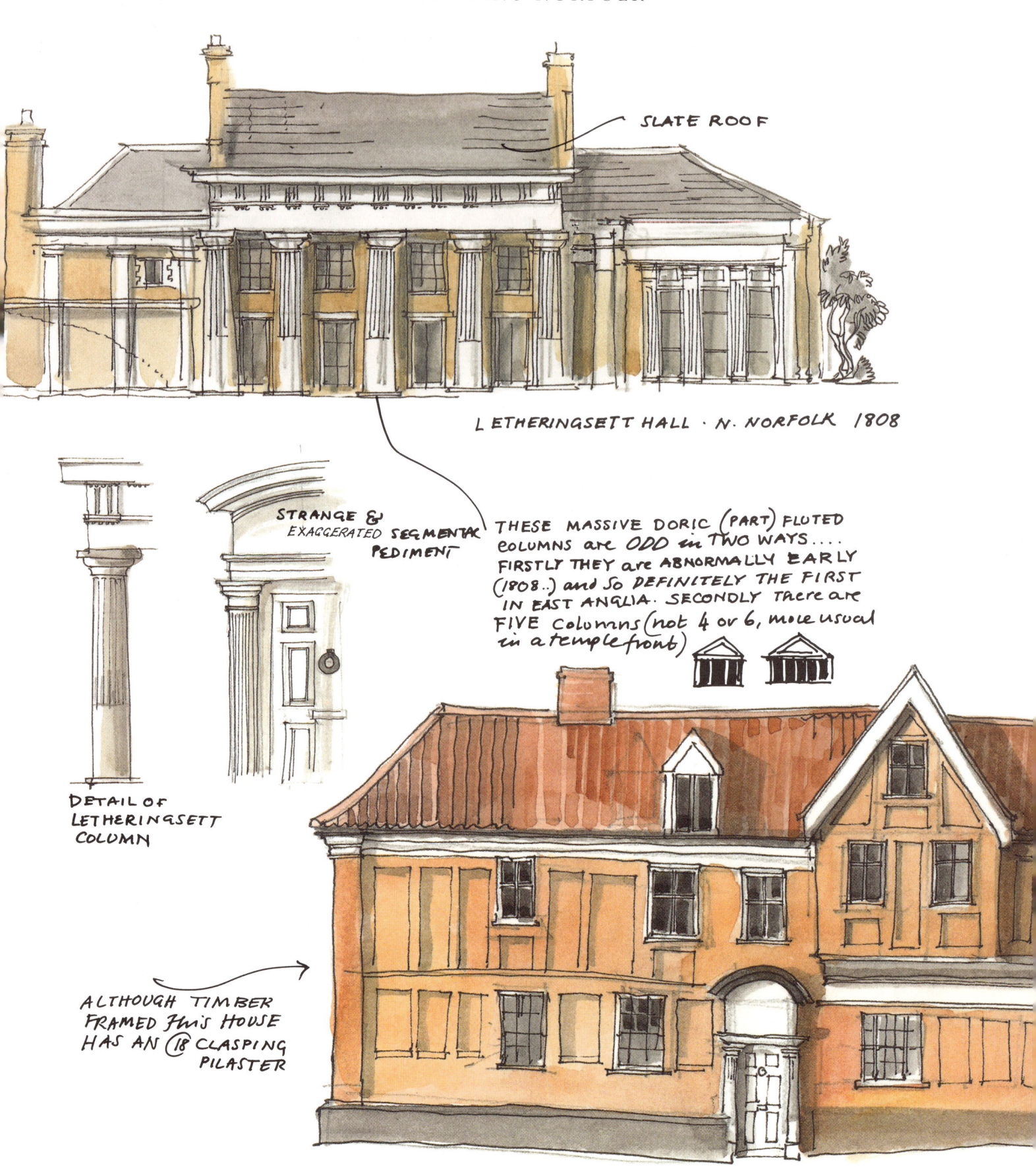

SLATE ROOF

LETHERINGSETT HALL · N. NORFOLK 1808

STRANGE & EXAGGERATED SEGMENTAL PEDIMENT

DETAIL OF LETHERINGSETT COLUMN

THESE MASSIVE DORIC (PART) FLUTED COLUMNS are ODD in TWO WAYS.... FIRSTLY THEY are ABNORMALLY EARLY (1808..) and so DEFINITELY THE FIRST IN EAST ANGLIA. SECONDLY There are FIVE columns (not 4 or 6, more usual in a temple front)

ALTHOUGH TIMBER FRAMED this HOUSE HAS AN C18 CLASPING PILASTER

CHURCH FARM · E · HA.

62

BUILDING NORFOLK

THIS IS THE EAST GABLE of DENVER HALL of about 1520

IT IS A POCKET-VERSION OF E. BARSHAM...

STEPPED GABLE

DECORATED PINNACLES

STRANGE PEDIMENT Pevsner calls it "WAVERING" but it is not quite as free-form as that...

CHEVRON DECORATION

TERRACOTTA PANELS

HOOD MOULD

OGEE PLAQUE

FOUR LIGHT CROSS CASEMENT

63

BUILDING NORFOLK

This is a page of ARTS & CRAFTS, VERNACULAR REVIVAL HOUSES of the early C20. NORFOLK is well off in this field & I MIGHT equally have illustrated KELLING Hall, another BUTTERFLY PLAN HOUSE or HAPPISBURGH HALL designed by DETMAR BLOW

1903.

THIS IS VOEWOOD HOUSE, JUST OUTSIDE HOLT. It was designed by E.S. PRIOR who had worked in the offices of NORMAN SHAW. The ARTS & CRAFTS movement grew out of the GOTHIC REVIVAL in the 1870s and its exponents made great study of ENGLAND'S VERNACULAR BUILDINGS...

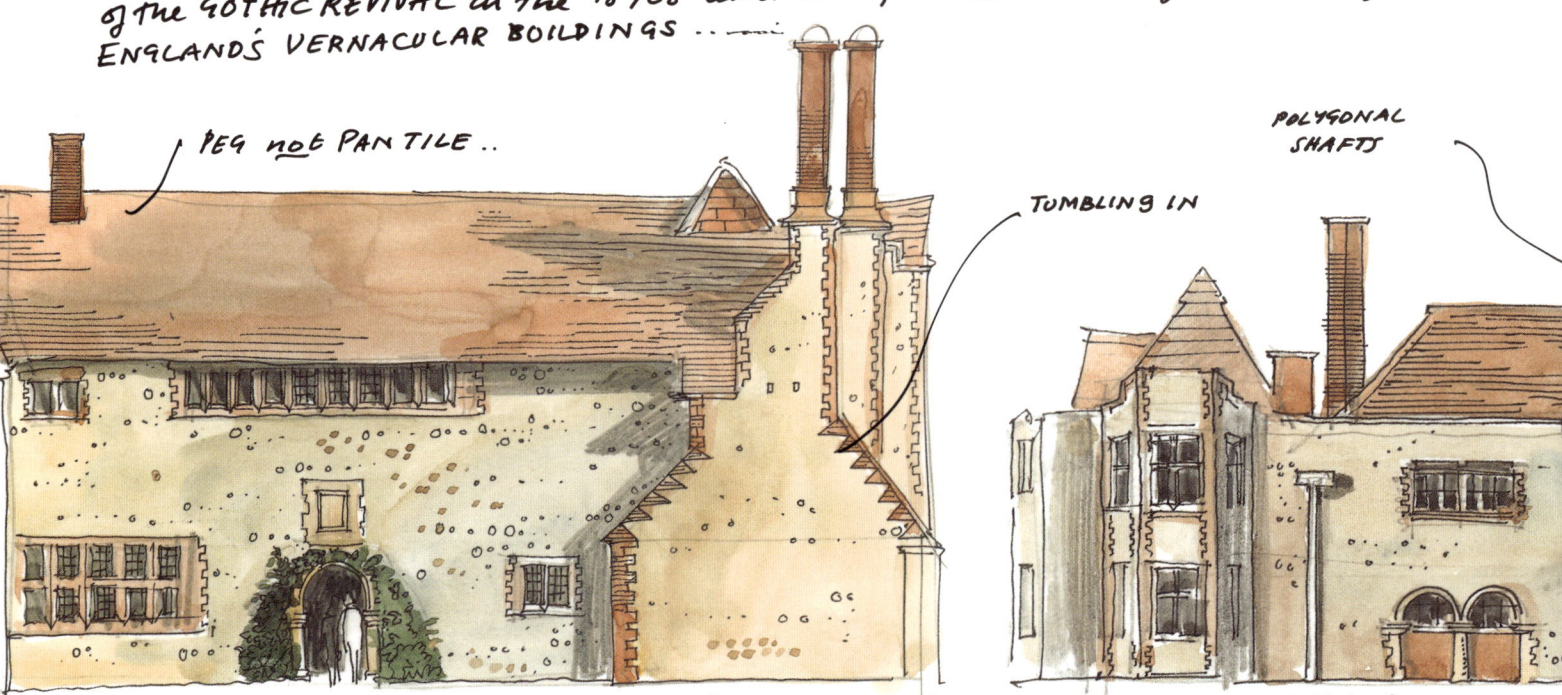

PEG not PANTILE..
TUMBLING IN
POLYGONAL SHAFTS

The SUCCESSFUL BANKER LORD HILLINGDON commissioned OVERSTRAND HALL from LUTYENS in 1899. Austere but with many stylish if mannered quotations from the Norfolk vernacular.

..... PRIOR was concerned with the VERY LOCAL MATERIALS & first excavated the site for VOEWOOD. This produced GRAVEL, SAND & FLINT, so unsurprisingly the house is of CONCRETE construction ... plus almost EVERY OTHER LOCAL or *nearly* LOCAL MATERIAL.

HERE IS A DETAIL SHOWING some of these Materials - TILES. layed in herringbone pattern, brick flint & west Norfolk Carr-stone

- Thin bricks
- diapering
- Carrstone

JOGGLED LINTEL

ONLY A FEW YEARS EARLIER LUTYENS had built a rather unsatisfactory house for Lord BATTERSEA. Lady B, née ROTHSCHILD wanted a new house by this successful Architect but her husband was OBDURATE and she had to make do with converting two existing VILLAS.

THIS BANQUETTING house/PAVILION in the wall is however entirely LUTYENS & fairly NORFOLK-like as well

7. NORFOLK'S COUNTRY HOUSES

Following the Reformation the emphasis on building shifted away from churches to country houses. Until the break with Rome in 1536 and subsequent suppression of the monastaries, the focus of architectural effort was ecclesiastical. If you wanted to express your wealth or status, it was through the church. Since eighth- and ninth-century Christianised Saxon times, the thegn (local leader) had seen in the parish church a vehicle through which to establish his credentials as landowner and local leader. Throughout the Middle Ages great benefactions had flowed from private individuals to the church. Monastic establishments and institutions like the great Hospital of St Giles in Norwich were all endowed and built in this way, and even as the sixteenth century began there was still considerable spending on parish churches. Henry VIII's cataclysmic reorganisation of the Church in England changed all this at a stroke.

First, the monastic foundations which had played such a vital part in the management of the country and which actually owned over 30 per cent of the land were dissolved. This meant that a large amount of property, land and buildings was put up for sale by the Crown ,which had expropriated it, or allocated to individuals loyal to the state. Consequently a new class of landowners appeared in the countryside: often lawyers or others holding political office, bringing new blood and importantly non-agricultural money to their new parishes. Second, while some abbey churches were transferred to their parish as parish churches, the majority were sold for building stone, and there are many houses in Norfolk whose stone has come from demolished religious houses.

The new landowner, equipped with an ex-monastic estate, was, in time, ready to build, and this time the desire found itself expressed in his own house. This development was not immediate. Huge personal reserves had been expended on the acquisition of the new properties, and in most cases it was 50 or more frequently 100 years before the 'great rebuilding' began – houses like Blickling (built by the Hobart family), Stiffkey (built by Sir Nicholas Bacon, who was Queen Elizabeth's Lord Keeper of the Great Seal), Rainthorpe , Heydon, and Great Witchingham.

New houses were not only built on ex-monastic property. The sixteenth and early seventeenth centuries saw new money being directed to secular houses already standing. Felbrigg in 1612 and Barningham in 1617 were built on existing estates, examples of modest Jacobean splendour utilising the newly modish Renaissance detailing of their period. Like the pre-Reformation houses of Oxborough, Mannington and Middleton Tower, these are characterised by the use of Norfolk brick as the principal building material. The soft apricot-coloured brick keeps these houses within the vernacular in a way that later houses like Houghton and Holkham are not.

The great early seventeenth-century house of Norfolk is Raynham. Its Dutch gables and well-lit rooms must have been inspired by Sir Roger Townsend's Grand Tour in 1620, which took in the Netherlands as well as Italy. The combination of Holland's bright brick buildings with Renaissance Rome and Palladio's villas and churches in and around Venice combine in this unusually early classical English house. Townsend took his mason, William Edge, with him to the Netherlands and during this time began the building work using stone from the nearby dissolved Coxford Abbey for foundations. Sir Henry Spelman, whose house at Wolterton was soon to be rebuilt under the later ownership of Sir Horace Walpole, wrote in 1632 that the 'stately house' had been built 'using none of the Abbey stone around it'. Is this an indication that design was becoming, for the first time, more important than materials, defence or other practicalities, and if so is this the first house in Norfolk where architecture was king? Raynham marks the move from old to new. From now on Norfolk's country houses would be classical.

Ryston reinforced the trend in 1672 and Melton Constable followed in 1687; and at the beginning of the eighteenth century came Kimberley, Langley and then Norfolk's two palaces: Holkham and Houghton. These last two are the county's prize exhibits – confident, grand expressions of mature Palladian classicism standing in complete and all-enveloping parks. These were idealised classical landscapes each with drifting herds of fallow deer. Holkham is the larger and rather more austere. Nikolaus Pevsner's claim that the yellow brick of which it is built is reminiscent of Tuscany does not really cut the mustard; however, as an exercise in English Palladianism on a massive scale but cleverly articulated both vertically and horizontally, it is unbeatable. This book does not cover any interiors, but as Holkham is such a complete intellectual project of Enlightenment design, it would be dotty not to mention the extraordinary colonnaded Marble Hall, it is actually made of alabaster, with white marble stairs rising to a ballustraded gallery; this gives onto three series of rooms running in corridorless enfilades past tall windows, every one of which frames a perfect pastoral landscape. The park is cleverly planted with holm oaks that, being evergreen, keep the view from those windows bosky all year.

Houghton is more conventionally beautiful and also more concise, although considerably more expensive to build, costing £200,000 to Holkham's £97,000. Colen Campbell's design of 1730 is refined and elegant with a well-defined piano nobile above a heavily rusticated ground floor. The towers on the pavilion at either end visually link Houghton with its slightly less architecturally distinguished predecessors, Langley and Kimberley; but it is most notably visually distinctive because of its isolation in its landscape. Cut off from its stable block, the park comes right to its plinth, and there is no visible barrier at all between the house and Lord Pembroke's pavilion, the waterhouse, some 500 yards (450 m) away.

At the opposite end of the scale is Honing. This modest five-bay red-brick house of three storeys was built in 1748. Fifty years later it was slightly modified by Humphrey Repton for the Cubitt family, who still live in the house. Its park, although scarcely 50 acres (20 hectares), is so cleverly planned with perimeter belts and clumps that the landscape is as complete as that of Holkham or Houghton, even if, instead of Pembroke's temple, its only folly is a thatched conically roofed pavilion designed by Repton and hidden in the woods. The house is tall and distinguished with a semicircular bay on one side; the centre three bays are protruding with a cartouche and fanciful rococo swags in the pediment and discreet stone cornice and plat band. This last feature, no more than 9 inches (23 cm) deep, is the only result from Repton's revision of the building in the 1790s. Despite its modest size – it cost only £1,000 to build – it is definitely a country house and not a manor, villa or similar lesser structure.

Smaller country house building continued throughout the eighteenth and early nineteenth centuries, but Norfolk does not have a truly great late eighteenth-century house, a Kedleston or a Heveningham. But there are good houses of this date. Matthew Brettingham's 1740s house at Gunton was trebled in size by the Wyatt brothers in the 1770s while working nearby at Holkham; Shotesham and Letton were designed by Sir John Soane in the 1780s, and the charming Gothic Beeston St Lawrence was built in 1769.

The nineteenth century saw Donthorne's works built. W. J. Donthorne was a local architect born and working in Swaffham. His early Gothic Cromer Hall was built in 1829. It is an extraordinary confection: pinnacles, gables, battlements and Gothic detailing, all in fine flintwork, knapped and galleted. The imposing entrance is guarded by two stone knights who have a Toad Hall-ish grandeur and surprising longevity. Hillington Hall was built between 1824 and 1827. It was another Gothic piece, a slightly heavier handed treatment with hefty porte cochère and battlements. These are only visible in photographs as it was demolished in 1946, but its lodges and walls remain.

One of the most mournful houses in Norfolk is Bylaugh Hall. It is not, nor ever was, a beauty. It is a hefty neo-Elizabethan pile with towering mullioned windows that sit in massive bays with towers of chimney stacks at the corners. It was until very recently a ruin guarded by pigs and their keepers, whose tin shacks surrounded the house. Even now, subject to a rather compromising programme of restoration, it still feels like an utter folly. Perhaps this is linked to the story of its conception. The brother of the builder, Sir John Lombe, won the estate from its previous owner, Richard Lloyd, as a gambling debt in 1796. It was not until 1850 that Lombe commissioned this building from Charles Barry Junior and Richardson Banks. When completed it was the very last word in contemporary luxury, with stable block and 750 acres (300 hectares) of new park all enclosed within a brick wall, most of which still stands. For only fifty years the house was occupied enjoying the modern amenities; after that a sucession of tenants lived at Bylaugh until it was sold after the First World War. Over the next thirty years it crumbled until its roof was removed in 1950.

The current owners have begun the job of conversion to a hotel/conference centre. Inside, incongruous and undersized reproduction furniture sits uneasily in one great room; a bold attempt to partially restore the central hall — with some parts of the walls visibly left as found — is unconvincing. The stables, by Barry, have also been subject to some works providing a bland and ill-proportioned series of rooms, but outside the elevations are being retained. A Herculean task is being embarked upon, but whether its setting can be saved as well it is hard to know.

Another house converted to a hotel, with all the institutionalisation that is inclined to bring, is Lyndford Hall. This was also built in the 1850s for an industrialist and is huge, rambling and neo-Jacobean, brick with stone facings and shaped gables. To come across this white elephant lurking in the gloomy coniferous plantations of Thetford Forest, heralded by an avenue of Wellingtonias, is astonishing. The final approach is through a splendid entrance courtyard, then into a series of huge rooms looking out over a formal parterre stranded among the black ranks of Sitka spruce.

The agricultural collapse of 1875, which seems to be relevant to every section of this book, might have stopped all country house building, but the adoption of the breech loading shotgun in the 1860s gave rise to the practice of shooting driven pheasants in increasingly large numbers. Before this, shooting had been a relatively gentle pastime, two or three friends walking through the coverts with spaniels or perhaps with pointers on the stubbles — a scene familiar from a million melamine place mats. Now larger parties of eight or nine sportsmen might come to shoot with wives and servants and stay for as little as that product of the railway age, the 'Friday to Monday'. These parties wanted to shoot 400 or 500 birds every day and often substantially more. East Anglia was, and remains, ideally suited to this, the dry climate suiting the pheasant, a native of Asia from the Caucasus to Japan, and the partridge. So new industrial and City money came to Norfolk either as tenants of existing houses whose impoverished owners, stripped of their high farming rent rolls, were delighted to leave or as builders of their own new mansions. Pickenham was built by a magnate in the world of prefabricated garden sheds, and the Mr Green who built Kenhill had made his fortune in Wakefield manufacturing boilers, particularly the successful and much adopted 'Green's Economiser'. Perhaps Norfolk's best is the post-agricultural-boom house of Sennowe Park at Guist.

In 1898 the Sennowe estate was bought by Thomas Cook, whose travel agent grandfather had founded the eponymous business that produced his fortune. Cook lit on Sennowe as the subject of his attentions and hired George Skipper, then Norfolk's leading architect, to remodel it. Less than fifty years previously the late eighteenth-century the house had been altered by Decimus Burton; now in 1906 it was to undergo a transformation more dramatic by far. The east front is seventeen bays long and is as profoundly articulated as could be contrived and also as elaborately decorated without ever becoming heavy handed. It is built of brick with cream stone dressings and is a virtuoso essay in Edwardian glamour. Back from the house stretch generous stables behind a flourish of an archway, and towering behind in the woods is the water tower with octagonal pavilion on top of a massive cornice. The tower is 30 x 30 feet (9. x 9. m) in ground plan and feels immense; its top two storeys are the tank, ensuring enviable water pressure to this day.

This is the swansong of the Norfolk country house. The First World War ended the world it was built for, and since 1918 country houses have been on the back foot. Some have bucked the trend: Holkham and Houghton are thriving and open to the public, and about half of the rest are still inhabited, some by the families that built them. But during the interwar years and the 1950s nearly 100 houses were lost. Some were plain and unexceptional – Victorian Thursford and Woodbastwick are not great architectural losses – but some are older and a great deal more interesting, such as eighteenth-century Elmham Hall or sixteenth- and early seventeenth-century Beaupre, lamented even in the 1930s when it was demolished. Some large nineteenth-century piles have gone more recently; Weasenham Hall, a subsidiary Coke property, was demolished in the late 1990s due to the poor quality of the original building. Others are so compromised as to be almost unrecognisable. Stratton Strawless Hall, home of the Marshams since the fourteenth century, has lost its second floor, been rendered down and converted into flats, and is now approached by a bathetic avenue of spindly silver birches. A similar fate has befallen Rackheath Hall; the main elevations have survived, but at the rear undistinguished suburban villas fill the old pleasure grounds and the remnants of the park are now scrub and rough grazing.

Conversion to multiple occupancy is not always a bad thing. Gunton Hall seemed utterly doomed when it came to the attention of Kit Martin, the doyen of splitting up a great house, in 1980. It had been the home of the Harbords, Lords Suffield, since the seventeenth century, but the agricultural depression and inheritance tax had left the last of the family to live there, Lady Doris Harbord, in a nearly ruined shell and occupying two rooms at the back of the house. The estate had shrunk from 20,000 acres (8,000 hectares) at its nineteenth-century peak to 100 acres (40. hectares) of park around the house.

The main rooms at the front of the house were burnt out after a fire in 1882 and never rebuilt.

Martin has cleverly reworked the sprawling eighteenth-century house into a series of still grand homes, utilising the well-proportioned rooms and Brettingham's and Wyatt's graceful elevations. The front two apartments are so generous in size and proportion that they seem large country houses in their own right. Further back towards the stables and kitchen yards, smaller houses have been created, the entire building being utilised. At the same time all subsidiary houses, including Park Farm where Martin himself lives, have been completely and brilliantly restored.

This project is signally different from Rackheath Hall: it has been done in such a way as to improve and preserve this important and outstanding grouping of buildings in their landscape and has not in any way compromised the integrity of the site. This may have been detrimental to the overall financial return on the development but visually leaves the estate unusually intact. With the significant help of the picture dealer Ivor Braka and Charles Harbord Hamond, son of the current Lord Suffield, 1,000 acres (40 hectares) of park have been reclaimed from arable farming. Hundreds of fallow, sika and red deer now graze the sward; in fact, the view of Gunton Hall from the road is a perfect eighteenth-century print.

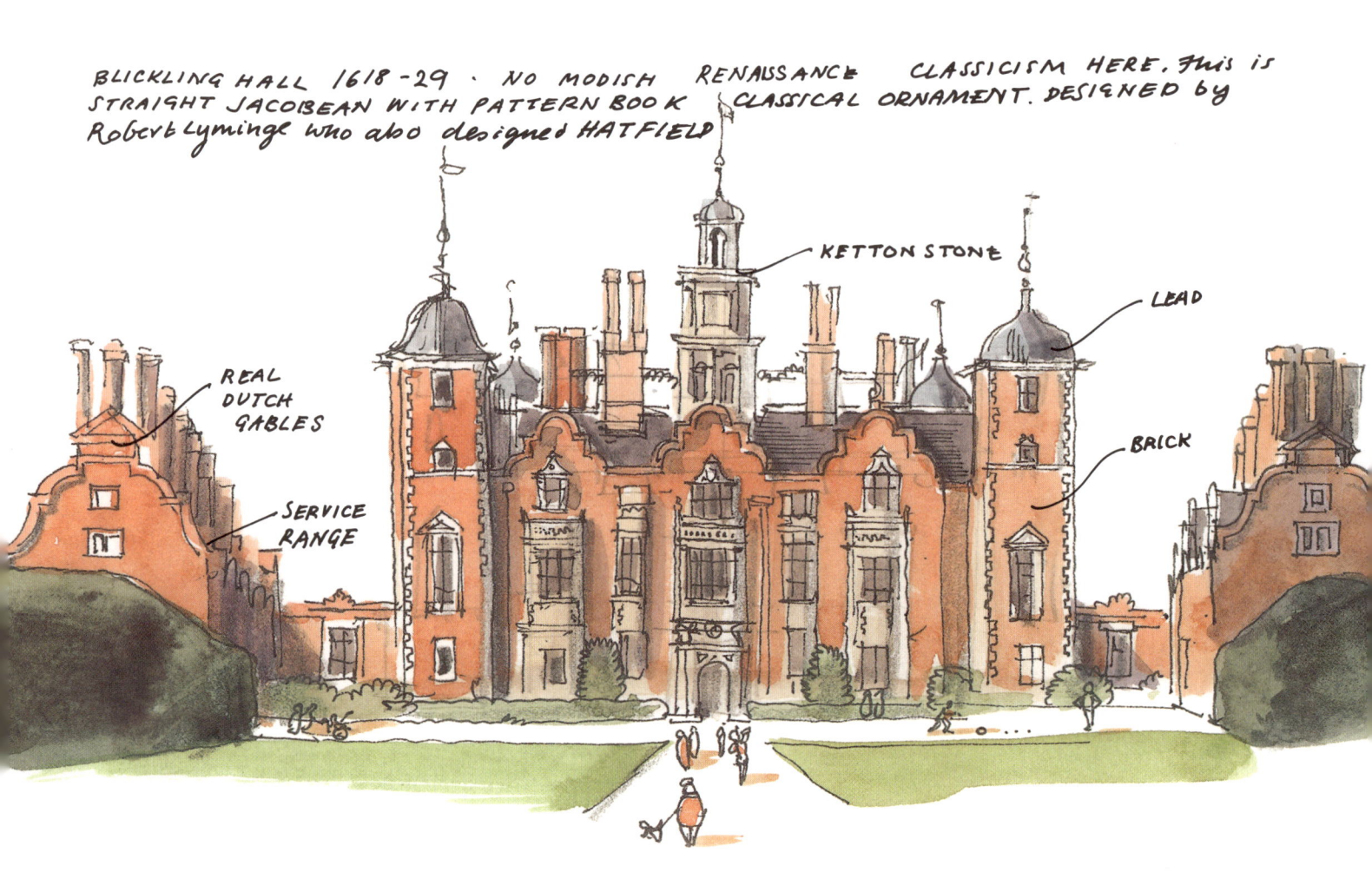

BLICKLING HALL 1618-29. NO MODISH RENAISSANCE CLASSICISM HERE. This is STRAIGHT JACOBEAN WITH PATTERN BOOK CLASSICAL ORNAMENT. DESIGNED BY Robert Lyminge who also designed HATFIELD

- KETTON STONE
- LEAD
- REAL DUTCH GABLES
- BRICK
- SERVICE RANGE

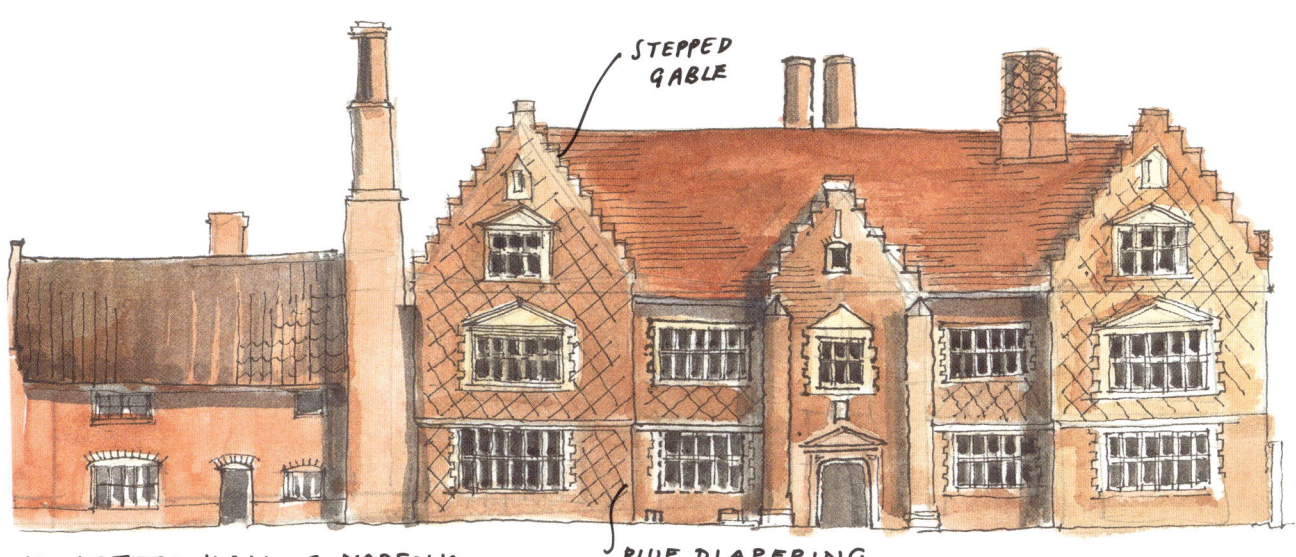

KIRKSTEAD HALL · S · NORFOLK
1614

STEPPED GABLE

BLUE DIAPERING

BARNINGHAM HALL built for Sir Edw PASTON in 1612 – A ROMANTIC PILE VISIBLE from ACROSS ITS PARK at MATLASKE · N. NORFOLK

BUILDING NORFOLK

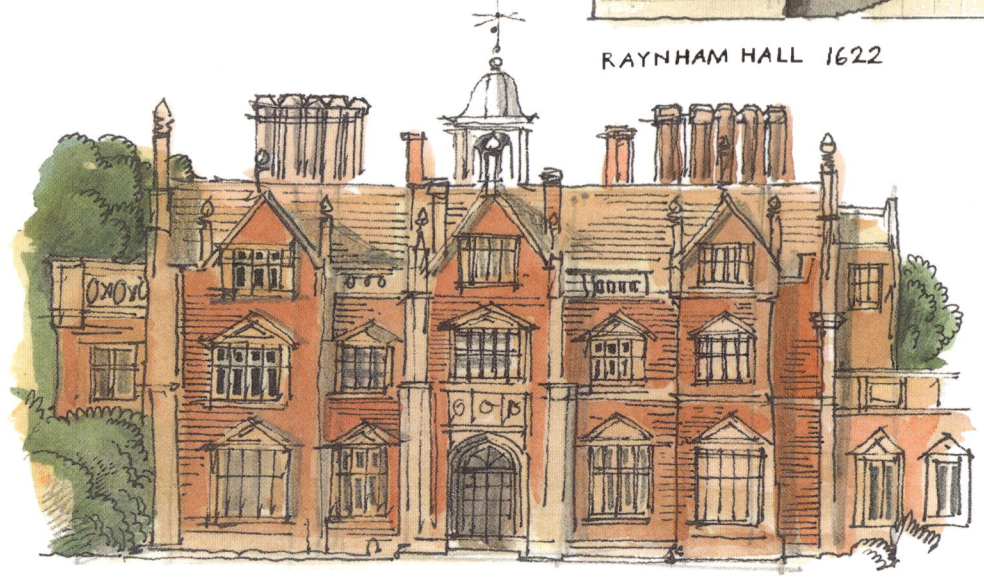

RAYNHAM HALL 1622

HEYDON HALL, a Perfect house in a Perfect LANDSCAPE 1581-4 BRICK with cemented Dressings..

MELTON CONSTABLE - is hidden in its Park. It is the only house illustrated in Kip's book of 1708. BUILT BY Sir JACOB ASTLEY after 1664 but is UNINHABITED. See it in the 1970 film of the GO BETWEEN decorated with JULIE CHRISTIE & ALAN BATES.. Its future is uncertain...

BUILDING NORFOLK

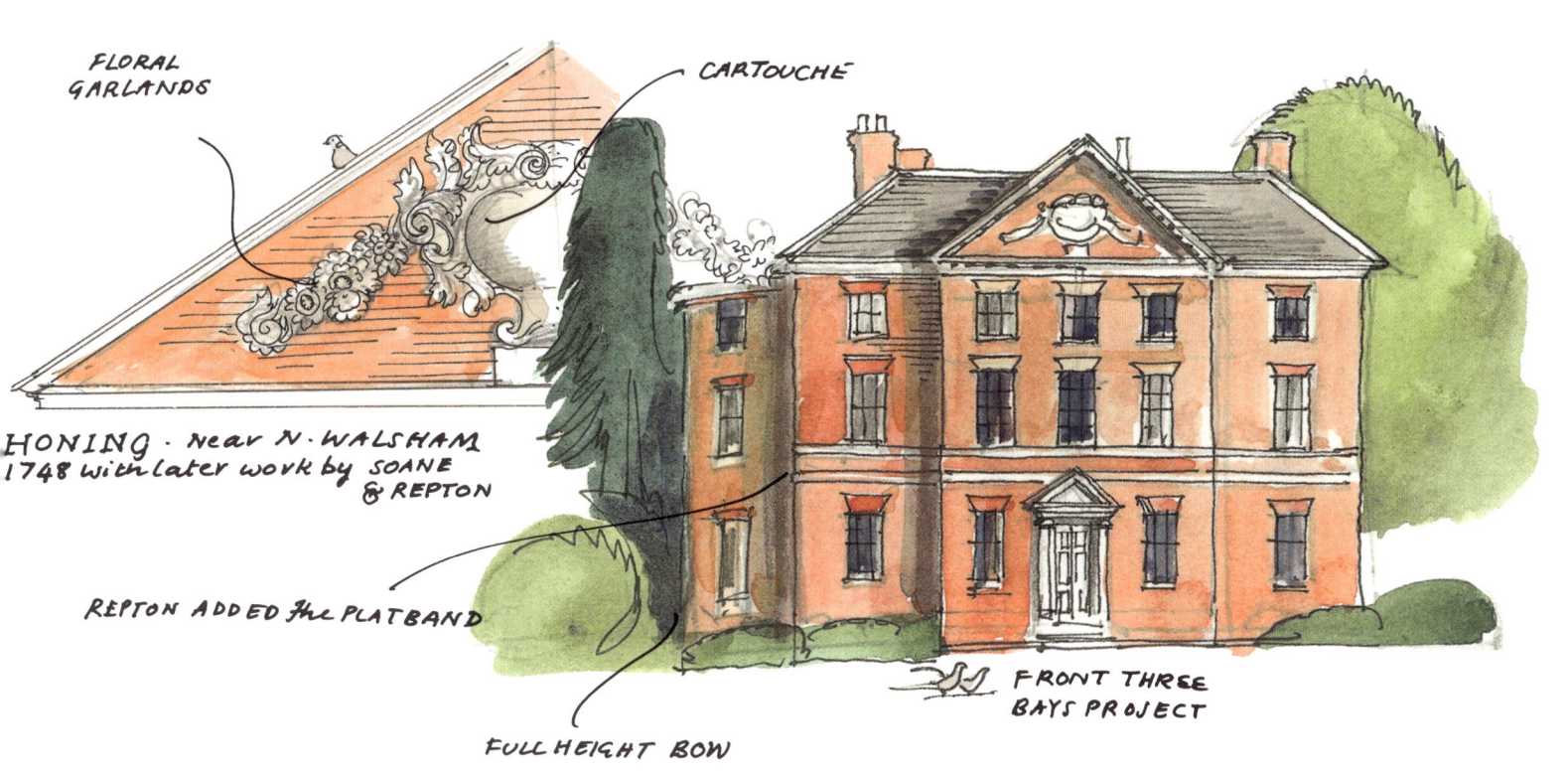

FLORAL GARLANDS

CARTOUCHE

HONING · near N. WALSHAM
1748 with later work by SOANE & REPTON

REPTON ADDED the PLATBAND

FULL HEIGHT BOW

FRONT THREE BAYS PROJECT

HIPPED ROOF with DORMERS

STONE QUOINS & DRESSINGS

ASHLAR (smooth square stone) faced ground floor

BUILDING NORFOLK

HERE ARE the BIG ONES.. HOUGHTON 1722 CAMPBELL, GIBBS & KENT
for Sir ROBERT WALPOLE. OPEN to the Public

- BALUSTRADE
- LANTERN
- DOMES (They are by J. GIBBS)
- YORKSHIRE STONE
- GIBBS WINDOW

STABLE BLOCK of HOUGHTON

HOLKHAM HALL. 1720s. built for THOMAS COKE & DESIGNED by him, WILLIAM KENT, Lord BURLINGTON & MATTHEW BRETTINGHAM
STONE LAID 1734..... COMPLETED 1761
(COKE DIED IN 1759)

KENT & COKE TOURED N. ITALY TOGETHER

- VENETIAN WINDOW

BUILDING NORFOLK

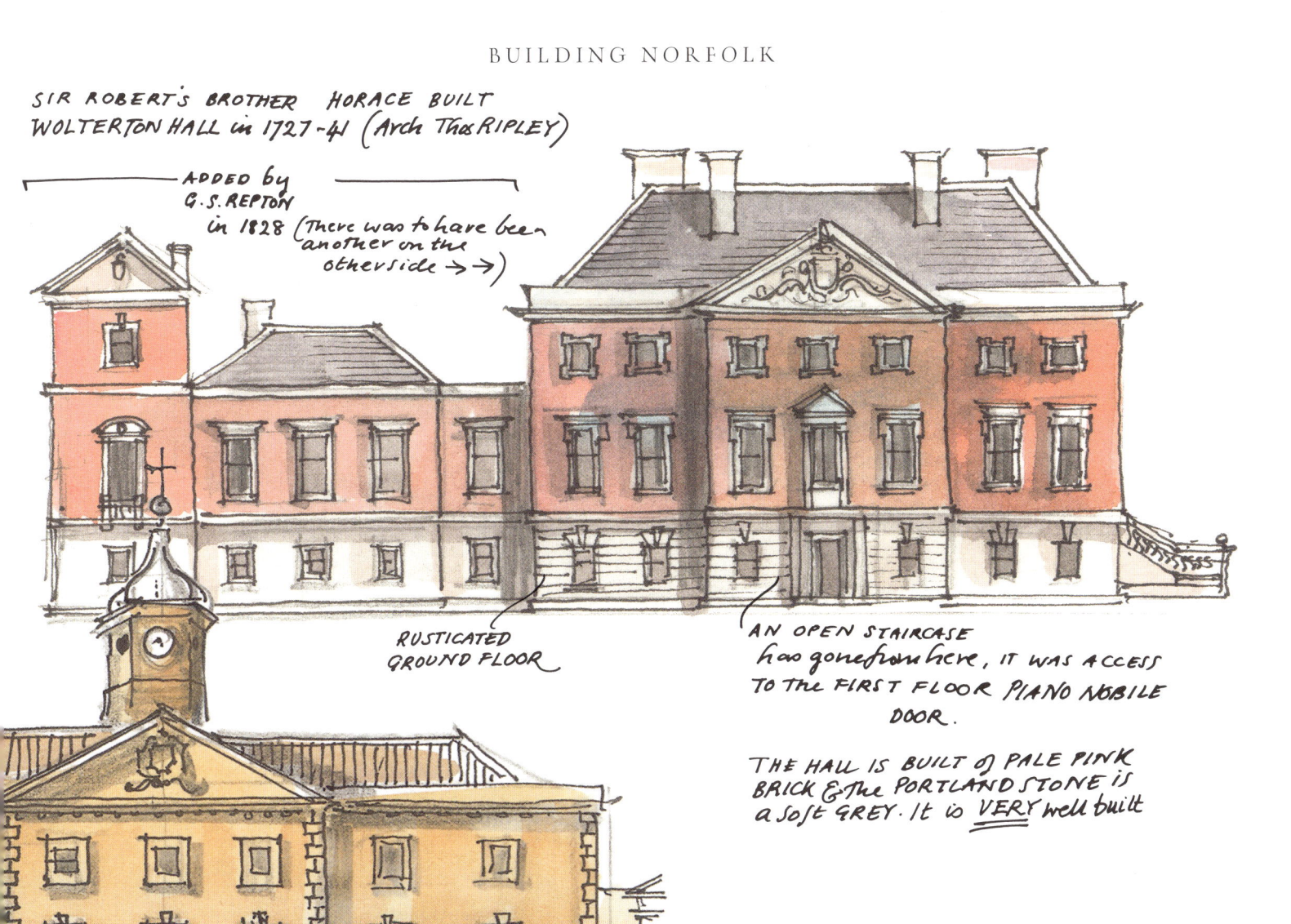

SIR ROBERT'S BROTHER HORACE BUILT
WOLTERTON HALL in 1727-41 (Arch Thos RIPLEY)

ADDED by G.S. REPTON in 1828 (There was to have been another on the other side →→)

RUSTICATED GROUND FLOOR

AN OPEN STAIRCASE has gone from here, it was access to the first floor PIANO NOBILE DOOR.

THE HALL IS BUILT OF PALE PINK BRICK & the PORTLAND STONE is a soft GREY. It is VERY well built

PEDIMENTED WINDOWS

RUSTICATED GROUND FLOOR

BUILDING NORFOLK

ABBEY HOUSE · LITTLE WALSINGHAM 1806-16 for Rev H. LEE-WARNER

REMAINS of DORMITORY of ABBEY

GUNTON PARK built for Sir Wm HARBORD & DESIGNED by MATTHEW BRETTINGHAM in 1742 later S+J. WYATT 1780-85

BUILDING NORFOLK

CROCKETED FINIAL
BATTLEMENTS

BEESTON ST LAWRENCE 1787. A GOTHICK BOX

WALLS of SQUARED KNAPPED FLINT

BOLD GRECIAN PORCH... This one has 4 great Columns not 5 like LETHERINGSET on PAGE 62..

1829/30

TOWERS C1740s

PAVILIONS - SALVIN 1840

The house below is BYLAUGH HALL 1849-52 Charles Barry Jun & Richardson BANKS. It is a BIT of a BEAST.. but POWERFUL & neo Elizabethan. see HIGHCLERE, the work of BARRY'S FATHER. IT IS BUILT of STONE over BRICK as the EXPOSED MASONRY in the GREAT HALL SHOWS..

GATE PIER at SENNOWE.

BUILDING NORFOLK

PORTE-COCHÈRE

SENNOWE HALL 1774 then DECIMUS BURTON 1855 but MOST SIGNIFICANTLY GEORGE SKIPPER 1908 built for Thos Cook, GRANDSON of Thos Cook The TRAVEL AGENT. The last Great House in NORFOLK

RESTLESS KEYSTONE

LOBED ARCHITRAVES

EDWARDIAN BAROQUE. - generous & good humoured

SHERINGHAM PARK 1812 · H·REPTON

8. ESTATE BUILDINGS

Norfolk, particularly the north-west of the county, is dominated by large estates. This is less so in the south and east, as previously discussed, as higher land values and proximity to Norwich established a pattern of smaller landholdings that has continued until the present day. The estate is the preserve of *polite* architecture not least because where there was an architect employed to work on the big house, there would be a likelihood of his involvement in smaller projects close to hand, such as lodges, gateways, stables, follies and other ancillary buildings.

Perhaps the most noticeable of these is the lodge. It has particular importance as it is the first indication to the observer of the presence of the great house and hence must set the tone. In some ways this is a reflection of the relationship between house and gatehouse in the sixteenth century, although these also contained living accommodation or at the least rooms for the use of visitors and in some cases for bailiffs or other officers of the house. These were often such a focus for architectural creativity that they became as important as the house itself: the gatehouse of East Barsham is bejewelled with niches. With octagonal piers and terracotta decoration throughout, it is as entrancing as the manor itself.

Lodges proper do not begin to appear before the advent of the Romantic park. Kip and Knyff's *Britannia Illustrata* (1708), the finely engraved survey of England's country houses in their landscapes, shows only one house in 'Norfolkshire' – Melton Constable – but in common with all the other houses it shows no lodges in the conventional form. Even the grandest palaces like Chatsworth in Derbyshire are approached by a gate in the park fence along a public road that was as yet undiverted and often close by the house. Perhaps the closeness to the public road meant that a lodge was unnecessary as the gates could be controlled from the house itself.

As the formal parterres and allées of the seventeenth and early eighteenth centuries were swept away in the search for the Romantic and more naturalistic parkland of Brown and Repton, so the lodge marking the beginning of the drive that would wind speciously but prettily through the timbered park grew in significance, until by the nineteenth century even large rectories or suburban villas might sport a pair. The unlodged Melton Constable was lavishly appointed in 1810 with lodges bearing muscular Doric pillars and pilasters and colossal urns on rusticated piers, while Gunton is approached through Samuel and William Wyatt's massive classical portico. Other approaches to this house are marked with more modest lodges, but strangest of all is the half-folly, half-lodge: an observatory tower where a triumphant Doric arch supports two substantial rooms beneath a soaring pinnacle visible for miles. Sir John Soane designed the austere and elegant lodges to Langley, one a neat Doric booth the other more elaborate and surmounted by two elegant greyhounds lying in state above the motto *toujours fidele*.

Not all lodges reflect the houses they announce. At Barningham, the vertiginous Jacobean façade of the Hall is at odds with the rather friendly South Lodge in Matlaske designed by John Adey Repton in 1807. This rather light-hearted cottage semi-orné with fretted bargeboards and Hansel and Gretel gingerbread thatch welcomes the visitor and makes the austere pinnacled block of the Hall all the more dramatic when turning the corner into the park. At Hillington, Donthorne's historicist Gothic lodges of 1824 refer to a house since demolished and rebuilt in modest Queen Anne style. They are built with regular, dark chocolate brown slips of carrstone, as are several other estate buildings in the village.

More utilitarian structures were also the subject of architectural attention. The sawmill at Gunton is in itself a gripping bit of early nineteenth-century engineering. It is water powered, the energy provided by manipulating the flow of water between two lakes in the park. It drives six large vertical blades that slowly but inexorably saw the butt of a tree into seven slices. This is occasionally set to work and is well worth watching. But the building of 1820, while of timber and thatch, is distinguished with a regular pediment under a thatched roof. More workaday architecturally but outstanding for its size and simplicity is the wood store at Melton Constable. Simple trusses support the roof over an aisled barn 160 feet (50 m) long with one unbroken pantiled roof. Is this Norfolk's longest tiled and uninterrupted roof? A later building, the estate office at Honing, is an exercise in solid good building. In the light of that office's status as headquarters for the management of over twenty estates at the turn of the nineteenth and twentieth centuries, perhaps this was a form of advertisement for the service they would offer. It still houses the drawing office responsible for the design of hundreds of estate buildings of that date.

Most noticeable of estate buildings are those devoted to agriculture, in some cases (as at Holkham) a business so serious that model farms were established to promulgate improved methods of farming. Those at Holkham were designed by Samuel Wyatt, architect of Windsor Castle. They are covered in the next chapter about farm buildings.

Follies, temples and summerhouses are a field much studied, no doubt due to their status as miniature masterpieces. The waterhouse at Holkham is a perfect parkland temple sitting on a rusticated pedestal, while Holkham's vine house (Wyatt, 1800) is restrained and elegant with a Soanesque shallow arch. Thomas Cook was one of the few to bring serious amounts of outside money into agriculturally depressed Norfolk in 1906. In commissioning George Skipper to remodel Decimus Burton's house, he created Norfolk's most exciting Edwardian building, but his work was not confined to the house and fine baroque stables. He also built a whimsical summerhouse at the head of the lake in a diluted Arts and Crafts style, and most charmingly a small open steading to house the nanny's donkey, now sadly uninhabited. All these buildings, along with architecturally distinctive walls, gate piers, farm buildings and the estate cottages that were built during the nineteenth century, are very important in characterising the Norfolk countryside. The standard of building changes for the better on large estates, both in actual quality of work and in levels of architectural sophistication. Estate ownership also promotes a stasis, a lack of dynamism and a level of inertia, and consequently (and occasionally unintentionally) a strong force of conservatism and conservation. It is among estate villages that the best protected pieces of the rural built environment can be found.

This is well represented in Heydon. This is a planned and formal estate village built around an older village green and a fine fourteenth- and fifteenth-century church. In the early nineteenth century a formula was arrived at to provide workers' housing, presumably to replace poorer quality earlier buildings. These cottages are mostly in pairs of terraces, and in the case of one group they are linked to form one highly articulated run of cottages. The centre bays are beneath brick pediments and under an imperforate pantile roof. All the elevations have at one time been limewashed, and the remnants of this soften the appearance of the brickwork. Beyond the green is a row of small cottages backing onto the churchyard; the rectory is hidden by holm oaks, and a fine pair of gates and the dower house, with crow step gables and Earle arms, complete the picture. While none of these are individually outstanding — although the pediment terraces are unusual and very pleasing — it is the completeness of the setting that is extraordinary. This is a completely preserved environment, and while it is now in outstanding condition the most remarkable thing about it is that nothing jars or lets down the whole. This must be a result of estate ownership, total control over all the buildings, and most importantly a stifling of individual improvements that in the last fifty years would have led to a riot of porches, garages, garden walls, conservatories and other inappropriate accretions that would inevitably have compromised the village architecturally.

Heydon is a 'closed' village: one with single ownership . This characterises it both architecturally and as a community. The closedness stifles entrepreneurism and the expression of individual aspirations. The town of Little Walsingham, in any case unique due to its being the continuing focus of pilgrimage, has shared some of this status. The institutional ownership of the centre of the town by the abbey, and subsequent to its suppression, by the Walsingham estate, has meant that it is the sole example of a settlement in North Norfolk whose buildings are mainly pre-eighteenth century. Similarly, the National Trust's ownership of the market place in Aylsham must be a significant reason for its survival as a pre-nineteenth-century setting.

More showy and also more variegated is the village at Holkham. Pevsner is predictably lemon lipped in the first edition of *The Buildings of England: North-West and South Norfolk*: 'The north gates are of c.1850 and unfortunately in the Tudor style.' But among the cool and wise moderation of Samuel Wyatt, the fantastical extremes of the more full-blown neo-Elizabethan is surely a welcome contrast. The Reading Room is an eccentric massing of turrets, cupolas and star-topped chimneys, applied half-timbering, jettying and elaborate woodwork. This could only be estate work, an exaggerated version of the profoundly unvernacular cottage style also used in the village green at Woodbastwick. The most confident homeowner would never have proposed or accepted such a baroque design, just as the heavily chamfered Swiss cottage woodwork on the crazy porches of the two cottages on the Kimberley estate could only be the work of an inspired architect let loose by a generous landowner. Contemporary owner-built cottages are, by contrast, insipid and quotidien or at the best plain.

Sandringham's cottages and estate buildings, almost all of which were rebuilt in the first thirty years of royal ownership, are resolutely thorough. Using a patriotic British style, hood moulds and restrained Tudor or Gothic detailing, the Prince of Wales, later Edward VII, created a Sandringham style that by utilising local materials — flint, carrstone of varying colours, brick and pantiles — paid more than lip-service to the vernacular while in no way reproducing the poor quality cottages that had gone before. Evidence of these previous houses is easy to see in the 1800 survey of the neighbouring Houghton estate, much of which now lies within the boundaries of Sandringham.

Less showy estate work is evidenced throughout the county, only differentiated from owner-built cottages by its regularity, repetition throughout a village or group of villages, and by a plaque or tablet stating the date and initials of the holder of the estate at the time. Drawings in the Honing estate office show a model simple brick and pantile cottage used there and on many of the estates managed from that brick office. It is pleasing, unassuming and, while designed with economy and longevity in mind, is nevertheless decent, well proportioned and, again mainly through use of easily available local materials, recognisably Norfolk in style or at any rate East Anglian.

This approach was continued in the early years of the twentieth century by local authorities. The immediately post-First World War years saw the acquisition of land by the county council to establish county smallholdings and farms, all of which were built in a similar modest style. Later housing acts, particularly in the late 1920s, gave rise to more council housing in villages, replacing what was seen as badly substandard rural housing. These are for the most part dull, 'anywhere' housing with drab rendered elevations and the council's initials and date on the front. Later pre- and post-war council housing tended to adopt a more agreeable watered-down Arts and Crafts design inspired by groundbreaking work at Letchworth Garden City, with hipped roofs and pantiles the only reminder of regional type. Here the local government takes on the role of estate owner, unimaginative but decent, and building houses that are decidedly larger than their modern housing association equivalents.

THE READING ROOM
HOLKHAM VILLAGE

LODGE to DONTHORN'S HILLINGTON HALL (Demolished) 1828. LODGE SURVIVES..

carrstone slips

Lodges to GUNTON PARK. Wyatt

BUILDING NORFOLK

THURTON LODGE · LANGLEY · SOANE 1784

CHURCH LODGE · MELTON CONSTABLE 1810

ANOTHER LODGE at GUNTON - ELABORATE USE of BRICK & FLINT & PICTURESQUE Thatch

BUILDING NORFOLK

COADESTONE OVAL PATERA

CARVED STONE DOG

VISITING DOG

CHEDGRAVE LODGE · LANGLEY Sir John SOANE 1784-90

ITALIANATE DECORATIONS

GIANT DORIC PILASTERS

OBSERVATORY TOWER 1830 · GUNTON PARK

BUILDING NORFOLK

TUSCAN COLUMNS

HANWORTH LODGE · S + W · WYATT — GUNTON PARK

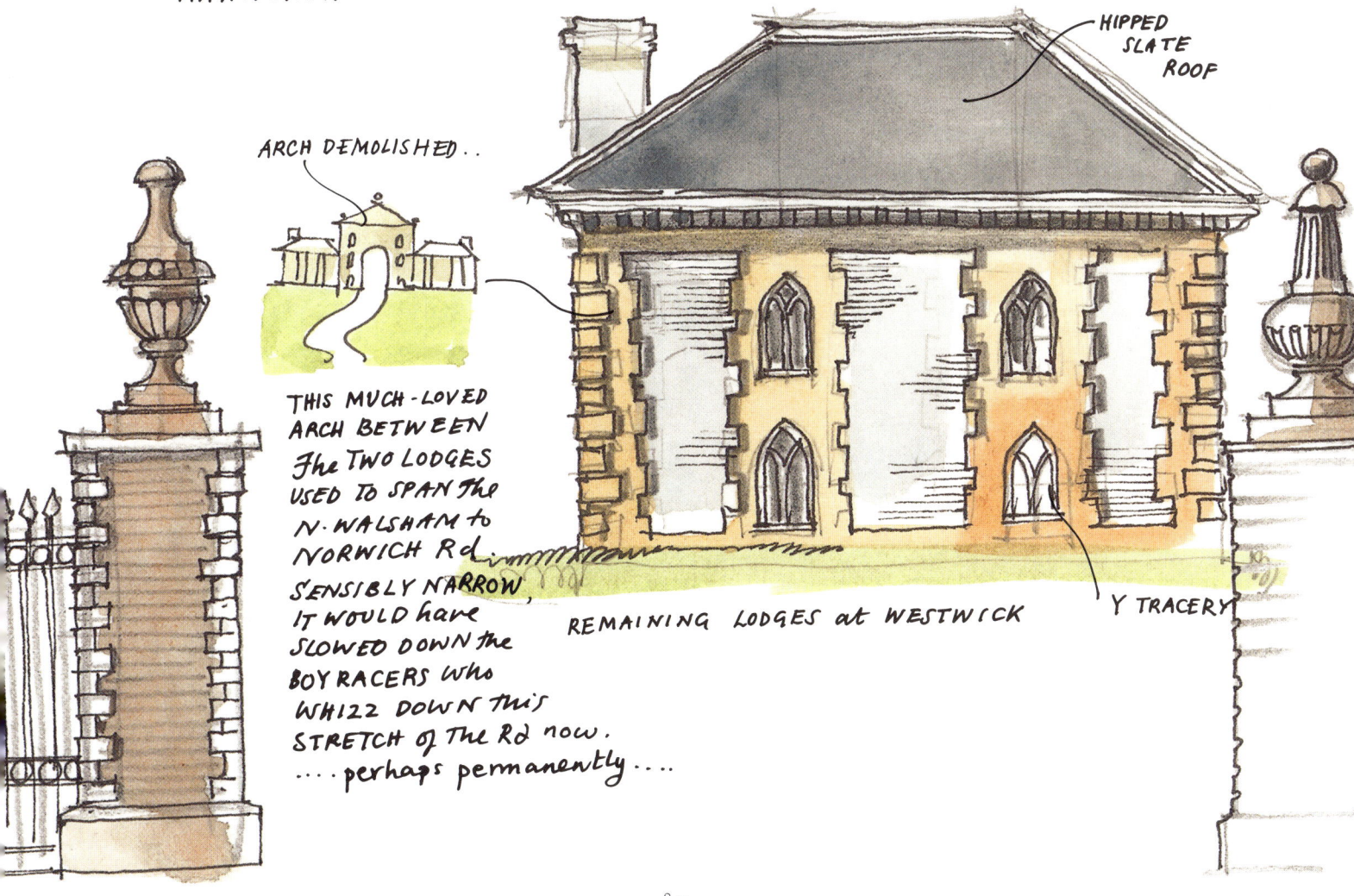

HIPPED SLATE ROOF

ARCH DEMOLISHED..

THIS MUCH-LOVED ARCH BETWEEN the TWO LODGES USED TO SPAN the N. WALSHAM to NORWICH Rd. SENSIBLY NARROW, IT WOULD have SLOWED DOWN the BOY RACERS who WHIZZ DOWN THIS STRETCH of THE Rd NOW.
....perhaps permanently....

REMAINING LODGES at WESTWICK

Y TRACERY

87

BUILDING NORFOLK

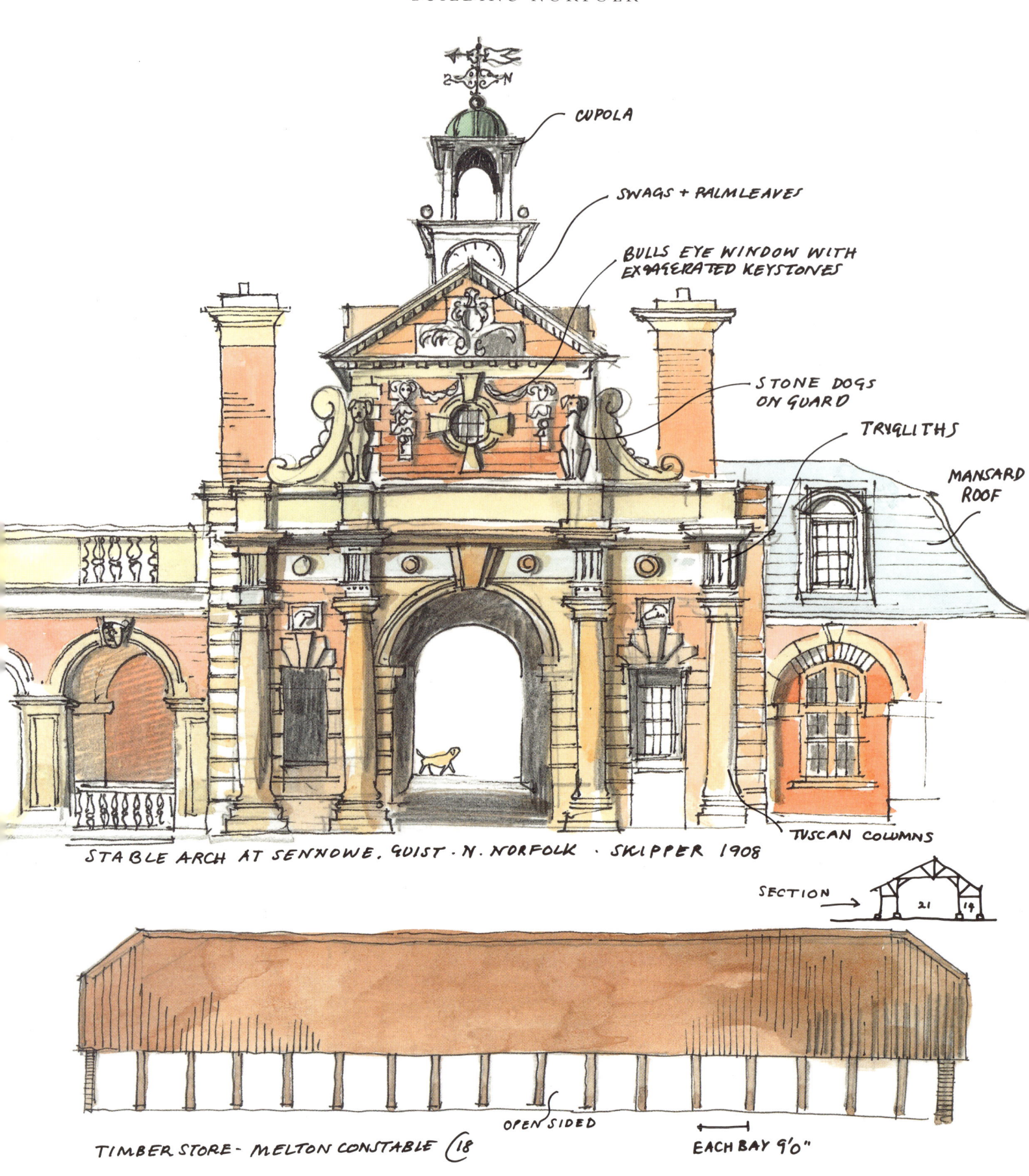

- CUPOLA
- SWAGS + PALM LEAVES
- BULLS EYE WINDOW WITH EXAGGERATED KEYSTONES
- STONE DOGS ON GUARD
- TRYGLITHS
- MANSARD ROOF
- TUSCAN COLUMNS

STABLE ARCH AT SENNOWE · GUIST · N. NORFOLK · SKIPPER 1908

SECTION

TIMBER STORE - MELTON CONSTABLE C18

OPEN SIDED

EACH BAY 9'0"

88

BUILDING NORFOLK

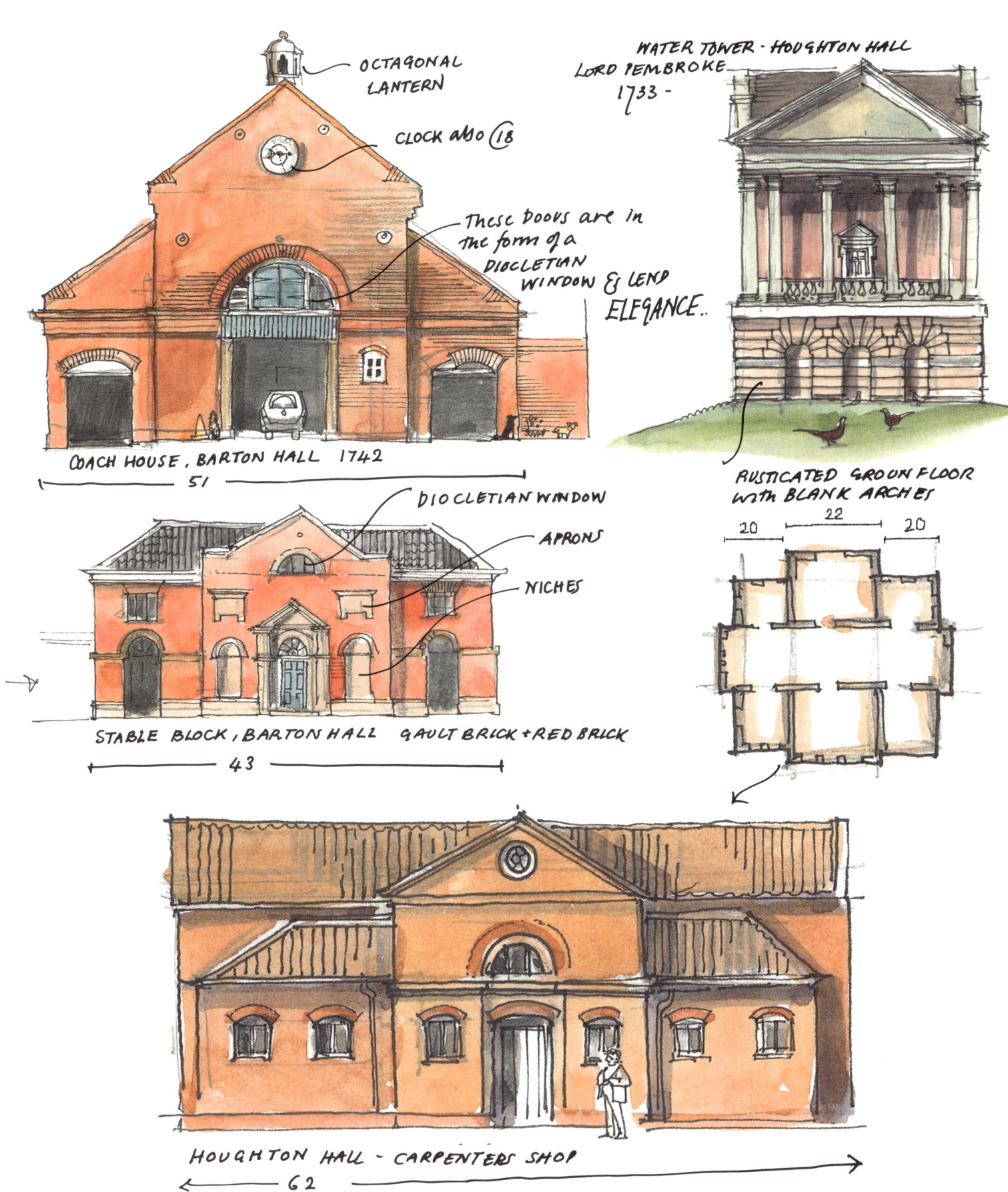

Coach House, Barton Hall 1742 — 51
- OCTAGONAL LANTERN
- CLOCK also C18
- These doors are in the form of a DIOCLETIAN WINDOW & lend ELEGANCE..

Water Tower - Houghton Hall, Lord Pembroke 1733 -
- RUSTICATED GROUND FLOOR with BLANK ARCHES

Stable Block, Barton Hall — Gault Brick + Red Brick — 43
- DIOCLETIAN WINDOW
- APRONS
- NICHES

20 · 22 · 20

Houghton Hall - Carpenters Shop — 62

89

BUILDING NORFOLK

CLOCK TOWER HEYDON

CLOCKTOWER AT GUIST ERECTED TO CELEBRATE THE SILVER JUBILEE OF GEORGE V in 1935

GATE PIER @ SENNOWE 1905

BOAT HOUSE 1910 AT SENNOWE GUIST. carved on a beam..
"this is your home. look for no other"

BOAT HOUSE
GONTON PARK
2002
built on old footings
as an ARTIST'S
STUDIO ~ it has a view
of the 40 acre GREAT WATER

BUILDING NORFOLK

STABLES at MODEL FARM · WYATT 1792   HOLKHAM

HIPPED OUTSHUTS

BRITAINS BEST BARN, the GREAT BARN, HOLKHAM HALL. WY

LUNETTES

BUILDING NORFOLK

CLASSICAL DETAILING

DOORS TO THRESHING FLOORS

1790 · GRAND & AUSTERE with RESTRAINED & MUSCULAR DECORATION

BUILDING NORFOLK

ORANGERY at LETHERINGSETT HALL   N. NORFOLK
This has just been re-constructed from a complete ruin

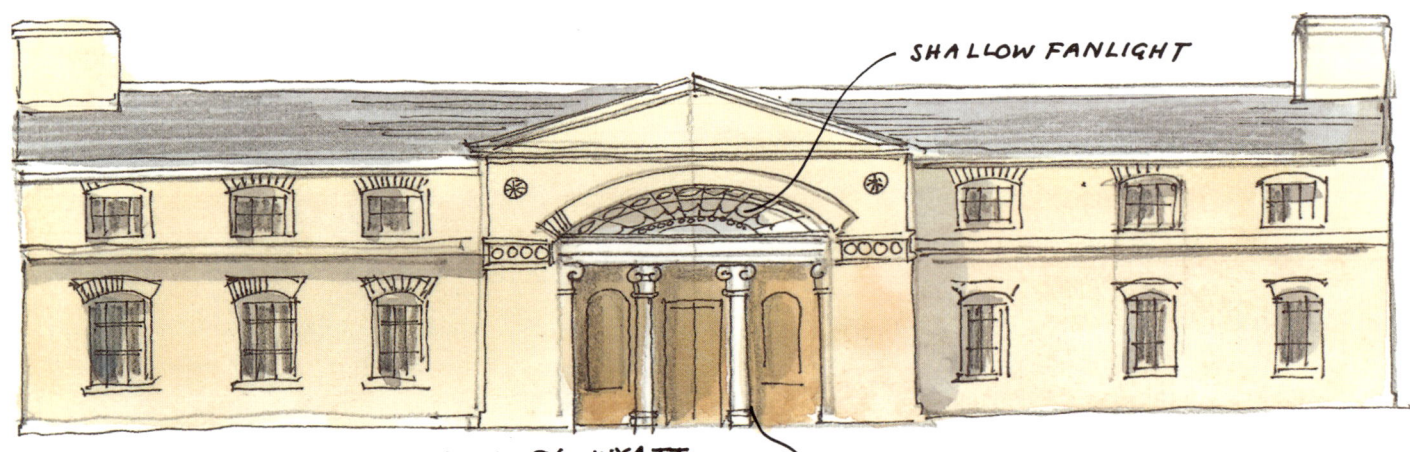

VINE HOUSE · HOLKHAM   1782-84 WYATT
SHALLOW FANLIGHT
IONIC PORTICO IN ANTIS

HONING ESTATE OFFICE 1880

BUILDING NORFOLK

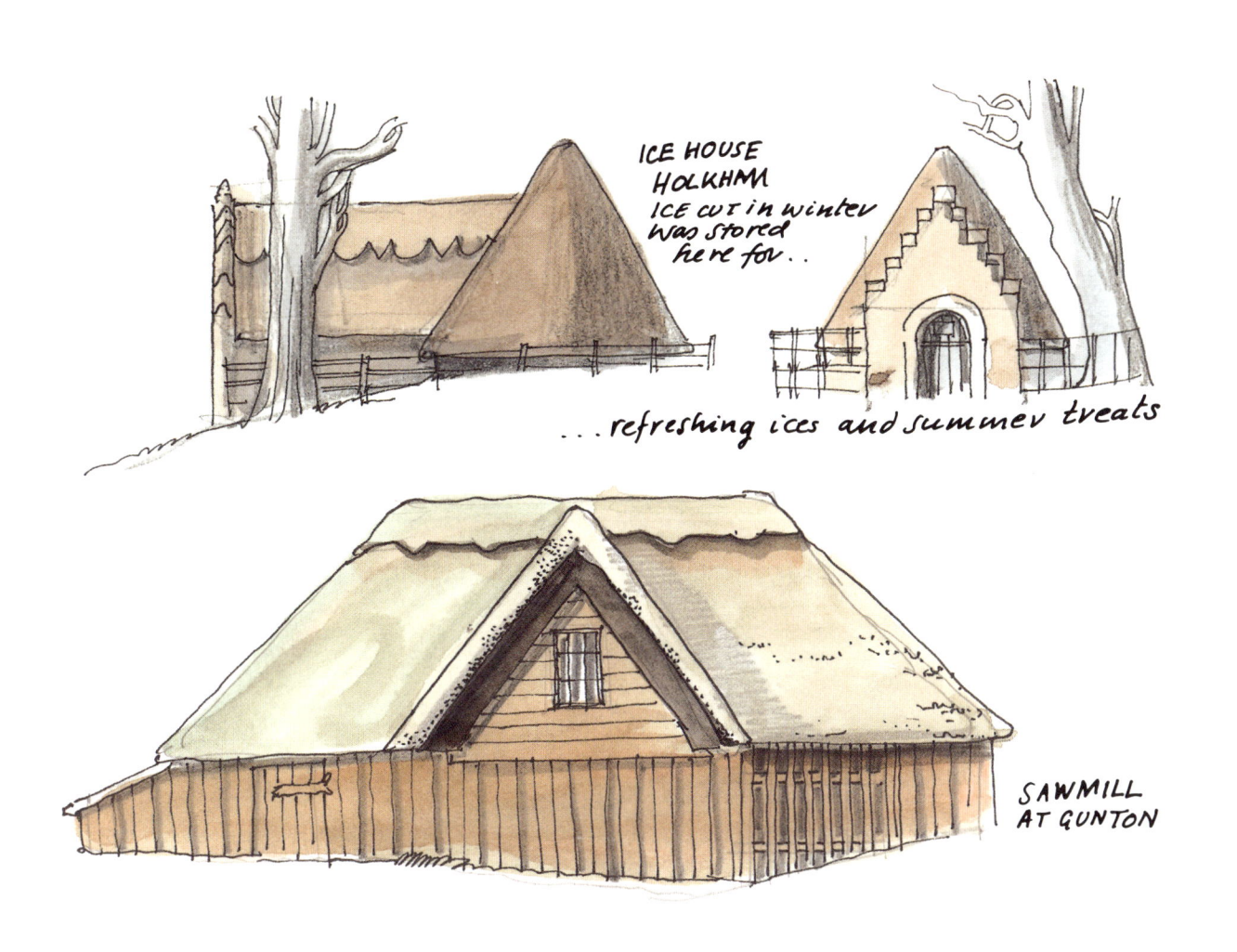

ICE HOUSE
HOLKHAM
Ice cut in winter
was stored
here for...

...refreshing ices and summer treats

SAWMILL
AT GUNTON

LARDER @ KENNELS at SENNOWE

95

BUILDING NORFOLK

GUIST POST OFFICE 1914 · SKIPPER

SHAPED GABLE, HERE IS CENTRE TO SHOP ELSEWHERE LINKS A PAIR OF COTTAGES

THESE MANNERED & COMPLEX GABLES and the EXAGGERATED PLAT BAND are A SOPHISTICATED INTERPRETATION of the VERNACULAR. EACH HOUSE IS SLIGHTLY DIFFERENT. THE POST OFFICE IS PARTICULARLY FINE WITH ITS CROWSTEPPED GABLE AND BOLD CHIMNEY STACKS. THE HEAVY BRICK EAVES ARE A FEATURE that LINKS all these BUILDINGS

HEYDON · ESTATE COTTAGES/SHOPS EARLY C19

JOLLY GOOD DOORWAY

BUILDING NORFOLK

WYATT LODGE at HOLKHAM 1821

ESTATE COTTAGES at WOODBASTWICK

COTTAGES AT SANDRINGHAM POST 1865

ORNATE LATE VICTORIAN PORCHES AT KIMBERLEY.

97

9. BARNS AND FARM BUILDINGS

The farm buildings of an area are a reflection of the value and type of agriculture practised in it. Norfolk has strong arable traditions, and although it has also produced milk, meat and, on the poorer heathland, wool, cereals have been its staple crop since Saxon times. This emphasis has affected its farm buildings, which are grander and more extensive than those of livestock rearing areas further west and north due to the large amount of machinery required for improved arable farming: drills, ploughs, harrows, cultivators and many tumbrils, the ubiquitous two-wheeled carts that moved dung, sugar beet and fodder from field to clamp or barn and vice versa. In 1950 there were a dozen tumbrils at Manor Farm, Worstead. Haywains and straw carts and flat-bedded trolleys completed the substantial vehicle count, all of which needed to be stored under cover. With these came the horses. There were also 22 cart-horses (Shires and Suffolk Punches) in their stables in 1955, which in turn necessitated tack rooms to keep and care for all the harness and storage above for feed. Finally, there were bullock yards and dairy buildings, the first open-fronted supported with oak posts, the second with stalls for each individual milk cow.

As farming has changed – first in the eighteenth-century Agricultural Revolution and later through the rich 'high farming' years of 1840–75 and yet again in the post-1945 intensification of agriculture – these buildings have been through many conversions. As mixed farming has become increasingly uncommon, many of the lesser buildings have simply fallen into disrepair and been demolished, along with countless labourers' cottages that housed the farm workers whose jobs have also disappeared during these changes. Wolterton estate employed 26 people on 2,000 acres (800 hectares) in 1970 and now employs 6. Worstead, a farm of a similar size, has dropped from 23 to 6.

The sale particulars of Matlaske Hall from 1951 give a clear snapshot of the built components of a typical farm of the time. It was 366 acres (140 hectares), more than twice the then national average, and was a mixed farm, stock and arable. It comprised:

'fine large barn with partly boarded floor, two loose boxes, three loose boxes, warm sheltered cattle yard with eight-bay open shed and two loose boxes. Cart-horse stable and loft over, seven-bay cart shed and tractor house. Cattle yard and four cattle boxes and four-bay open shed, a range of sixteen deep bullock boxes with central passage and bings [these were feeding troughs supplied centrally by chute], turnip house, meal house, cattle yard with four boxes and six-bay open shed and a large barn.'

Earlier sale particulars from 1923, a period in which a huge amount of Norfolk changed hands due to death duties incurred from the First World War, show another two yards, subsequently demolished to make way for a Second World War airfield. These contained yet another eight boxes, yards, turnip and meal houses, and large barns.

In 2007 the picture is very different. Matlaske Hall is now part of a much larger and viable holding of 2,000 acres (800 hectares). The headquarters is on another farm three miles away. All but two barns and a small range of stables are gone. A farm labourer who still works on the land remembers demolishing the rest of the farmyard forty years ago. The best barn is illustrated below; it was built in 1770, perhaps an indication of the date of some of the other buildings. It is redundant but in good condition. The other barn is now a house and a cabinet making workshop. This record illustrates the number of traditional buildings that have disappeared from the county in the last fifty years.

Even the great threshing barns were made redundant — indeed earlier than most other buildings. These were noble buildings: the largest in each farm had large double doors in the front with corresponding but much smaller ones at the rear. This was to effect a strong through draught to winnow the corn, which had been stored in bulk with its straw in the lofts on either side, being threshed by hand with flails on the chalk or stone floor. This task took up many wet winter days. However, the invention of the threshing machine in 1810 totally changed this process. Corn was kept stacked in thatched ricks outside, awaiting the arrival of the thresher. This was a large machine, driven by steam, in one end of which sheaves of corn were introduced. At the other the clean grains of corn could be fed into sacks and stored. The great doors and floor became redundant, and these barns were internally adjusted to suit other purposes, such as the storage of corn or machinery or the winter housing of animals.

Some of the larger barns have been converted to house grain-dryers, but increasingly they are deemed inconvenient as tractors and equipment become even larger and farming practice becomes less varied, so non-agricultural uses are sought for them by their owners. Furthermore, as smaller holdings have been consolidated — the average holding in 1930 was 128 acres (52 hectares) while it is now 700 (283) — whole yards have fallen in disuse and seek a new purpose.

Early barns are timber framed. The black boards of the barn at Shottesham clothe an outstanding fifteenth-century oak frame with a wonderful set of reducing braces, the lowest pair broad and muscular. This is well worth looking at, though not signposted. A farm employee proudly showed us around a building on which English Heritage has rightly lavished a lot of money. Not far away near Long Stratton is a similar building, although this time not subject to the same degree of restoration and the frame more compromised with later additions. The barn at Baconsthorpe Castle is seventeenth century, was originally twice as long, and formed part of a complex of buildings around the castle, possibly with a matching barn opposite. With its strong buttresses there is something monastic-looking about this barn.

The barn at Matlaske already described was built in a time of agricultural prosperity during the first phase of the Agricultural Revolution. Its high building quality reflects this, and although it is a barn its fine proportions and graceful lines mark it as being very much a building of its period.

The model farm was a phenomenon of the late eighteenth and nineteenth centuries. Landowners were caught up in a powerful move to improve their estates. As most farms, once enclosed, were then let to tenants, it was through enhanced rents that these improvements would best be felt by the proprietor. High rents required the very best tenants, themselves entrepreneurs and farmers who were fully committed to the new agriculture. Attracting these desirable agriculturists required inducements, and while fine farmhouses might encourage marital pressure to take on a tenancy, it was farm buildings that would clinch the deal. So began wholesale improvements of barns and yards adhering to designs best suited to the new ways. These changes were principally taking place in arable country on the east coast of England and in the Borders. In Norfolk Holkham led the way.

Thomas Coke was the owner of the Holkham estate, and his life was given over to improving agriculture.

England's burgeoning population needed to be fed, and Coke wanted to produce more of that food. He was concerned not only with improving arable yields by rigid adhering to crop-rotation systems and marling (adding highly alkaline chalky clay to land to counteract acidity), but also with producing better farm animals. The poor Norfolk cattle were crossed with the larger and better made Devon bulls, while the native sheep, the rather lanky but tough Norfolk Horn, benefited from an infusion of robust but meaty Southdowns. Coke held land in hand, a home farm on which to experiment and demonstrate on his own terms some of these improvements. These demonstrations became the famous 'Shearings', proto-agricultural shows drawing attendees from all over the county, country and indeed beyond. Prizes and cups were awarded for varying classes of beast, crop or achievement: greatest number of watermeadow created, fattest wether (a castrated male) of the Leicester sheep breed, or greatest number of horses fed by swedes. These last were a crop introduced by Coke.

The centrepieces for these shows were the Great Barn and later the model farmyard at Longlands Farm. These buildings are far more architecturally sophisticated than the Matlaske barn. They are classical and echo Palladio's own agricultural work on the Brenta villas of the Venetian nobility in the sixteenth century. There, the high priest of neo-classical architecture had not only worked on the pleasure domes of wealthy aristocratic patrons, but as they were gripped by an interest in farming, he had also designed granaries and barns, often attached to the villa itself. At the Villa Emo at Fanzolo near Castelfranco del Veneto, the central three bays of this elegant villa are in fact a threshing floor surprisingly frescoed by Giambattista Zelotti in 1559 with a series of murals on the seasons featuring the first depictions of maize, recently imported from the New World and no doubt the height of modernity at the time. A ramp leads to the central doorway, on a gradient so shallow that carts bearing grain could easily be driven up them.whether corn was actually trundled into Palladio's fresco'd Sala is unknown but the implication is clear ; this is a building on a farm. Granaries stretch out in both directions, the building only furnishing accommodation when two towers on either end are reached. Despite serving two functions, farm building and great house, the villa is one grand architectural statement, a fusion of palace and farm.

Holkham's Great Barn is a classical temple to agriculture. With pediment, Diocletian windows, pilasters and an elegant cornice, this is as polite as architecture gets while retaining a muscularity appropriate to a farm building. The granary at Longlands Farm on the Holkham estate also pays homage to the Palladian villas. In this case the whole building stands elevated on a forest of Tuscan columns with a central pavilion with rather Italianate eaves — surely Britain's grandest granary?

The building of farmyards continued, and throughout the 'high farming' years there was a continuous process of improvement as agricultural incomes grew, fuelled by the rising demand for food from England's growing population both in the increasingly industrialised North and in the metropolis. This boom crashed in 1874, when the American railways linked the corn-growing prairies with the exporting ports of the east coast and cheap American corn began to be landed by the thousand tonne in Liverpool, Glasgow and Milford Haven. Low production costs in the Midwest and ease of transport undercut British prices, and it became increasingly uneconomic to grow wheat here. Land fell out of production and the emphasis drifted to livestock, but soon this too fell foul of imports as the development of refrigerated transport brought Australian, New Zealand and American meat within reach of British markets. There was still farm building during this depression but at much reduced levels.

Although the great days of the Edwardian shooting parties were still to come, as were many large houses built to accommodate their participants, the late nineteenth and early twentieth centuries actually saw the dismantling of many of the large estates built up in the previous two centuries. Farm building continued during this later period but did not reflect any viable return on investment, rather a *folie de grandeur* on the part of new money coming into the countryside.

The introduction of death duties, exacerbated by the losses in the First World War which caused some families to lose two or more sons in that four-year period, further diminished estates, as did the vindictive nature of the Liberal and later Labour governments' attitudes to landowning in the first half of the twentieth century. Holkham shrunk from 42,000 acres to 22,000 (17,000 hectares to 9,000) and Gunton from 12,000 to 1,000 (5,000 to 400). In 1925 half of the land in the county was said to be for sale.

The days of the model farm, in fact of any significant farm building, were over, and until the intensification of agriculture following the Second World War the great barns, stockyards and granaries gradually fell into disrepair. R. W. Ketton-Cremer, in his very personal and revealing history of Felbrigg, describes the tatty condition of the farms and houses on that estate when he inherited it from his father in 1922. Fields were undrained, woods unthinned; in fact, frequently farms were unable to find tenants at all.

In the 1920s and 1930s – during the period of greatest agricultural depression – there was an influx of farmers from outside the county purchasing land en masse. Opportunistic farmers arrived from the east of Scotland: Patersons, Cargills, Alstons and Neills, who were to control large areas of Norfolk.

Similarly, farmers from land-poor Holland arrived. The company Anglo-Dutch Farming erected several barns like the one in Foulsham. These were a totally new shape, foreign to Norfolk, tall and with an uninterrupted span. Despite being built in the early 1950s these are all still in use today. The same cannot be said of other pre-1970s buildings, all of which are just too small for today's tractors and farming techniques.

The change in the scale of agriculture has left a huge number of redundant buildings. While many were demolished plenty more survive, and as property prices have risen so has their viability as subjects for conversion. Hundreds have been transformed into houses with varying levels of success. I will cover this later in the book. But it seems likely that over the next twenty years almost all the remaining traditional farm buildings will need to find new uses.

BARN AT HOUGHTON

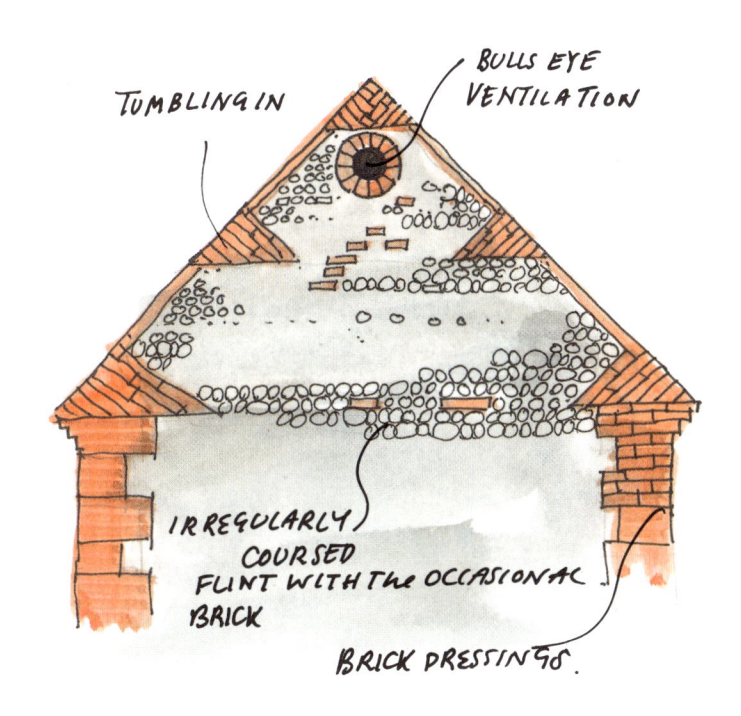

- BULLS EYE VENTILATION
- TUMBLING IN
- IRREGULARLY COURSED FLINT WITH THE OCCASIONAL BRICK
- BRICK DRESSINGS

BUILDING NORFOLK

HOUGHTON

BARN & CART SHEDS at QUIDENHAM

ALBERMARLE ARMS & DATE 1906

CLAY INFIL IN TIMBER FRAME

C16 NEAR LONG STRATTON

102

BUILDING NORFOLK

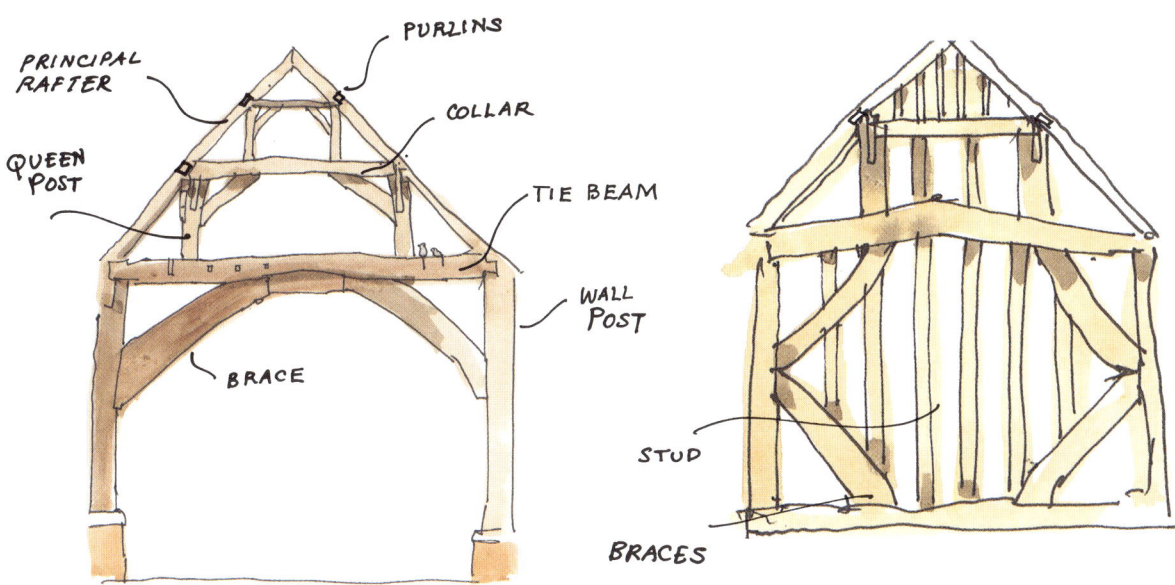

BARN at SHOTTESHAM

PRINCIPAL RAFTER
PURLINS
COLLAR
QUEEN POST
TIE BEAM
WALL POST
BRACE
STUD
BRACES

MATLASKE HALL BARN 1790

103

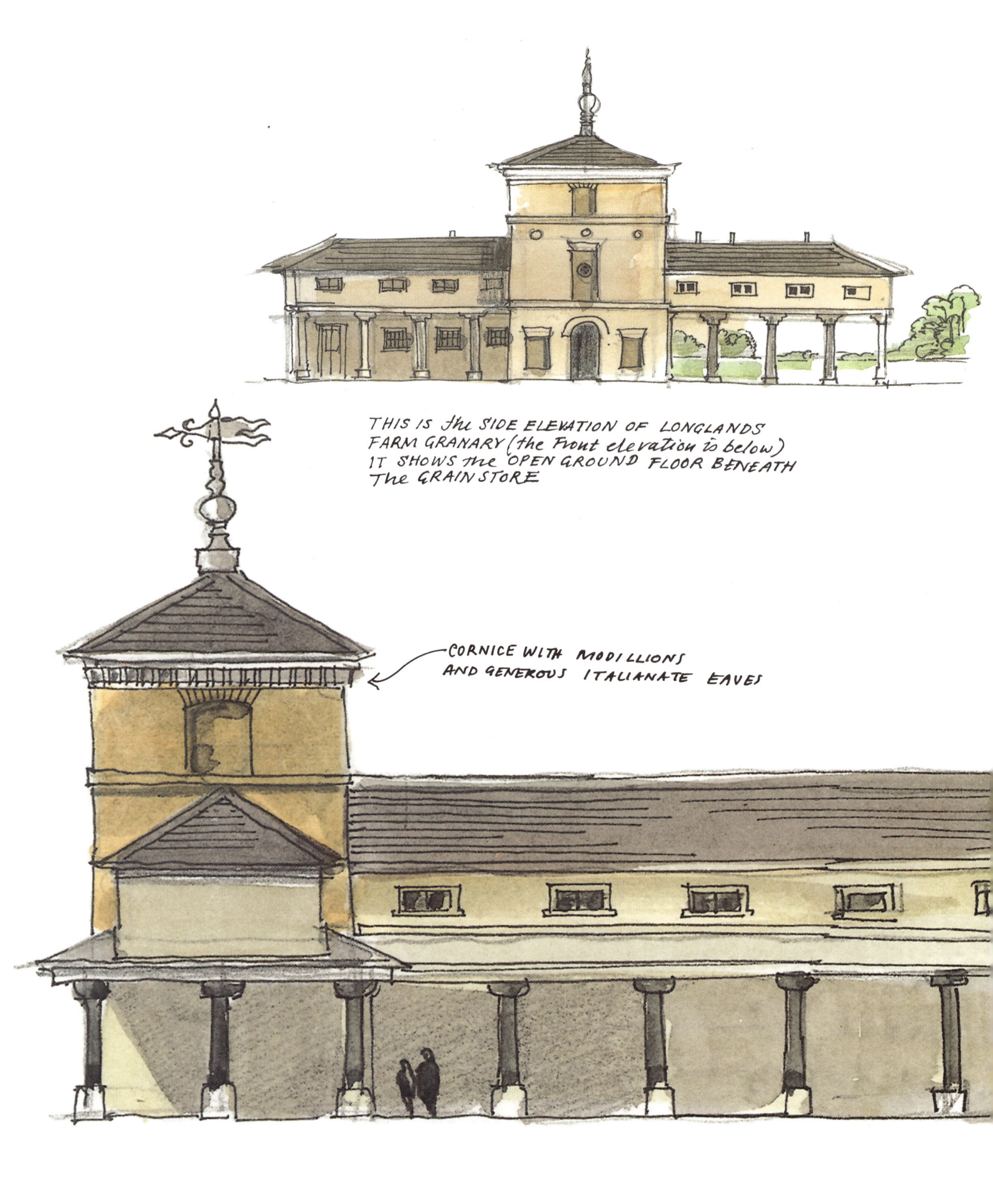

THIS IS the SIDE ELEVATION OF LONGLANDS FARM GRANARY (the Front elevation is below) IT SHOWS the OPEN GROUND FLOOR BENEATH THE GRAIN STORE

CORNICE WITH MODILLIONS AND GENEROUS ITALIANATE EAVES

BUILDING NORFOLK

J. WYATT 1795 BARN AT LONGLANDS FARM HOLKHAM

CLOCK IN GABLE

G.A. DEAN 1860 — THE GRANARY AT LONGLANDS FARM · HOLKHAM
ALSO DESIGNED the BARNS at MODEL FARM & in 1898 PUBLISHED A VOLUME of COUNTRY HOUSE · LODGE & FARM DESIGNS

105

BUILDING NORFOLK

THIS RANGE OF BARNS at BRANTHILL FARM

BULLOCK YARD at SANDRINGHAM — BUILT TO A HIGH STANDARD UNLIKE CONTEMPORARY ISOLATED RANGES OF BUILDINGS

SHED @ SIDESTRAND OF SUCH HIGH BUILDING STANDARDS + UNSHOWY but FAULTLESS DESIGN .... IS IT LUTYENS?

COLTISHALL & DATED 1756

BUILDING NORFOLK

CASTLE FARM · BACONSTHORPE (17) WAS THATCHED (WAS ONCE TWICE AS LONG)

HOUGHTON

This is the BARN Referred to on page 101 and of DUTCH Design. It is CLEARLY DIFFERENT from its CONTEMPORARIES WITH SINGULAR PITCH & SPAN

← 84' →

10. ALMSHOUSES

Almshouses are a class of building on their own. They are the tiniest of cottages, in fact sometimes so small that even the most modest pensioner's needs cannot be met and the internal divisions need to be replanned. However, architecturally they are often of great significance, the focus of a lot of decorative attention and used as a vehicle for visible expenditure. In post-Reformation England there was a need for a new channel for charitable expenditure in the absence of the guilds, chantries and other ecclesiastical institutions that had previously served this purpose. Almshouses suited this admirably. They were conspicuous, in the heart of the community, and thus clear of any suspicion of popishness, and capable of supporting large and beautifully modelled shields, escutcheons or plaques bearing the name and hagiographic description of the donor coupled with noble sentiments favouring abstinance and general decent behaviour among the fortunate inmates. Almshouses were built in Holkham village in 1757 and were endowed with income from some agricultural land. These were to house up to thirteen pensioners. In 1848 they were restored by the great gloomy gothicist S. S. Teulon.

Almshouses, although not necessarily connected with a specific church or chapel, often wear semi-ecclesiastical vestments. The Beetley almshouses of 1838 are in a nondescript British style, hood moulds and two centred arches in Tudor porches beneath a patterned slate roof, the only local feature a pair of stepped gables, a nod to the vernacular. At Meeting Hill, Worstead, the restrained terrace of cottages is clearly of a piece with the Baptist chapel of 1829 and its manse. Strangely, Pevsner, even in the 1997 edition, does not dwell on this extraordinary grouping, a Nonconformist settlement apart from the village dominated, even loomed over, by its massive Perpendicular cathedral of a church. Nearly 200 years later the buildings remain — they are visually intact as no major alterations have taken place — but this brave Baptist world has not materialised; the almshouses have been sold off, as has the manse, and the school is derelict. Thirty years ago children from Worstead went to the Baptist Sunday school, collected by Mr Roper in a mini-bus, but perhaps that was the last gasp of Nonconformist utopianism. It is now only a shell.

Earlier and more architecturally elevated is the Fisherman's Hospital in Great Yarmouth. This was not a private institution but paid for by the corporation of Yarmouth in 1702. It is reminiscent of the Seamen's Hospital in Mile End Road in London, a gracious courtyard and central portico with hexagonal lantern above. On either wing is a Dutch gable and, above, very decorative dormers with swooping bargeboards. Visually there is a very strong Dutch connection here both in design and in the high quality of the building. Amsterdam has a great tradition of almshouses. They are called 'hofjes' and are found throughout the city. I have shown one here with the rather unlikely symbol of a turnip over the door. Inside the gate is a very small yard with houses round it. These small courts of almshouses were established by successful merchants and vary terrifically in size, some being as large as a modest Oxford college quad while others comprise no more than six cottages.

The Howard almshouses at Castle Rising were built in 1614. They were founded by the Duke of Norfolk's younger brother, the Earl of Northampton, who also founded almshouses at Clun and in Greenwich. Not only are these an extremely well-preserved and picturesque set of buildings, marred slightly by the addition of an indifferent nineteenth-century chapel that projects at the rear, but they are part of an attractive and complete grouping. They are opposite the fine Norman church, and close by are the rectory and several other good barns and cottages all made of brick and carrstone. Behind are an attractive garden, wash houses and well-tended allotments, beyond which damp meadows stretch to woodland. Unbelievably a notice by the door calls for applications for residents; perhaps there are some archaic and restrictive rules for pensioners who wish to be admitted – otherwise there would surely be a long waiting list.

The nineteenth-century range of almshouses in Downham Market in the form of a colonial bungalow was built to celebrate the diamond jubilee of Queen Victoria. These could be in any town in southern England with no reference to the Norfolk vernacular whatsoever. The same could not be said of the Royal Norfolk Regiment almshouses on Mousehold Heath in Norwich. These decorative cottages on a curving ground plan have shaped gables and heavy quoining. In the top of each gable is an oval plaque bearing the name of a soldier from the regiment who received the Victoria Cross. Strangely, these were built in 1949, although their appearance might place them thirty years earlier.

FISHERMAN'S HOSPITAL
GREAT YARMOUTH · 1702

BUILDING NORFOLK

ALMSHOUSES are a monument to the PIETY and general good works of the DONOR. SO they are designed with the ARCHITECTURAL IMPORTANCE DUE TO A MINOR PUBLIC BUILDING.

THE HOWARD ALMSHOUSES CASTLE RISING 1614 (COST £451) BUILT BY EARL OF NORTHAMPTON. ALSO GOOD VIEWED FROM THE REAR

EARLY C19 CHURCH BUNGALOWS / ALMSHOUSES @ BRISLEY · MID NORFOLK

EACH PLAQUE IN GABLE WITH DETAILS OF REGIMENTAL VCs

BATES V.C.

UNLIKELY CURVED GROUNDPLAN

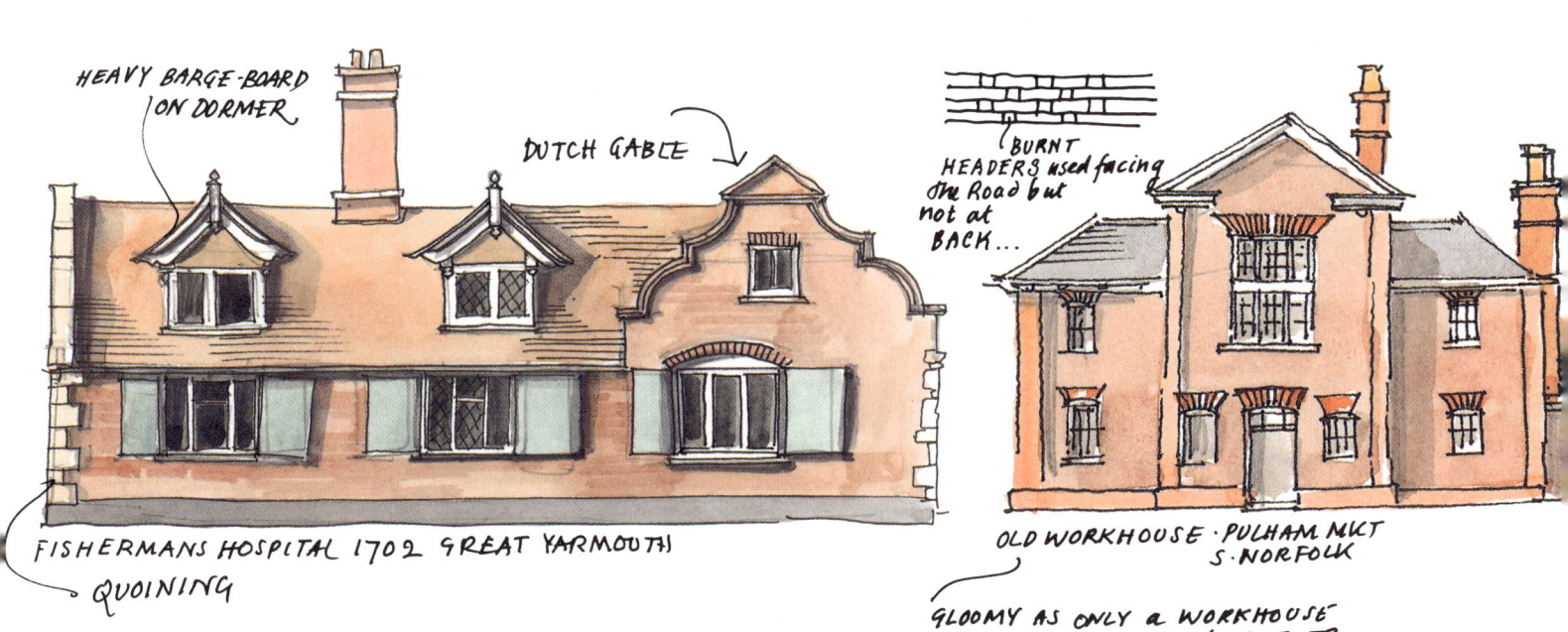

BUILDING NORFOLK

- HEAVY BARGE-BOARD ON DORMER
- DUTCH GABLE
- BURNT HEADERS used facing the Road but not at BACK...

FISHERMANS HOSPITAL 1702 GREAT YARMOUTH
QUOINING

OLD WORKHOUSE · PULHAM MKT S. NORFOLK

GLOOMY AS ONLY A WORKHOUSE CAN BE - WOULD THEY be BETTER DEMOLISHED?

TERRACOTTA PLAQUE

RETREAT ALMSHOUSES at DOWNHAM MKT · W. Norfolk. Built to mark the 60th Year of Q. Victorias Reign

1838 BEETLEY
HOOD MOULDS
UN-VERNACULAR SLATE

III

11. INNS

The spiralling downfall of the pub is well documented. Atomisation of communities, television, wine, the cinema, the rise of feminism and the New Dad, and most recently the excoriatingly active policing of the drink driving laws and controls on smoking have all played their part, as no doubt has the series of overconfident and lurid makeovers so many have been subjected to. But historically the pub has been socially and architecturally significant. Norwich was alleged to have a church for every week of the year and a pub for every day. The former is unlikely ever to have been true, particularly after the Reformation thinned out religious establishments in the city in the sixteenth century, but perhaps the latter is more convincing. A walk down King Street shows an extraordinary number of houses to have been pubs and/or breweries, and while these may not have all been simultaneously pulling pints or scattering sawdust, the fact of their having existed is inescapable. Similarly, in every village where one pub stumbles on, there were once two or three hostelries. Before the great improvements in rural housing in the nineteenth and twentieth centuries, the overcrowded rural slums were well worth escaping for the evening and the pub was the sitting room of the village, the only place where entertainment could be found. Cottages which are now considered so small that two are knocked into one to accommodate a retired couple were once inhabited by families of eight or more children, and even walking about the child-strewn floors must have been a challenge after bedtime.

Where a community is large and lively enough, pubs survive. Aldborough manages to sustain two establishments in a more or less successful way, a testament to the strength of the community and its size providing enough drinkers to walk or bicycle to the pub. Until the advent of the railways rural transport was slow and unreliable, and journeys that are now taken two or more times a day were major undertakings. This called for inns as staging posts on long journeys and as meeting places for those away from home, in many ways the diametrically opposite function of the village escape pub.

One of the finest coaching inns in Britain is that at Scole near Diss. The White Hart is a tremendous brick tour de force. The A140 that goes from Suffolk via Norwich to Cromer has ancient origins: large parts of it are Roman – it connected two great military establishments, one at Caistor St Edmund (then Venta Icenorum) and the other just north of present-day Ipswich – and it has been in continuous use ever since. Scole marks the half-way point between Ipswich and Norwich so was ideally situated for passing trade, which was substantial. Despite quite thorough internal alterations, it is easy to see past this and imagine its generous parlours full of seventeenth- or eighteenth-century travellers, pewter tankards foaming, heavy rummers full of claret, broiled mutton chops, and hoydenish serving girls with opportunistically disorganised lacing to their bodices, or a hunting breakfast of the sort drawn so beautifully by Cecil Aldin in *Mrs Tickler's Caravan* (1931).

On the roadside elevation there are five brick shaped gables, two with segmental pediments and three pointed. They surmount eleven very unequal bays divided by giant order pilasters; the whole façade is clasped together by generous brick quoins. The windows are large and differ from one another in size and form, for this building has developed over 350 years. Now lost is the original ornate inn sign that stretched right across the main road, quite a usual device for large establishments of this type. At the rear are wide openings forming a giant loggia and leading into the parlour and rather old-fashioned Elizabethan staircase. They face an elegant range of early nineteenth-century stables across what is now the carpark but was once a clattering stable yard. These must replace an earlier set of stables as they would always have been an important function of the inn. This is one of the finest buildings in Norfolk, and as so often the interior requires imagination to reconstruct among the mitred napkins, hotelware and Velour ballroom chairs. But as I sat drawing on the wall opposite, bemoaning the end of *Vanity Fair*-type rollicking hospitality and the demise of all things good, an incredibly sweet girl came out with a cup of tea and a biscuit and faith in the inn was restored.

The Black Boys in Aylsham is very different. Although deep inside it may also be mid-seventeenth century, it is early eighteenth century from the market place. Giant order pilasters support a heavily carved baroque frieze with putti frolicking among the fronds. (This sounds splendid, but actually you need to look quite hard to see beyond what at first sight does seem to be a rather a coarsely painted and ordinary sort of a building.) The tall first-floor sash windows are those of the old Assembly Room. While no rival to the urban splendour of Thomas Ivory's Assembly House in Norwich or the elegance of King's Lynn, this was its regional equivalent. Tidy minuets were tripped in here, matches made and no doubt plans discussed for the Norwich–Cromer toll road and other eighteenth-century projects. This was a centre for a very local social whirl but perhaps drawing from far enough away to fill the Black Boys' bedrooms.

Great houses also spawned inns. At Blickling the house that the bricklayer Joseph Balls had built for himself in 1693 was turned, in 1740, into a pub. There was enough business then from servants of visitors to the big house and its own staff to justify the establishment. This is still the case, although it is now National Trust employees and the many thousands who visit the property who prop up the twenty-first-century bars. At Houghton this was also the case. The New Inn sat opposite the gates to the park. It was built in 1720, roughly speaking at the same time as the big house. In fact, that date makes it one year before the earliest date of the Hall, so perhaps it was built first – maybe even to accommodate the architects Colen Campbell, Thomas Ripley and later Gibbs and Walpole himself, the client. Were the fine details of the house actually drawn on those parlour tables? Either way within 100 years the pub had ceased to function, quite conceivably because towards the end of the eighteenth century the estate had fallen into disrepair, crippled with the cost of its own construction. Despite a brief period at the beginning of the nineteenth century when the new owner, the Marquess of Cholmondeley, lived at Houghton while his Cheshire home Cholmondeley Castle was being rebuilt, the estate continued to fall. Trees were felled for timber and the park ploughed up, so it is no surprise to find that by 1845 the King's Head had become a farmhouse. So it has remained and now houses the agent for the estate, its beery past indicated only by its distinguished elevation. The process of conversion of private to public house and back seems to be a constant one.

Two more pub buildings are the Saracen's Head at the gates of Wolterton, distinguished by its recognisable abnormally generous eaves, and Model Farm at Holkham. The Saracen's Head is still busy although it no longer serves pints to estate servants (there are barely any left anyway). Model Farm has had a more varied career. It was first built in 1790 as accommodation for farmers and other interested parties attending the great 'Shearings' that Coke held from 1780 to 1814. Across the yard a refined and elegant model farm was also built in cream Holkham brick, much pedimented, corniced and quoined. So numerous were these visitors that Samuel Wyatt extended the already grandiose inn in 1800. It was then turned into a generous farmhouse but, later still, abandoned to use as a grain store, in which state it was when the current Lord and Lady Leicester decided that they would restore it, planning to move there when they left the Hall. Both these things have now happened, and Model Farm, house and farm buildings are in the finest fettle as dower house for the Holkham estate.

The renovation of the Red Lion Hotel in Cromer was a confident speculative investment in 1887 by its owner, John Smith of Kensington. This Gault brick Queen Anne/Pont Street Dutch makeover is elaborate and visually arresting both from the esplanade and from Jetty Street. It is an example of a building where the use of a sophisticated architect has taken it completely outside its local vernacular.

The Globe Inn in the Buttlands in Wells has recently undergone a serious restoration by its owners, the Holkham estate. Following the outstanding success of the revamped Victoria Hotel at Holkham, a once grey and dreary flint-faced estate pub that is now elevated to funky weekend haunt for Londoners drawn by the nearby four-mile-long sandy beach, dunes and the Hall. The Globe has been rethought, and the fine façade gripped by quoins and with heavily rusticated arched doorways has been rejuvenated.

All significant pubs needed stables both for their own use and for those of lucrative travellers. Those of the New Inn at Worstead, a mid-eighteenth-century building, are fine with storerooms above and are as well built as the pub itself.

The Crown Inn in Wymondham has a most singular door-case, with heavily lobed architrave, a broken pulvinated frieze and hollow pediment. In an otherwise plain though good eighteenth-century façade, this must have been a form of advertisement, as is the crazy thatched dining room at Acle. To work and attract a clientele, these have to be recognisably *public* houses and sometimes more than a sign is employed.

ELABORATE DOORCASE at COLTISHALL

BUILDING NORFOLK

WHITE LADY (of easy virtue?...)

BLACK BOY

HIPPED & BLACK-GLAZED PANTILE ROOF

The BLACK BOYS INN in AYLSHAM, N. NORFOLK.

HIGHLY DECORATED FRIEZE
There was an ASSEMBLY ROOM INSIDE

GIANT ORDER PILASTER

WYMONDHAM Pub in Mkt STREET.

SHAPED GABLE

THE KINGS HEAD. COLTISHALL

CLASPING PILASTERS

JETTIED UPPER STOREYS

BRITONS ARMS · ELM HILL NORWICH

HALL FARM HOUGHTON. WAS THE NEW INN of 1720. THE EARL of OXFORD was PUT UP there in 1737 (to inspect building?) until 1800 The main gates to the hall were opposite. It remained an Inn until 1832

HERE IT IS ILLUSTRATED IN The 1800 SURVEY of HOUGHTON

2 CASEMENT WINDOW

NR CAISTOR.

WHITE PAINTED BRICKWORK

THE GLOBE INN, the BUTTLANDS · WELLS See PAGE 176

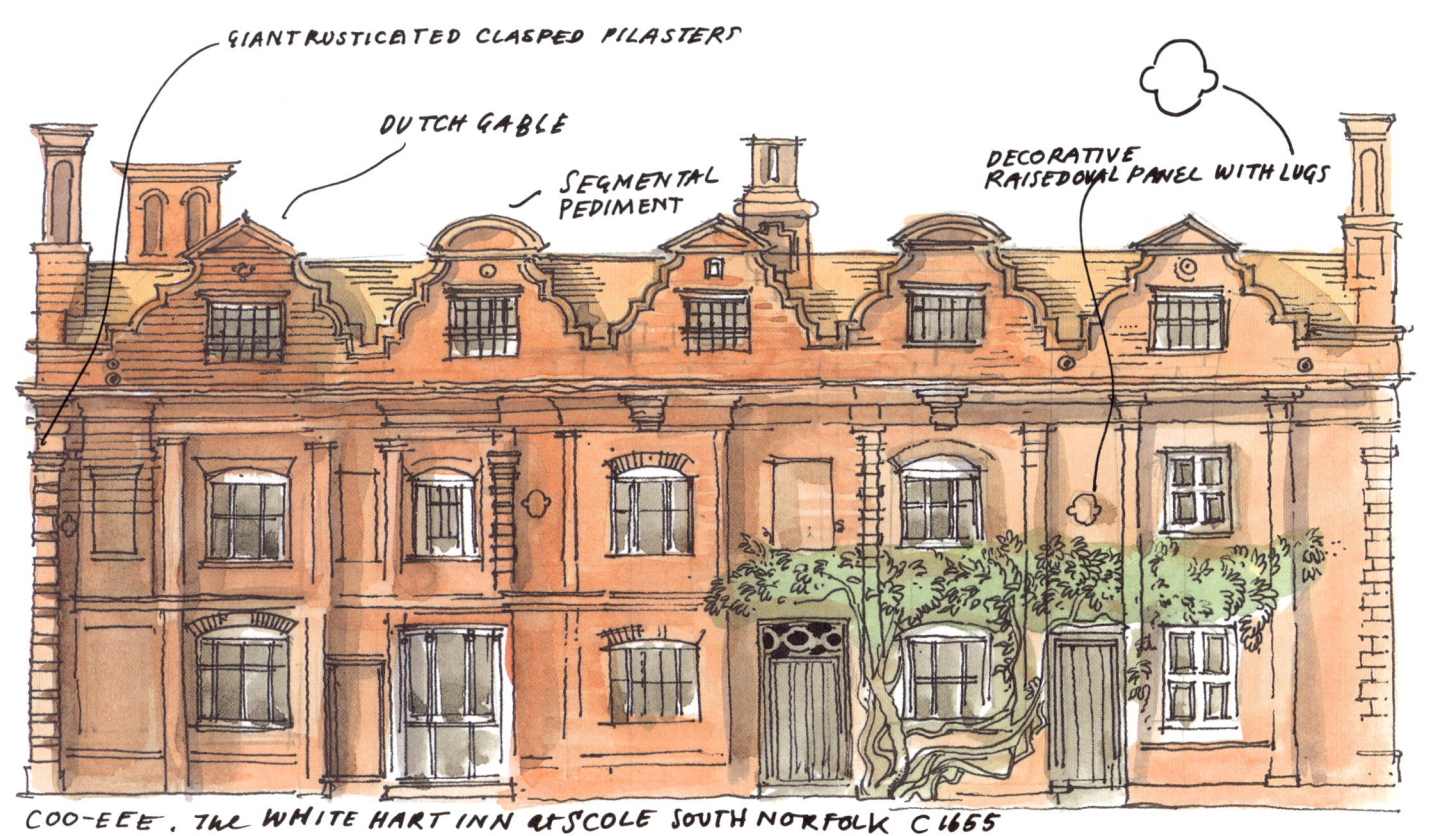

RUSTICATED ARCH

BAY WINDOW

GIANT RUSTICATED CLASPED PILASTERS

DUTCH GABLE

SEGMENTAL PEDIMENT

DECORATIVE RAISED OVAL PANEL WITH LUGS

COO-EEE. The WHITE HART INN at SCOLE SOUTH NORFOLK C.1655

BUILDING NORFOLK

- STONE KEYSTONE
- CRAZY & DERY AIRY PEDIMENT
- LOBED ARCHITRAVE
- PLINTH

DETAIL OF WYMONDHAM PUB
FIELDED PANELS

THE GREYHOUND WYMONDHAM 1580
DEPRESSED ARCH
DEPRESSED SMOKER
ARCH TO YARD

THE NEW INN, WORSTEAD. N. NORFOLK. STABLES

MODEL FARM HOLKHAM
was originally the NEW INN
WYATT 1786

SASH WINDOWS
IN RECESSED
ARCHES

THE CROWN HOTEL on the
BUTTLANDS. WELLS NEXT THE SEA
WAS SOCIAL EPICENTRE of C18
WELLS

QUOINS

THE CROWN

12. PARSONAGES

The Rectory, The Vicarage, The Old Parsonage: all these addresses are redolent with associations, literary and architectural. Isolated, spacious and calm, a far cry from the hard strivings of the farmhouse but without the formal expectations and landowning responsibilities of the great house or manor. The parsonage is desirable. Architecturally the definition is less precise as there have always been houses for priests and continue to be so, although the current vicarage, egalitarian and unshowy, will have little kudos when it becomes the New Old Vicarage. The parsonage of P. G. Wodehouse, Dornford Yates or Agatha Christie is most definitely Gothic while Jane Austen's is restrained and Georgian, but before the great age of the country vicar there had also been medieval priests' houses. Methwold is sixteenth century with stepped gables; Great Snoring is fifteenth but was originally the Hall.

Medieval and Tudor priests had very varied fortunes. Some were attached to great monastic establishments or colleges, but others relied for their modest stipends on the agricultural income of their glebe, the land apportioned for the benefit of the priest in each village. This was normally as strips of land in the open fields alongside their parishioners. Remnants have remained until very recently; the sale particulars of the Matlaske Hall estate of 1923 contain a map on which are shown three strips of glebe, each a remnant of a pre-enclosure open field. These had survived at least 200 years longer than the field syastem of which they were subdivisions; indeed, the particulars state that the estate is the tenant of the rector in respect of these small enclosures. In 1951 the estate was sold again, but by this time only the track that leads from the Hall to the northernmost strip remained. This survived until 2007 when in a fit of neatness it too was bulldozed away, unknowingly obliterating a clearly visible physical reminder of the link between medieval parson and village.

In the sixteenth century many poor priests had no house but lodged close by. In 1584, only 600 out of a total of 9,000 parishes in England yielded enough income to support a priest educated enough to preach. Glebe land allocations in Norfolk were fairly generous, an average of 39 acres (16 hectares). This was enough to provide the rectory with the majority of its food for the year; in addition to this the parson's income was augmented by the tithe – by the eighteenth century converted into a financial transaction and no longer paid in kind.

The reduction in infant mortality during the eighteenth century produced a greater number of surviving sons in landowning families. The actual numbers of children born did not decrease commensurately, producing an excess of male family members. Throughout the sixteenth and seventeenth centuries the post of country parson had been filled by scholars searching for patronage, often living in extremely basic conditions. Anthony Bax in *The English Parsonage* gives the example of the curate of Cobham in Kent who in 1772 'lodges at present at the Leather Bottle. No family like to have him.' But it was increasingly the case that the patron of the living, usually the local magnate, would look to the living he was accustomed to provide, augment it and redirect it to one of his own younger sons. Bax again: 'One of the gentleman's sons is presented with the living, which from its value, and the goodness and situation of its parsonage house, is no bad establishment for a younger son, even of a family as wealthy as his.' This was not a completely satisfactory solution, as the previous incumbents had been happy to live in modest circumstances deemed unfit for these aristocratic young priests. This new style of candidate instigated a wave of rectory and vicarage building never seen before, which was strengthened by an Act passed in 1826, but even this did not sort out the grievous lack of accommodation for rural parsons. An ecclesiastical commission of 1831 found 2,878 parishes with no parsonage house at all, although this was undoubtedly in no small part due to the practice of pluralism, by which one priest might hold two or more livings. This became almost the norm. In the early nineteenth century Cobbett wrote that in England 332 parsons held 1,496 parishes and that 500 more parsons held 1,524 more. This practice became increasingly contentious as the eighteenth and nineteenth centuries progressed.

As pluralism was gradually stamped out, new resident priests moved to the rural parishes where large, generous gentlemen's residences at least the size of small manor houses were prepared for them. This in turn made the livings more and more attractive to the young gentlemen in need of occupation and income, so much so that the spiritual side of the job was almost an irrelevance. Rev. Charles Adams wrote in 1700: 'Mr Abdy that was minister died ... my cozen Jack Nicklas is to have his living, so he is to go into orders with speed, this good living has made him declare his resolutions of being a minister.' That this was such an opportunistic vocation was perhaps not worthy of comment. What is fairly certain, however, is that no incumbent now takes the job attracted by the modest stipend or the cramped modern vicarage built in the corner of its predecessor's garden.

Eighteenth-century rectories in the county were classical in style: Holt in 1770, Baconsthorpe in 1795 and Foulsham in 1790. This changed in the nineteenth century: first to Italianate – Salle in 1857 and Somerleyton and Wickmere in 1858 – before moving towards full-blown Gothic Revival following the publication of John Ruskin's *Stones of Venice* in 1851. Then followed some Edwardian rectories like Blakeney. What all these buildings have in common is that they are polite and not truly vernacular, frequently being the only architect-designed building in a village. Consequently, particularly in the case of later nineteenth-century examples, the parsonage is the only building that is completely alien architecturally from its neighbours.

This influx of gentry priests, as well as sometimes bringing a strong strain of evangelism into the Church of England, brought a welcome injection of energy both intellectual and more importantly economic to that institution. The significant investment in property provided a long-lasting and irresistible perk no longer enjoyed by the clergy today.

Did these substantial houses, country houses in miniature, each with its own stable block and barns, whispering cedars and gravel drive, play a significant role in establishing the priestly dynasties that provided future incumbents throughout the nineteenth and twentieth centuries? They certainly produced one of the defining features of rural Britain, part of the village axis of church, manor house and vicarage that is the focus for middle-class life in the country.

The demise of the grand rectory was not mourned by all. Wickmere Rectory, built for the Rev. T. Beauchamp in 1858, was considered impractical in 1953. It is not particularly large. It has 12 rooms and 8 acres (3 hectares) of garden and paddock, but its size was a source of annoyance to the then rector and his wife, who remember it as being draughty and impossible to heat except for the kitchen, which housed a new Aga, a recent gift from the patron of the living, Lord Walpole. Their move to a smaller modern rectory was a huge relief and they never regretted the change. The house was sold for £2,000 and immediately split into two smaller houses. It remained divided, a family living in each half and all but an acre sold to a local farmer who kept pigs in the stables and gig shed for the next twenty years. It was only with rising prosperity and improving transport connections that the property seemed to become viable again, and it was sold and returned to single ownership.

This is a familiar and completely representative story. Coston Rectory was sold by the Church in 1959 for £1,500 and Little Melton in 1955 for £1,200. These prices were low even for that time, reflecting the poor condition of these buildings. In common with the rest of the country, many of these rectories and vicarages had been built only 100 years earlier, their brief period of occupation reflecting the rapid rise and fall of the status of the parish priest.

The post-war parsonages are barely worthy of architectural mention. A wild swing away from their spacious predecessors led to a collection of profoundly undistinguished and frankly inadequate small houses. These are for the most part too small to hold even the smallest PCC meeting; perhaps this helped to marginalise the parish priest. The insignificance of his, or her, house now makes them a less overtly public person, surely a bad thing when the Church is in decline.

EAST HARLING RECTORY POLYCHROME BRICKWORK

LIVELY ASYMMETRY
STEPPED GABLES

BUILDING NORFOLK

WICKMERE OLD RECTORY · N · NORFOLK · 1858

THIS WAS WHAT THE MIDDLE 3 BAYS LOOKED LIKE BEFORE MODIFICATION BY A GERMAN BOMB... FEB 1941 — IT WAS BUILT IN 1840

BACONSTHORPE OLD RECTORY LATE C18

FOULSHAM OLD RECTORY POST 1770 THEN 1840s (1790)

PIERCED TERRACOTTA BALUSTRADE

13. CHURCHES

Norfolk's churches are the buildings most commonly associated with the county. They are quite simply the best in Britain. Perhaps this is not as absurdly bold a boast as it might appear at first glance. Of course, all counties have fine ecclesiastical buildings, whether medieval or nineteenth-century Gothic Revival, but it is East Anglia, and Norfolk in particular, that has numerical supremacy if nothing else.

From the eleventh to the sixteenth centuries there were 928 churches in the county, of which 878 remain today, 620 in active service, the rest in various states of decline from utter ruins like Sco Ruston to carefully maintained redundant churches like North Barningham. This is the greatest density of medieval churches in Europe and hence the world. Why is this so in a place that now seems so incredibly underpopulated? Norfolk, as we have already touched on, was once a much busier powerhouse, both of trade and proto-industrialised weaving, but also (and most significantly in the case of churches) in late Saxon times it was the most densely populated part of England.

This population density was the product of mass immigration. Waves of northern Europeans left the chilly German shores of the Baltic in search of richer and unexploited farmland. They landed first on this eastern coast and found in the area level and easily farmed land equally suited to growing crops or rearing livestock. Settling here, Saxon thegns became estate owners; and when in the seventh and eighth centuries Christianity was brought to England these same estate owners felt, on conversion, the need to erect the first East Anglian churches. They were initially built at the side of the landowner's house, and the parishes established around them were consequently coextensive with the Saxon estates. Being a thickly populated part of England, this also became the most densely churched as well. So not only are the austere isolated churches that punctuate the Norfolk countryside an unrivalled architectural and archaeological resource, they are also an thrilling reminder of the county's pre-Christian past. The early churches may have been built on the sites of earlier pagan temples both to benefit from the continuity of a site of worship and to emphasise the triumph of the new religion. St Augustine and the early Christian missionaries were exhorted by Pope Gregory to 'destroy the idols' and to have 'holy water sprinkled into the temples, altars built and relics set there. So the people will have no need to change their places of concourse. And where they were wont to sacrifice oxen to demons in this matter, also there should be some substitution of solemnity.'

The Church in England was originally controlled from minsters. These were large central churches, centres of administration from which priests sallied out to preach. The minsters were established by local Anglo-Saxon kings and survived the attacks of the Vikings, but became less important as the parish system became better established and each parish had a resident priest.

None of these original buildings remain, neither churches nor minsters. Indeed, they were probably wooden structures and short-lived. Claims that the round towers so prevalent in Norfolk have Saxon origins are unconvincing, although recognisably late pre- or immediately post-Conquest stonework is visible in several. An example is the pointed-topped windows in the tower of Little Snoring. The Norman conquerors built more substantial stone structures. The seat of the See moved from Thetford to the administrative centre of Norwich, and a new Norman bishop, Herbert de Losinga, began work on the cathedral church of the Holy Trinity in 1096. This is, of course, the county's greatest church: towering and muscular, full of bold Romanesque decoration, and soon the centre of a great monastic establishment with its complex of attendant buildings. It is not the only surviving early Norman church in the county. Hales in the south is a miniature and very perfect example; so is the monastic remnant, now parish church, at Binham, and the much restored west end of Castle Rising, while perhaps the grandest tower in all of Norfolk is that of North Lopham with five storeys of blind arcading.

Thomas Rickman (1776–1841) was the architectural historian whose researches into the churches of England led him to recognise the divisions in style in those buildings. It was he who coined the expressions Norman, Early English (E. E. for short), Decorated and Perpendicular. Norfolk's churches display all these styles, but the county is poorest in the E. E. and its great outburst of building is in the Late Decorated and Perpendicular. Like the other 'wool churches' in Gloucestershire and Somerset, it is the soaring naves lit with clerestory windows above that characterise these great churches. Salle, Walpole St Peter, Terrington St Nicholas, Worstead and Tunstead are among the most impressive, where the unusually sunlit interior is as thrilling as the exterior. Smaller buildings are no less outstanding. Little Witchingham, although redundant, is earlier (thirteenth century) and still a spiritually moving place, its immaculately restored wall paintings giving some idea of the elaborate decoration that originally covered the walls of every parish church. This tells in bold and clear visual imagery the stories that an illiterate rural congregation subjected to services in Latin could not otherwise follow. There are many fragments of paintings elsewhere: in Crostwight a 10-foot (3-metre) high St Christopher towers over you, while at nearby Edingthorpe he is attended by six saints.

These frescoes are of historical interest and often very beautiful, but they remain essentially primitive; indeed, even the fragments remaining in Norwich Cathedral, surely the highest status ecclesiastical building in the county, have little of the refinement of their Florentine or Sienese contemporaries. Why were we so primitive? Was it a culture that did not value the visual? This seems unlikely given the complexities of high medieval Gothic architecture with its elaborate vaulting, arcading, crocketing and sophisticated massing of columns. The humanist scholar Poggio Bracciolini, whose life was devoted to the study of classical texts and the civilisation of the ancients, a man for whom sophistication counted, was not impressed by his visit to Britain in 1429. He wrote:

The nobles of England deem it disgraceful to reside in cities and prefer to live in country retirement. They reckon a man's nobility by the size of his country estate. They spend their time over agriculture and traffic in wool and sheep.

Perhaps this rural focus might account for the lack of attention to the visual arts.

There is one great exception to this: the painted rood screens unrivalled in quality and number elsewhere. These screens that divide the nave of the church from the chancel or choir had a significance now lost. They supported the Holy Rood, a representation of Christ crucified. The large and often heavily decorated cross was a focus for prayer and a constant visual reminder for the illiterate parishioners of the Crucifixion at the centre of their faith. Little wonder, then, that the supporting screen was also the focus of much decorative painting and at a level of sophistication far beyond that achieved in the wall paintings close by. Screens at Cawston, Horsham St Faith (which also has an outstanding painted pulpit), Barton Turf and Worstead are all decorated with carefully painted saints. Best of all and most elaborate is that at Ranworth in the Broads: its angels' wings are as beautifully feathered as any northern International Gothic angel.

The fourteenth and fifteenth centuries saw the greatest output of church building and improvements. This was its swansong. The Act of Supremacy in 1534 by which Henry VIII was made supreme head of the new Church of England, and the dissolution of the monasteries and sale of their properties in the late 1530s, saw a dramatic change. Until this date the church was the focus for almost all architectural expenditure, whether by a local landowner or tradesman. Gifts of roofs, screens and new windows continued right up to the break with Rome. After this, however, the church lost out to secular projects, and future investment and display of personal wealth was redirected to the manor and great house and civic buildings.

Two great destructions of church interiors occurred within a century: first, the Reformation via Henry VIII's realignment of the Church followed by the continued Protestant policy under his son Edward VI; and, second, the even more destructive Puritan modifications that ensued during and after the Civil War. These cataclysmic attacks, divided by Archbishop Laud's early seventeenth-century reversions, sent the altar table spinning around the church depending on the current liturgical orthodoxy. This rumpus has left a mark on the fabric of Norfolk's churches today: the broken head of a lute-playing church band member on an oak pew-end at Wickmere, the heavily scratched out face of St Thomas a Becket on the screen at Worstead, and countless other minor and major defacements are a powerful reminder of the destruction that was caused by these seismic changes in the Church, although not all saints were equally reviled. St Gregory, for example, with his triple tiara, was perceived as particularly popish and invoked more frantic destruction than less inflammatory figures. Another focus for attack was the actual rood beam, gallery and carved figures: these were invariably destroyed while the screen itself, although frequently moved west, was rarely lost entirely.

Despite the wholesale destruction there was still later sixteenth-century church building, like the charming all-brick and all-of-a-piece St Peter's church, Hoveton, or the tower of Twyford on the Norwich to Fakenham road, or the surprisingly secular square-topped Perpendicular windows inserted into Binham when it ceased to be a priory and became the parish church. However, by and large church building had stopped.

The period from the Restoration of Charles II in 1660 until the accession of Victoria to the throne in 1837 was not one in which church building played a great part, although there remained a fairly continuous squirely input directed more towards furnishings and monuments. This was a period of high church attendance, for although the Reformation changes had been imposed on the parishes from above, at local level there was a degree of independence that allowed a parish priest to accommodate the customs of his congregation. However, a complete rearrangement of the interior was not at all uncommon – most frequently the addition of box pews as at St Mary's, Worstead. These afforded accommodation with comfort for worshippers who were subjected to much longer services than today. This was a preaching-based liturgy and services would last up to 1½ hours and be non-eucharistic (that is, they would not involve taking Holy Communion). The weekly celebration of the Eucharist was considered popish, and offering communion at Christmas and/or Easter was perceived as being quite observant enough. The focus of the service was now the sermon, often a published sermon read out loud, and consequently the pulpit gained in importance. Two- or even three-decker examples were installed, one for preaching, one for reading and one for the clerk. There is a very good example in the restrained 1809 refit of St Mary the Virgin, Bylaugh.

This was the age of pluralism: the custom of a priest taking charge of two parishes or more, and more importantly the incomes from those livings. This practice was considered undesirable as it inevitably led to the priest being geographically divorced from at least one of his parishes, part of the inexorable drift away from the late medieval phenomenon of the church as centre of the village. This was not just greed. Clergy incomes were, at the beginning of the eighteenth century, extremely modest. The average income for a parish priest in Norfolk of £70 per year was not much above the then poverty line of £50; indeed, in England as a whole, over half of the livings were below this level. In 1704 this problem was in part alleviated by the establishment of Queen Anne's Bounty, a fund to augment poor clergy's incomes. This was to have a significant impact on the fabric of Norfolk, allowing an increasing amount of money to be spent on improving the parsonage.

This was also the age of the country house. Villages were moved as part of grand landscape projects, sometimes leaving the church isolated in the new park. Felbrigg near Cromer looks at its old parish church across its now tatty parkland, while the last vestiges of the village of Wolterton were swept away by Horace Walpole, brother of Sir Robert of Houghton, when he began to build Wolterton Hall in 1727. The parish was united with neighbouring Wickmere in 1737, and the former church began its rapid slide into ruination. Eighteenth-century engravings of many of Norfolk's churches show extreme dilapidation, chancels abandoned, roofs patched, windows filled in with brick. Indeed, picturesque ruins of churches, like those of cottages, were important elements in the Romantic landscape. Rendering fell off and was not reapplied, crumbling towers were reduced in size, but the Gothic style was utterly out of fashion, considered primitive and backward looking, and not worthy of attention by the squire, who found himself more concerned with other estate buildings and improvements to his house. The nave of the church was the responsibility of the parish, which had no funds available, and the priest – who would often be a salaried vicar not a freeholding rector with benefit of the living – would also be more concerned with the education of his children and the building of an improved parsonage than with keeping an unfashionable Gothic church in fine condition.

The advent of a reinvigorated nineteenth-century Church of England came not a moment too soon for the fabric of its church buildings. There had, of course, been some eighteenth-century church building. St George's in Great Yarmouth is, although deeply compromised by its conversion to a theatre in the 1970s, a recognisable Georgian town church, but this is an exception. The Cambridge Camden Society and the Oxford Movement, a group of Oxford clerics and academics who included John Keble, John Newman and Edward Pusey, a distinguished patristic scholar, believed that they would take the Church back to early Christianity, a Church of the Apostles. Newman, who in 1845 went one step further and converted to Rome, led this movement with the artistic guidance of Augustus Pugin (1812–52), another convert to Roman Catholicism. Pugin believed that the Gothic style was the only true Christian architecture, glorifying medieval pre-capitalist society as the ideal and vilifying the classical style as overtly secular, pagan and ill-suited to ecclesiastical use. Norfolk is perhaps the county least affected by the Victorian mania for church rebuilding, although few churches did not undergo a substantial refit during the second half of the nineteenth century, with varying degrees of damage to the old building involved. New roofs were installed, new furniture carved and screens re-erected. Internal fittings became seen as increasingly important, reflecting the Oxford Movement's emphasis on liturgy and ceremony.

There was an increasing irony in this overhaul, for while this was a movement from within the Church and not a politically imposed change like those of the sixteenth and seventeenth centuries, it coincided with a drift away from the parish church. Attendance levels fell dramatically. The changes to the rural community effected by the Agrarian Revolution had led to a significant proportion of the parish becoming landless labourers with little devotion to an institution that was perceived as the preserve of the landowner and grand tenant farmer. They moved towards the Nonconformist churches: Wesley's Methodists, the Baptists and Congregationalists, all movements strong in Norfolk and connected with the incipient farm-workers' unions. Those beautiful oak pews with lovingly carved reproduction poppy heads and cursive decorated ends were fated to be forever unpolished by the labourers' restless bottoms.

Fine examples of complete nineteenth-century churches include Glandford, highly decorated and almost completely rebuilt in 1896; Edgefield, a cool and brightly sunlit neo-Perpendicular box using materials and some of the actual architectural components of the demolished old church; At the other end of the scale the great brick barn of St James, Great Yarmouth, of 1869, or the more vernacular in treatment but still utterly foreign St Peter's, Sheringham, built by the Upcher family of Sheringham Park to accommodate the burgeoning tourist trade they were so keen to encourage as major landowners and developers in the town. Strangest of all is St Michael and all Angels, Booton. This spiky Gothic fantasy looms menacingly over the unexceptional country behind Cawston. Elegant elongated towers with clustered pinnacles stick up at either end of this peculiar ship of a church. A fantastically decorated porch leads into a similarly captivating and extreme interior. It was the work of the then parish priest, Rev. Whitwell Elwin, who recast the church in 1875 in a Gothic style in every way more light-hearted than was current in the theory-rich nineteenth century. The last significant church building in the county was All Saints, Bawdeswell. A restrained exercise in neo-Georgian, it is strangely urban and a little at odds with its neighbours but has a stylish interior and elegant detailing.

Norfolk is a county steeped in Nonconformism, was principally Parliamentarian in the Civil War, and has a tradition of independent mindedness. So it is no surprise that chapels are common and frequently of architectural interest. Like the church and the parsonage they are frequently more sophisticated buildings than their neighbours, drawing their inspiration from further afield. The Old Meeting House in Colegate is perhaps the best, even more exciting than the equally fine Octagon close by. The Old Meeting House looks very Dutch, and this is no coincidence as its congregation, led by Rev. W. Bridge, former rector of St George's, Tombland, had returned from religious exile in the Protestant Netherlands. Following the Act of Toleration of 1693 the congregation, comprised of rich Nonconformist tradesmen and Quaker bankers, built this perfect box with elegant brick pilasters, stone capitals and elaborate rubbed brick window dressings. Inside, all late seventeenth- and eighteenth-century chapels are austere with box pews and a gallery carried on wooden or iron columns. The focus of the interior is the pulpit from which God's all-important word would be preached, this non-eucharistic practice eschewing the altar altogether. The much smaller Oulton Congregationalist chapel also remains in use and has an uncompromised wooden interior. It is nominally open to the public, but serious hammering on the door of the nearby cottage rarely seems to raise the key-holding inmates. This building is fiercely undecorated without. Indeed, were it not for its unusual fenestration it might be a farmhouse. The peerless Walpole chapel in neighbouring Suffolk was, in fact, built out of such a farmhouse. Later and less elegant chapels continued throughout the eighteenth and early nineteenth centuries, to be followed by pared down Gothic prayer boxes, Italianate or even neo-Byzantine versions.

The sheer number of Norfolk's churches is such that some of their status will change in the future. Too many are badly attended and undersupported. However, the large sums awarded each year as grants from English Heritage, the Historic Churches Preservation Trust and other charitable institutions have meant that at no stage since the Reformation have Norfolk's churches been in such good architectural heart. This is in no small part due to the guidance of the Norfolk Churches Trust, a charity established by the late Lady Harrod through which local government money is channelled in the direction it is most needed and through whose grant aid hundreds of churches have been maintained or restored. There remains, however, a huge question as to their future. English Heritage stresses the importance of buildings having a use, and in many cases this is hard to demonstrate in a remote rural church. The rival centre of the village hall has much to answer for, usurping as it does the function of the nave of the church as a civic and community centre. Perhaps there will be a secularisation of some less architecturally significant church interiors, leaving the chancel sacred but allowing the rest of the building to fulfil part of its original function as meeting place. Maybe children's parties, over-60s lunches, quizzes, yoga groups (or worse) and meetings will fill the cleared nave all week and the church move back to centre stage in the village.

BUILDING NORFOLK

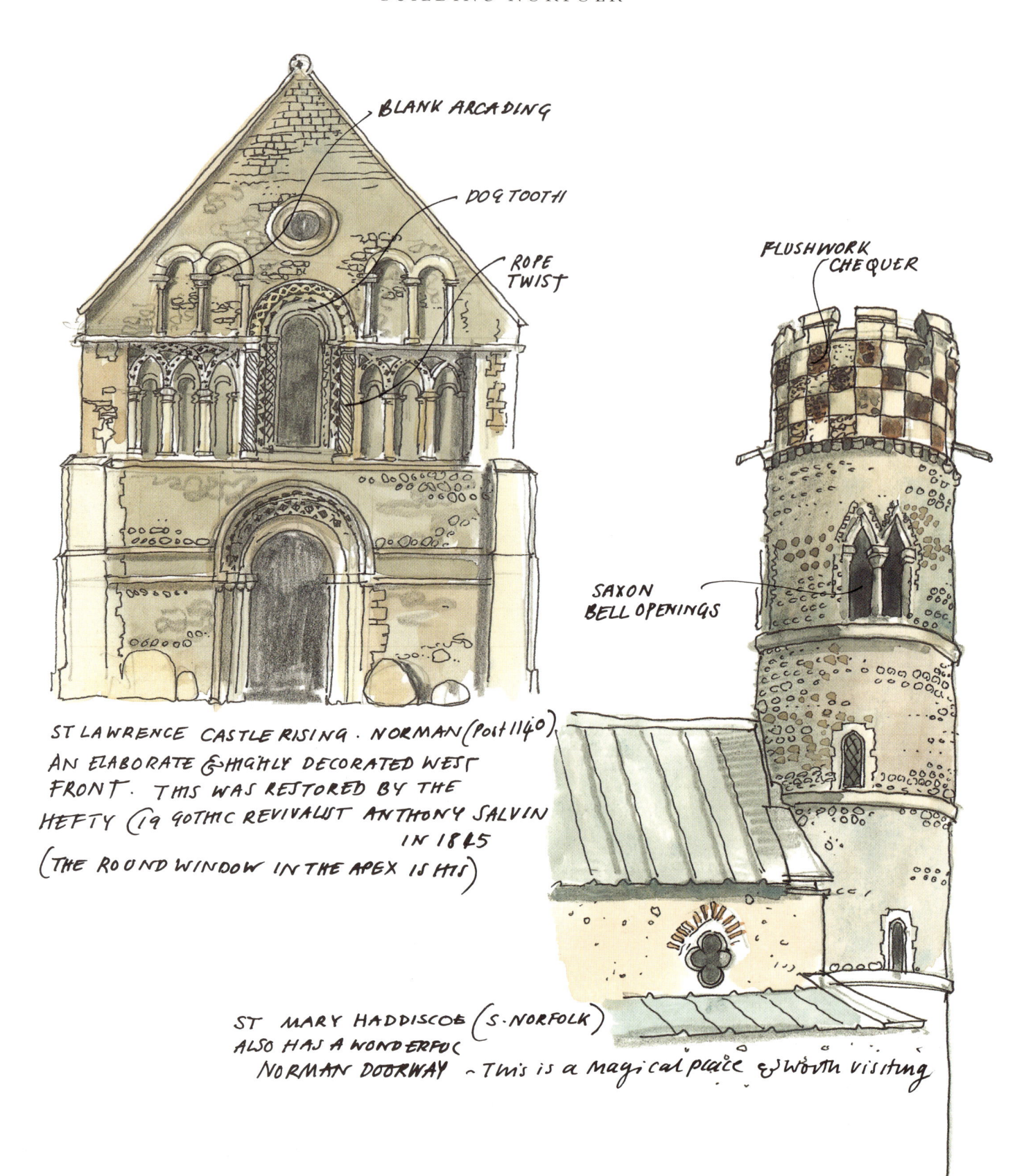

- BLANK ARCADING
- DOG TOOTH
- ROPE TWIST
- FLUSHWORK CHEQUER
- SAXON BELL OPENINGS

ST LAWRENCE CASTLE RISING. NORMAN (POST 1140). AN ELABORATE & HIGHLY DECORATED WEST FRONT. THIS WAS RESTORED BY THE HEFTY C19 GOTHIC REVIVALIST ANTHONY SALVIN IN 1845 (THE ROUND WINDOW IN THE APEX IS HIS)

ST MARY HADDISCOE (S. NORFOLK) ALSO HAS A WONDERFUL NORMAN DOORWAY - This is a magical place & worth visiting

130

BUILDING NORFOLK

ST ANDREW QUIDENHAM

ROUND TOWER with OCTAGONAL UPPER STOREY of 1400

SPIRE

PINNACLE FINIAL

MUSCULAR NORMAN c/1120 BATTLEMENTS (16)

ARCADING

LATE MEDIEVAL BUTTRESSES

ST ANDREW · SOUTH LOPHAM (S.E. NORFOLK) a five star building.

131

BUILDING NORFOLK

Pointing very flush so less rubble exposed

coursed pebble

BUILDING NORFOLK

This ruin at the side of All Saints Weybourne on the N. Norfolk coast was an Augustinian Priory of approx 1200. The tower, with its triangular headed bell openings shows that it was built incorporating parts of an earlier Saxon building

At various later dates the present church has also grown among fragments of the priory

BUILDING NORFOLK

ANGELS AT PRAYER

SCREEN

ST AGNES CAWSTON 1414 + EARLIER

84' A LONG UNINTERRUP[TED]

ST ETHELBURTS, THURTON
S. NORFOLK.

1330 WINDOW

FLUSHWORK IN PARAPET

SQUARE TOWER ILUSTRATES that FLINT TOWERS without major imported stone NEED NOT BE ROUND

ALL SAINTS BEESTON REGIS — ON THE CLIFF and beset by caravans...

134

BUILDING NORFOLK

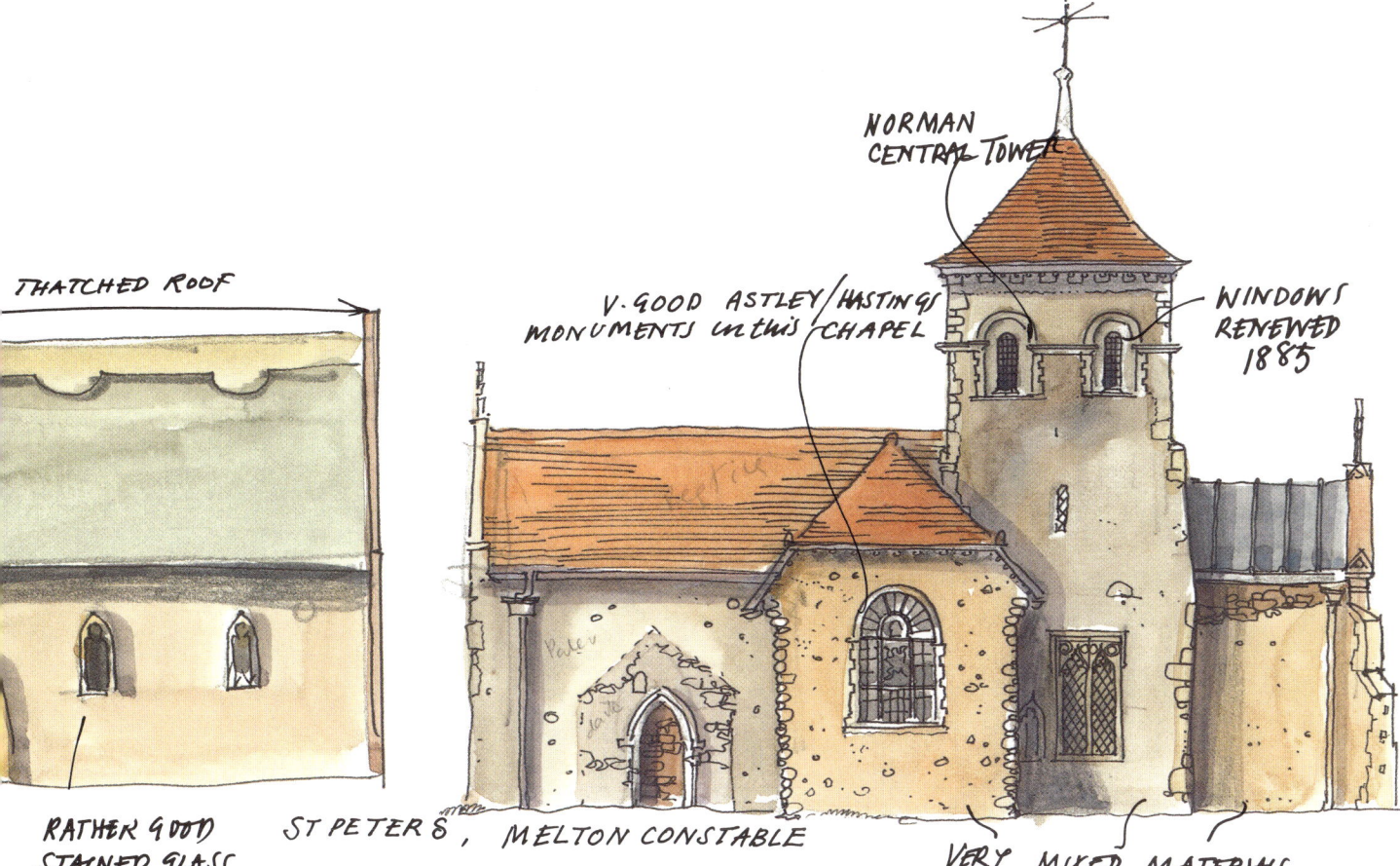

THATCHED ROOF

NORMAN CENTRAL TOWER

V. GOOD ASTLEY/HASTINGS MONUMENTS in this CHAPEL

WINDOWS RENEWED 1885

RATHER GOOD STAINED GLASS RE-USED IN OTHER WINDOWS

ST PETER'S, MELTON CONSTABLE

VERY MIXED MATERIALS CARRSTONE, FLINT, BRICK, PEG TILE LEAD ETC

SHARRINGTON ALL SAINTS — THE LARGE ARCHES WERE THE FORMER AISLE OF A LARGER INCARNATION — SMALLER & BRICK etc INFILL of APPROX 1820

135

BUILDING NORFOLK

PLATE TRACERY

A BARN of a CHURCH · ST PETER, SHERINGHAM. built for HOLIDAY PRAYER

← The (TWO) WEST TOWERS ARE PLACED DIAGONALLY.

CROCKETED FINIALS GALORE

TRULY ODD & EXCITING, ST MICHAEL & ALL ANGELS BOOTON. DESIGNED by the RECTOR Rev WHITWELL ELWIN 1875-1891

BUILDING NORFOLK

ST ANDREW, GUNTON · R. ADAM 1770. AUSTERE & ELEGANT and the KIND OF CHURCH that caused the GOTHIC REVIVAL 60 years later..

TWENTY SIX YEARS LATER LORD SUFFIELD OF GUNTON HALL COMMISSIONED...

...ST MARGARET, THORPE MARKET - FOR WORKERS OUTSIDE his PARK · DAINTY C18 GOTHIC

137

BUILDING NORFOLK

THESE ARE THE FIRST PANTILES USED IN NORFOLK

V REFINED LOBED BRICK ARCHITRAVE

THE OLD MEETING HOUSE · COLEGATE · NORWICH 1693

ORIGINAL CASEMENTS, SASH WINDOWS CAME MID 18

CONGREGATIONAL CHURCH IN BRISTON

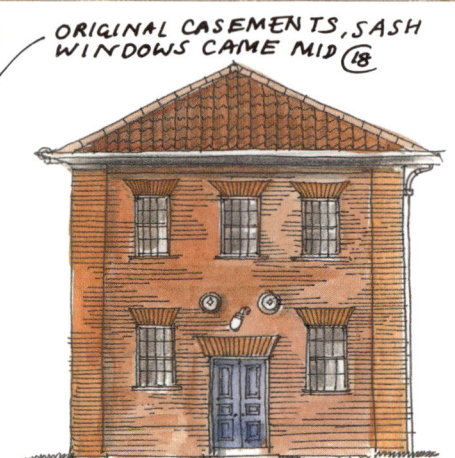

METHODIST CHAPEL HINDOLVESTON

17 WC 75

OULTON CHAPEL 1728 - This also had casement windows. It is built under a DOUBLE PITCHED ROOF but where the middle wall would be in a double PILE house, there are only WOODEN COLUMNS

IT HAS A CALM & AUSTERE INTERIOR

SHAPED GABLE

138

THESE TOP THREE ARE ALL at MEETING HILL at WORSTEAD · N-E Norfolk
Almshouses above Chapel and Minister's MANSE BELOW. These and three
other buildings form a fine GROUP of NONCONFORMIST church and its
dependencies of 1829

MEETING HILL CHAPEL

MANSE AT MEETING HILL

LUNETTE WINDOWS

PANTILES, a nod to the VERNACULAR

METHODIST CHURCH IN a very MANNERED BYZANTINE STYLE · EDWIN LUTYENS 1898
HE WAS WORKING NEARBY AT THE PLEASAUNCE (see Page 65)

14. GOING DUTCH

How Dutch is Norfolk building? Many of its characteristics are attributed to Dutch influence: the early use of brick, pantiles that began to usurp thatch as the roofing material in Norfolk in the eighteenth century, the ubiquitous Dutch and stepped gables, Dutch master builders and architects, and buildings specifically influenced by models in Holland like the customs house in King's Lynn.

But a trip to the Netherlands rather refutes some of the strength of these links. Vernacular building types in the equivalent towns in the Netherlands are very clearly different from any found in Norfolk or in any other English county. For example, the large pyramidal roofed farmhouses, the strange combination of pantile and thatch in one roof, and the frequent use of a large central dormer in the roof of a single-storey house are all building types that are absent in Britain. Brick sizes and bonds, church types, the high-necked gable that so characterises the short façade town houses of Amsterdam, Haarlem or Hoorn are all so different from their English counterparts.

Brick size is one of the most significant differences between the countries. English brick sizes have not always been standardised. The earliest Roman bricks were huge and flat, up to 18 x 18 x 1½ inches (46 x 46 x 4 cm), and can be seen in the well-preserved walls of Burgh Castle near Great Yarmouth built 1,600 years ago. There was no further brick building until the Middle Ages, and the earliest medieval bricks were still substantially thinner than modern sizes, those in the fourteenth-century walls of Norwich being 10 x 5 x 2⅛ inches (25 x 12.5 x 5.5 cm). It was not until the brick makers' charter of 1571 that a statute brick of 9 x 4½ x 2¼ inches (23 x 11.5 x 5.5 cm) emerged. After the Restoration in 1660 brick sizes became smaller again, and they remained small until the Brick Tax levied per thousand bricks ensured that sizes grew again to 9 x 5 x 3 inches (23 x 12.5 x 7.5 cm) . These may seem unimportant and insignificant, but they have a huge impact on the visual effect of a wall.

However, there are some very real links with the Netherlands. Visually this is perhaps best summed up as an ease with bricks and their use. The Scole Inn at Oxburgh or Blickling Hall or the tower at Clifton House in King's Lynn with their moulded brick decorations, brick pilasters and aprons all demonstrate this well. And while brick making was prevalent in most of the eastern counties from the Thames to the Humber from the Middle Ages onwards, it was only used for high status and swagger buildings. It was in the transference to a more workaday material for small manors, farmhouses and small barns that the Dutch style became most noticeable in Norfolk, although the latter categories are more likely to be of the late seventeenth or eighteenth century in date.

There had long been trading links with Holland. Since the Hundred Years' War with France (1337–1453), England had done business with its other North Sea trading partners. These trading towns, known as the Hanse or the Hanseatic League, were a loosely aligned collection of nearly 200 ports and trading towns as varied and widely scattered as Cracow, Lubeck, Amsterdam, Stockholm and Danzig. Theirs was an alliance of convenience formed to maximise the advantages of trading arrangements and enclaves in other large cites like London, Novgorod or Bergen. Such relationships existed between the merchants of the Hanse and the conveniently eastward-looking towns of Lynn, Yarmouth and Norwich. In King's Lynn today the name lingers on in Hanseatic House, a courtyard house of the sixteenth century, once the headquarters of this trade. From the fifteenth century Flemish or Dutch brick makers had crossed the North Sea to undertake building commissions. Sir John Fastolf used Flemish craftsmen to build Caistor Castle near Yarmouth in 1432–6.

The sixteenth and seventeenth centuries saw the arrival of great numbers of immigrants from the Low Countries. So numerous were these 'strangers' that they became at one time nearly 30 per cent of Norwich's population, and they were not limited to the city alone, significant numbers filtering out into nearby weaving towns like Worstead and North Walsham. These were hard-working Protestant refugees from the unbending Catholic rule of Spanish regents, and they introduced further skills from across the North Sea and with them new building materials. The pantile or 'Flanders Tyle' was a significant improvement on flammable and deteriorating wheat or reed thatch and, from the late sixteenth century, became generally desirable. But it was really in the seventeenth century that architectural links revealed themselves. Robert Lyminge, himself of Flemish extraction, built Blickling and then Felbrigg in 1604 and 1610. These houses sport fine Dutch gables and make use of classical ornament all taken from Dutch pattern books. Later in 1640 the great big-Whig Sir Roger Townshend built Raynham Hall with its two highly sophisticated gables and refined brickwork with Portland stone casings; meanwhile the mayor of Lynn commissioned the Merchants Exchange, now the customs house, on a thoroughly Dutch model with great light windows between elegant Ionic pilasters and a towering cupola receding into the sky. All these Norfolk buildings have the stamp of Holland on them. Perhaps it is fanciful to suggest that in Nonconformist East Anglia not only did the Protestant refugees find a home compatible with their beliefs, but the brightly lit, well-fenestrated houses of their homeland also felt at home in this neighbouring flat land.

The similarities between the two places become greater in their more rural areas. Travelling north from Amsterdam via Hoorn you reach Enkhuizen. This town sits right on the boundary between the bleak North Sea and the Isselmeer, the man-made lake created when the Zuiderzee project was completed in 1930. After an initial slump in its fortunes, the town became a tourist destination hugely augmented by the foundation in 1960 of the Zuiderzee Museum. This is a collection of fifty small houses moved from all over north Holland and re-erected in the form of a small seaside fishing village. Its canal-side streets are lined with perfectly preserved village houses, cottages and workshops all with authentic interiors – some even with eel-based stew steaming on the paraffin stove or with a small flock of malodorous goats grazing outside. These unexceptional buildings, brick and pantiled or with painted bargeboards, and their flat and uneventful landscape have more in common with the marshes of South Norfolk and their marshman's cottages, a mere 150 miles across the sea, than do their urban equivalents. There are identical cottages lying low in the Halvergate marshes where the same winds bring the same widgeon, plovers and geese to graze the same winter marsh.

It is in these marshes and in the vast fens of marshland west of King's Lynn that the great Dutch drainers, most famously Cornelius Vermuyden, worked to safeguard Norfolk farmers from flood. From the seventeenth century onwards, huge drainage projects changed wilderness into productive farmland for enterprising landowners; and, to preserve this, strings of drainage mills were built in the Dutch style.

Norfolk's buildings are not Dutch. Different street plans, narrower façades and different brick sizes and bonds all make them distinctive. If anything, the closest Dutch architectural connections are with the carefully built brick buildings of seventeenth-century America. Williamsburg in Virginia or the barns of New England, while specifically New World, refer more closely to their Netherlandish forerunners than do the refaced medieval houses of Aylsham or Walsingham.

BUILDING NORFOLK

BLICKLING & the first DUTCH GABLE 1618 - 1629

ORCHARD FARM
NR FRAMLINGHAM
EARL

(BAFFLE ENTRY) see Page 48

BUILDING NORFOLK

DUTCH GABLE i.e. with pediment

SHAPED GABLE ie without

1686 AYLSHAM OLD HALL

MARSHAM

1740

BINHAM

COLTISHALL

COLTISHALL

1624

BUILDING NORFOLK

NONE OF these except the warehouse ARE ACTUAL TYPES FOUND IN NORFOLK

HOIST FOR GOODS

TUMBLING IN

1672 (AUSTERE STYL)

BROUWNESGRACHT (A)

NIEUWLELIE

THATCH
PANTILE
BRICK

DUTCH HOUSE TYPES ABSENT IN NORFOLK

BARN TYPES from N.HOLLAND not found in NORFOLK

This house has a barn behind under the same Roof

Some Cottages in The Broads are a BIT LIKE THIS

BUILDING NORFOLK

LONG NECKED GABLE

TURNIP ~ SYMBOL OF DONOR OF THIS HOFJE
The Raepenhofje in AMSTERDAM

PA

T PRINSENGRACHT

There is a SIMPLE MESSAGE here. Norfolk & Holland have materials etc in common but have an ENTIRELY DIFFERENT VERNACULAR...

BARN / PASSAGE / HOUSE

T AN ENGLISH PE

There are DEFINITE similarities here between these two doorways, in particular the POLYCHROME RELIEFS

CUSTOMS HOUSE KING'S LYNN

HET ZONS HOFJE

FISHERMAN'S HOSPITAL YARMOUTH

145

15. TRANSPORT

If you sail from Wroxham along the river Bure to Great Yarmouth, turn right under the A12 and cross the expanse of Bredon Water to enter the Yare, you will in due course reach Norwich. There you will see the city through the eyes of a medieval merchant returning from the Low Countries. Along the way you may have made a short detour in Yarmouth and sailed along South Quay beneath that grand eighteenth-century parade, evidence of the town's mercantile success, then headed out towards the North Sea. Later along the reedy banks of the river you will spot the Roman walls of Burgh Castle to your left and pass most of the places that have seemed almost impossible to reach by road. The river Great Ouse, canalised and grand as it enters the Wash at King's Lynn, stretches across the infinity of the fens to Downham Market and on to Ely through areas completely inaccessible before the draining of the fenland.

Waterways were the great arteries of Norfolk's hinterland, as they were for most of lowland Britain until the nineteenth century. Sea-going vessels would unload into smaller craft when they could get no further, as the next stage of a journey by pack-horse would be laborious and slow. Even the minor rivers, the Tas, Thurne and upper reaches of the Wensun, were used as far as they were at all navigable. The advantages of a coastline that described half of the county meant that some towns like Wells-next-the-Sea were almost totally outward-looking in that their immediate hinterland was poor, sandy heathland supporting only a light agricultural population: its trade and wealth came entirely from the sea.

The river Bure becomes very modest indeed by the time it reaches Dilham. This made it unnavigable until the establishment of the North Walsham and Dilham Canal Company. A substantial investment of £30,000 produced 7½ miles of canal wide enough to take a Norfolk wherry. These were the indigenous sailing vessels that carried goods inland from the port of Yarmouth and transported agricultural produce around the inland river system. By 1826 the canal was open, connecting North Walsham to the river system. A system of staithes along the canal allowed access to a series of semi-industrial sites: for example, the bone mills at Antingham or the corn mill at Ebridge Mill, a building that survives today although derelict and currently awaiting conversion to alternative use. The arrival of the railway from Norwich in 1874 spelt the end of commercial viability for the canal, and it was sold in 1885 for £800. The last commercial load to be carried was in 1932, since when the canal has become overgrown and choked with weeds and rushes.

As noted before, the coming of the railways changed the fabric of Norfolk more than any other event in the nineteenth century, as it made industrially produced building materials, principally from the Midlands, instantly available throughout the county. The fact of the very late arrival of the lesser lines connecting Norfolk's hinterland with the regional centres meant that this dilution of the vernacular began to take effect only in the last two decades of the nineteenth century. This was twenty, thirty or even forty years behind the rest of the country and to a great extent explains the preservation of the market town in the county. Large hubs like Norwich and North Walsham acquired warehouses and rail yards, but the most peculiar of these railway developments was Melton Constable.

The railway network in the nineteenth century was controlled by dozens of operators whose lines converged at various points. One such was Melton Constable, the hub of the rural Norfolk railways and home of substantial train engineering works. In 1870 there was no village at Melton Constable. The tiny hamlet of Burgh Parva had 19 houses and 100 inhabitants, most employees of Lord Hastings, the proprietor. With the arrival of the Midland and Great Northern Joint Railway all this was to change. Adopting as its name that of Lord Hastings's nearby great house, the new village of Melton Constable quickly grew as the railway enterprise burgeoned. Yards, warehouses and a large engine building shed were erected, and Hastings released land for the development of railway workers' cottages which were built in 1882. The community continued to expand, until at its peak in 1911 the village had 1,200 inhabitants. More remarkable than this swift growth, however, was the architectural character of the settlement, for it illustrates most clearly the destructive effect of the railways on the local vernacular. Extreme convenience and cheap transport meant that *all* building materials were brought by train from the Midlands, where industrialised manufacture made them cheapest. The bricks, slate, and precast or manufactured architectural components are so recognisably not *of* Norfolk that the buildings could as easily be in Stoke-on-Trent. Hard bright red brick and alien Welsh slate are used in pattern book designs for quite high quality, industrial housing, and coming upon these unexceptional streets is always a surprise. Turning off the main road, this effect is amplified as you reach allotments or yards which feel decidedly northern. This is the clearest example of the effect of a change of transport on the built environment. Following the pernicious Beeching cuts of 1961, the station and the lines it served were closed; by 1964 the station had been demolished and the yards converted to an industrial estate, leaving the buildings as archaeological evidence of its brief surge to glory.

However, the railway has not entirely perished. Lines connecting Norwich with Yarmouth and Lowestoft through bleak but romantic marshland are heavily used. So is the unlikely and ineptly named 'bittern' line to Sheringham passing through Wroxham, Worstead and the beautifully restored station at Gunton (now converted to residential use). King's Lynn Station, with an unusually architecturally appealing curved glazed-in bar, is a more reliable route to London, making commuting from that town and its hinterlands more viable. Perhaps these lines will influence the sites of later development in the county.

Norfolk's road system has also served to prolong the architectural survival of the county as poor communications have acted as a damper on developement. To the south via the A11 is still frequently single-carriageway, while to the west the A47 is diabolically slow and unscenic. Driving around the county the overall lack of traffic is apparent, and there are large areas, those between the A140 Cromer road and the A1067 to Fakenham, where the driver is limited to remarkably minor roads and where even the most stalwart satellite navigation systems find their ingenuity severely taxed. Improvements will no doubt alter the relative isolation that an underdeveloped road system has provided, but until now this has limited the change from rural to satellite village to those settlements within ten miles of Norwich. Sprowston, Horsford, Horsham St Faith, Ringland, Taverham, Poringland and the Meltons circle the county capital and have all been subject to significant suburbanisation.

The last form of transport, air, has not had a major effect on the built environment, although the former RAF airfield at Horsham St Faith has served as a

BUILDING NORFOLK

substantial check to northern development, thus in part protecting the approaches to north and north-east Norfolk. However, transformed to a *relatively* modern regional civilian airport, it now serves as a reminder of Norfolk's recent strategic military past. Thrice daily return flights to Amsterdam have re-established the link across the North Sea between Norfolk and the Netherlands, once so significant, allowing day trips to Holland and international travel onwards from there.

The BERNEY ARMS MILL was built 1865 to grind cement clinker (This was chalky mud dredged from the bank of The R. Yare on which it stands.) Its use changed to Marsh drainage in 1886 and it was decommissioned in 1948

DRAINAGE MILL STRACEY ARMS

DRAINAGE MILL ON THE YARE (STEAM DRIVEN. Late (19) N'r STRUMPSHAW FEN

BERNEY ARMS MILL

DRAINAGE MILL @ CLIPSBY

148

BUILDING NORFOLK

SCS 1808

Having made such a thing about the difference between Holland & Norfolk this warehouse at Stalham Staithe is NOT UNDUTCH see its neighbour in Amsterdam for comparison

1909

More waterside warehouses at Stalham

Stalham Staithe

The Cantley sugar beet mill dominating the marshes around.

149

BUILDING NORFOLK

RAILWAY INSTITUTE

MELTON CONSTABLE after 1880..

INDUSTRIAL RAILWAY HOUSING
MELTON CONSTABLE

Railworkers Cottages
MELTON CONSTABLE

DOWNHAM MKT STATION 1847

This station served the WATTS NAVAL SCHOOL (founded 1873) This turned into The N. COUNTY SCHOOL in the 1890s Then became a BARNARDOs HOME - closing in 1955 It was demolished in 1960 but the beautifully restored STATION remains

COUNTY SCHOOL STATION 1886

150

BUILDING NORFOLK

TOLLHOUSE @ p 20

RAILWAY WATERTANK AT MELTON CONSTABLE

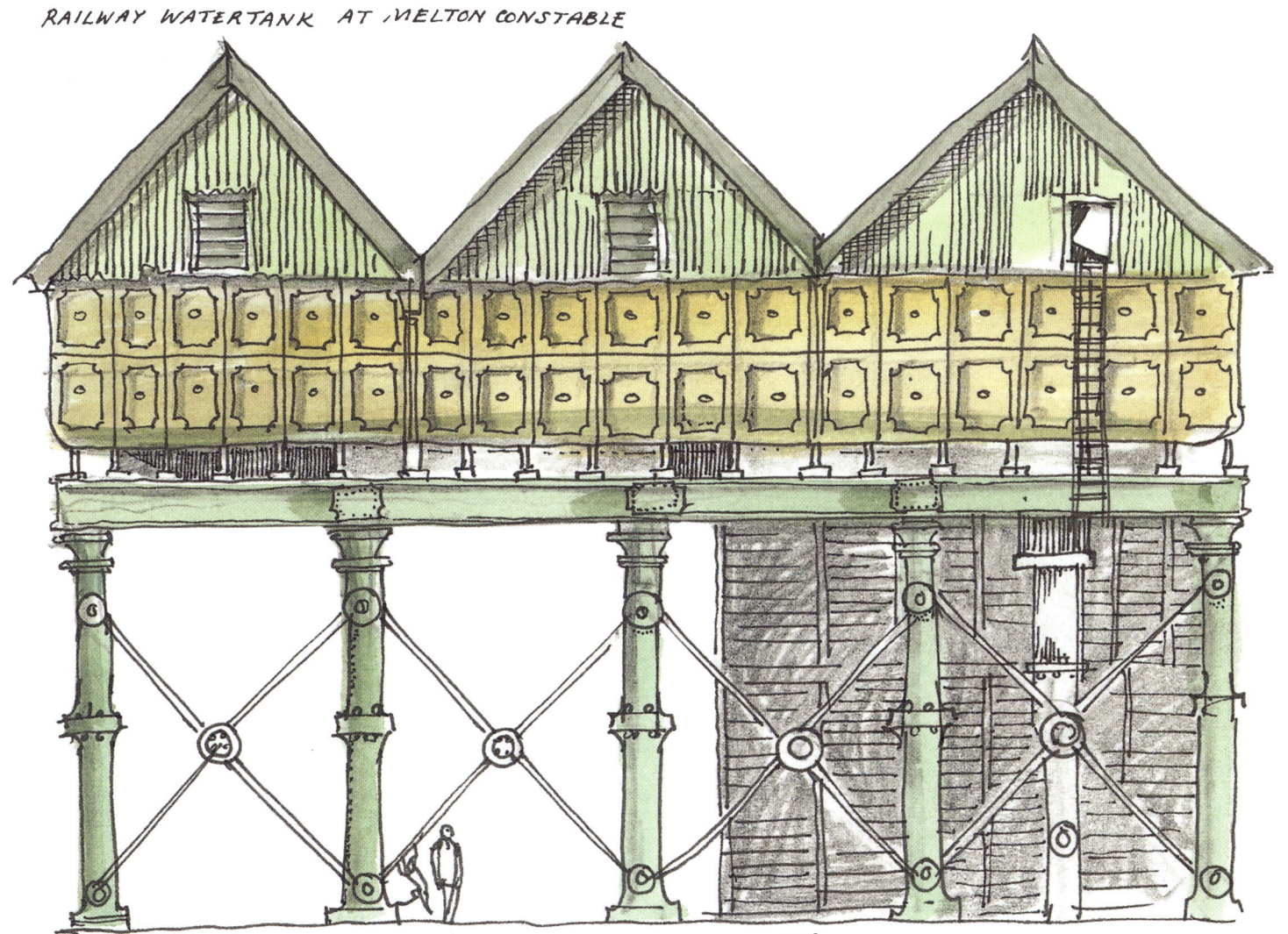

TATTY BUT V DISTINGUISHED - AN INDUSTRIAL TEMPLE 1882

16. TWO TOWNS: GREAT YARMOUTH AND KING'S LYNN

Corbridge's engraving of the West Prospect of Great Yarmouth was made in 1726. It shows the town from the landward side dominated by its two churches, the great medieval St Nicholas and the classical St George. The Quay is all but obscured by shipping unloading or passing on up the river Yare. The Gorleston side of the river is still hay meadow and grazing. Around the edge of the picture are shown twenty-nine town mansions, three or four storeys high with neat railings or formal gardens in front. They look rather like the best houses in Spitalfields in East London and are equally desirable. On the plan the rows running back from the Quay towards the market place and on towards the beach are clearly shown. This grid plan of sinuous main streets with smaller streets at right angles, the whole enclosed by a river on the landward side and the sea on the east, is likened by Pevsner to Manhattan. Although these two places are in character as different as could be conceived, the geographical similarity is good and certainly helps one to visualise Yarmouth. It has survived the years of nineteenth-century development, twentieth-century decay, a really thorough bombing by the Luftwaffe, and the usual ensuing post-war ravaging by credulous modernist town planners.

The plan may have survived but little of the grandeur of Corbridge's view has. The shops, away from the absolute centre, are tawdry and tired, and the shoppers also look more than a little frayed. Undeveloped until the nineteenth century when a series of speculative projects to the south began to appear, the seafront is remarkable in that one can currently drive the whole distance with almost no view of the sea. It is now seriously run down, and the great Edwardian fantasies – the Gem cinema, the Hippodrome and Barron's Amusements, put up as the Palladium – are now encrusted with low-budget fascias in garish day-glo colours and ill-conceived sign writing. Even the great St Nicholas, England's largest parish church, has a forlorn atmosphere of deep decay hanging heavily over it, its churchyard cleared and unloved, anti-vandal protection ever present, while the second church, St George, is now undergoing restoration after an architecturally unhappy sojourn as a traffic island and as a theatre, and is shrouded in rusting scaffolding.

Great Yarmouth has all sorts of architectural treats but they are well hidden: St James's church, a grand essay in Victorian decorated; the merchants' houses on the South Quay, a miniature version of the banks of the Neva in St Petersburg; the monument to Lord Nelson, precursor to his better known Trafalgar Square perch, this last lost in the anonymous wasteland of industrial suburb; Ralph Scott Cockerill's Fastolff House, an art nouveau extravagance; the tollhouses and the drop dead lovely Fisherman's Hospital of 1702.

In this respect Yarmouth is a great contrast to its western sister King's Lynn. King's Lynn is a showpiece. The walk – from the Tuesday market, a square European in scale, reigned over by the stately Duke's Head (1683), along the elegantly curving King and Queen Streets lined with prosperous merchants' houses, to St Margaret and the Saturday market and its surrounding medieval quadrangles, Hampton court and the Hanseatic warehouse – is as architecturally engaging as you could find in Britain.

The Quay is divided in the centre by the Purfleet, on the only remaining visible bank of which sits what must be one of Norfolk's best buildings, the customs house. This is a Restoration confection in butter-coloured Ketton limestone, all window and refined detail with an elevating, almost Dutch, cupola and weathervane. Facing it across King's Staithe Square is Bank House, a perfect early Georgian town house with two bays and a Gibbs door-case. The cornice has sprouted a baroque niche and rolled pedimented surround, lavishly bracketed and detailed. Bank House is only one of a group of idiosyncratic eighteenth- and late seventeenth-century buildings facing the Cut, which until the mid-nineteenth century brought so much shipping to Lynn.

Both these towns are economically depressed. Lynn has never recovered from the arrival of the railways in 1846 that wiped out the port's function as conduit for all goods to the county's hinterland. Its thriving whaling industry – the ships would sail from Lynn in March to return in July – was in decline from the 1820s onwards. Great Yarmouth, fattened on the miraculous draught of herrings that built the enormous town hall and banks in the late nineteenth century, buckled at the knees and collapsed when those shoals left the North Sea in the 1950s. The herrings were followed in short order by the holiday makers, who, lured by the unaccustomed *dolce vita* of the Mediterranean sun and food, also abandoned their traditional English seaside haunts, leaving Yarmouth high and dry.

Economic decline is not all bad. It is a force for conservatism, and a resistance to spending on assets that yield no income is a benign influence on the built environment until, of course, it begins to actually to fall down. It is a lack of money that has preserved the medieval plan of Yarmouth from the worst excesses of the post-war planners and kept unchanged the centre of Georgian-faced King's Lynn. (Indeed, the first time I visited Lynn it was swathed in eighteenth-century signage and artificial cobbles, and the costumed figures hurrying through the streets revealed that nearly all the town had been pressed into service as a film set.)

A lot of King's Lynn is lost. There was a well-meaning programme of slum clearance between 1933 and 1938. The *Lynn News* in 1933 quotes the vicar's 'thoughtful' sermon to the mayor and corporation as containing the phrase, 'Slum dwellers fare worse than gorillas.' The council planned to move nearly 2,000 people, 10 per cent of the then population, out of the yards that ran back from the main streets of the town rather as the rows do, or did, in Great Yarmouth. Archive photographs record these yards fully. Short rows of small houses appear to vary from early seventeenth century to late nineteenth. They do not all look to be in such very bad shape; indeed, they look as if they would now have become very desirable. A lot of the houses have steeply hipped roofs, and at this scale with old pantiles are very reminiscent of the smaller houses in rural Holland. No doubt this project would now be tackled in a more sensitive and preservationist way, and these urban cottages would, for the most part, have survived.

Such port activities as King's Lynn sustained have been further split by the emergence of the non-union port of Sutton Bridge further up the coast; here battleship-grey Russian freighters unload their fertiliser and collect corn, and while at Lynn there is still commercial activity further along the quay where timber from the Baltic is neatly stacked, it could not be described as a busy port.

Industry has spread around the edge of both towns. Yarmouth, home to the largest offshore oil port in Europe, has housed that oil's service businesses, and King's Lynn has a thriving food processing industry as well as all the usual edge-of-town retail concerns — but the fact remains that they are towns at the edge of Britain. Ever increasing fuel prices leading to expensive transport costs mean that they are badly situated for such manufacturing as continues in the country. Likewise the huge quantities of imports from the Far East are not landed at minor non-containerised ports like these, heading instead for the easy-to-access and well-connected ports of Felixtowe, Liverpool, Milford Haven and Ellesmere.

Tourism may well be the answer. It has served Yarmouth well in the past, but it seems more likely that King's Lynn — with its unspoilt townscape, outstanding buildings and a first-rate train service direct to King's Cross — will be the town to capitalise on this in the future. The train takes less than an hour to reach employment- and culture-rich Cambridge: perhaps this will make it a commuter town as well? With the glories of Holkham, Houghton and the Norfolk coast on its doorstep, perhaps a revitalised Duke's Head will accommodate high style holiday makers from London every weekend. Although relatively small, King's Lynn is, for its size, every bit as architecturally interesting as its erstwhile trading partners of Riga and Vilnius or the cities of Holland. Preserving the architectural heritage will be vital if this is to happen and the town rejuvenate.

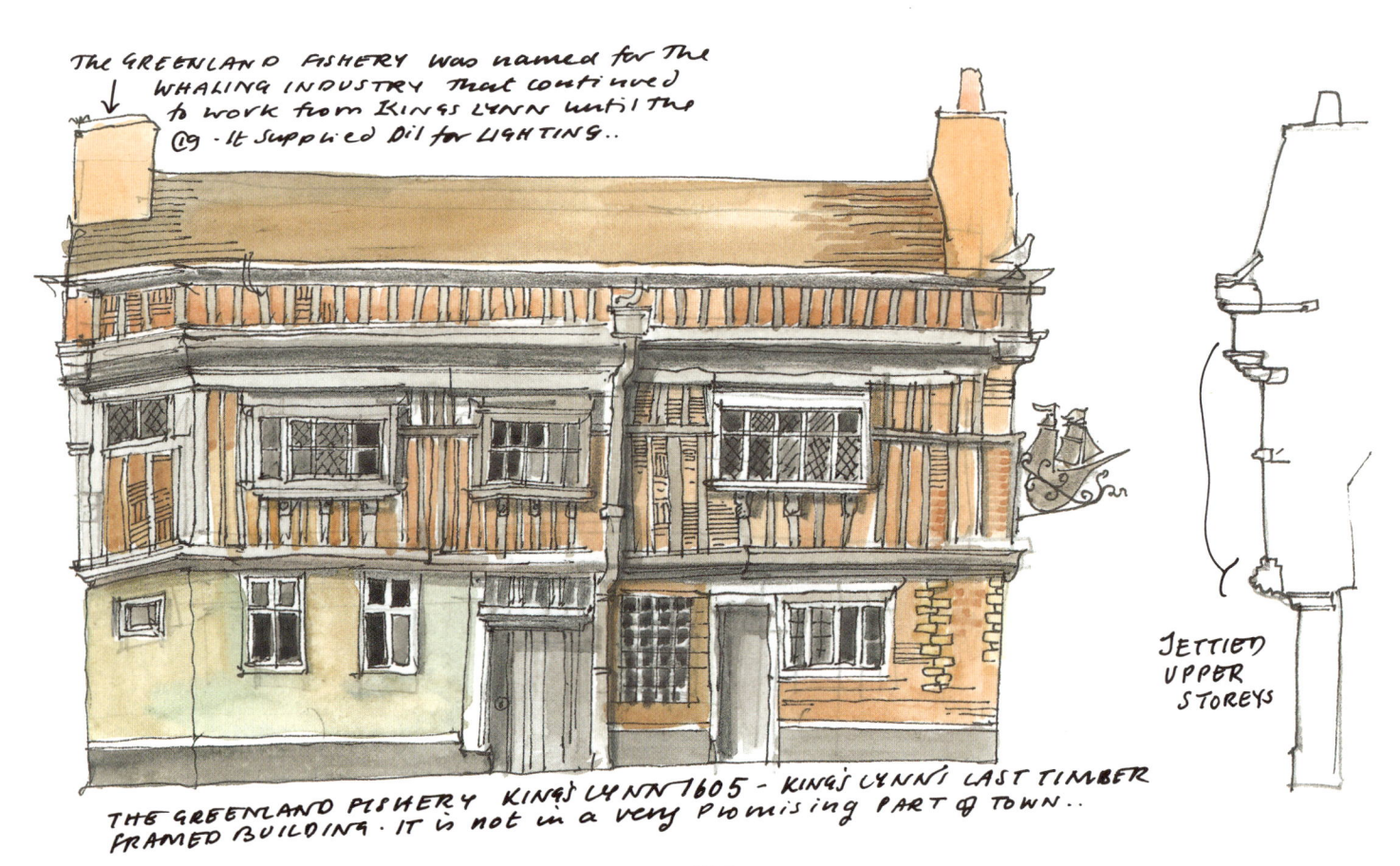

THE GREENLAND FISHERY was named for the WHALING INDUSTRY that continued to work from KINGS LYNN until the C19 · It Supplied Oil for LIGHTING..

THE GREENLAND FISHERY KINGS LYNN 1605 - KING'S LYNN'S LAST TIMBER FRAMED BUILDING · IT is not in a very Promising PART of TOWN..

JETTIED UPPER STOREYS

BUILDING NORFOLK

THE TOLLHOUSE
GT YARMOUTH - Every Period from C13 - C20. MUCH RESTORED. IT HAS BEEN PRISON, HOUSE, POLICESTATION, LIBRARY & NOW MUSEUM

NORTHWEST TOWER. GT YARMOUTH now houses an ARCHITECTS OFFICE (MEDIEVAL)

THORESBY COLLEGE EARLY C16. GABLES EARLY C18

155

BUILDING NORFOLK

OCTAGONAL TOWER was over the crossing of the FRIARY CHURCH

THIS IS NOW THE REAR ELEVATION but was originally the FRONT when the Tower faced this way towards the QUAY

BRITANNIA

GREYFRIARS TOWER · LYNN
The Remnant of the C13 & C14 FRANCISCAN FRIARY
Recently restored gardens surround the tower providing SCATEBOARDING OPPORTUNITIES

C16 TOWER · CLIFTON HOUSE KINGS LYNN

NELSONS MONUMENT YARMOUTH 1819 STANDS

TRAFALGAR SQ VERSION...
The Admiral sits by a coil of ROPE & A SHIPS BELL

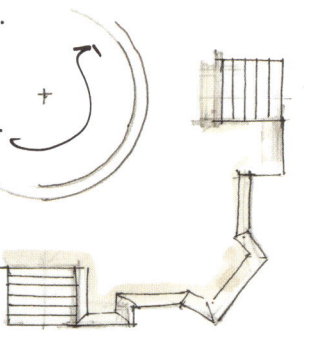

THIS MONUMENT celebrates the VICTORIES OF ST VINCENT THE NILE COPENHAGEN & TRAFALGAR

The NELSON MONUMENT is in STARK CONTRAST to its London SUCCESSOR of 1843. This one is stranded amongst FACTORIES in the OUTSKIRTS OF TOWN & was, until recently, shrouded in sand blown in to form a DUNE around its base.

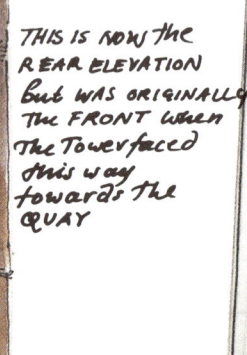

156

BUILDING NORFOLK

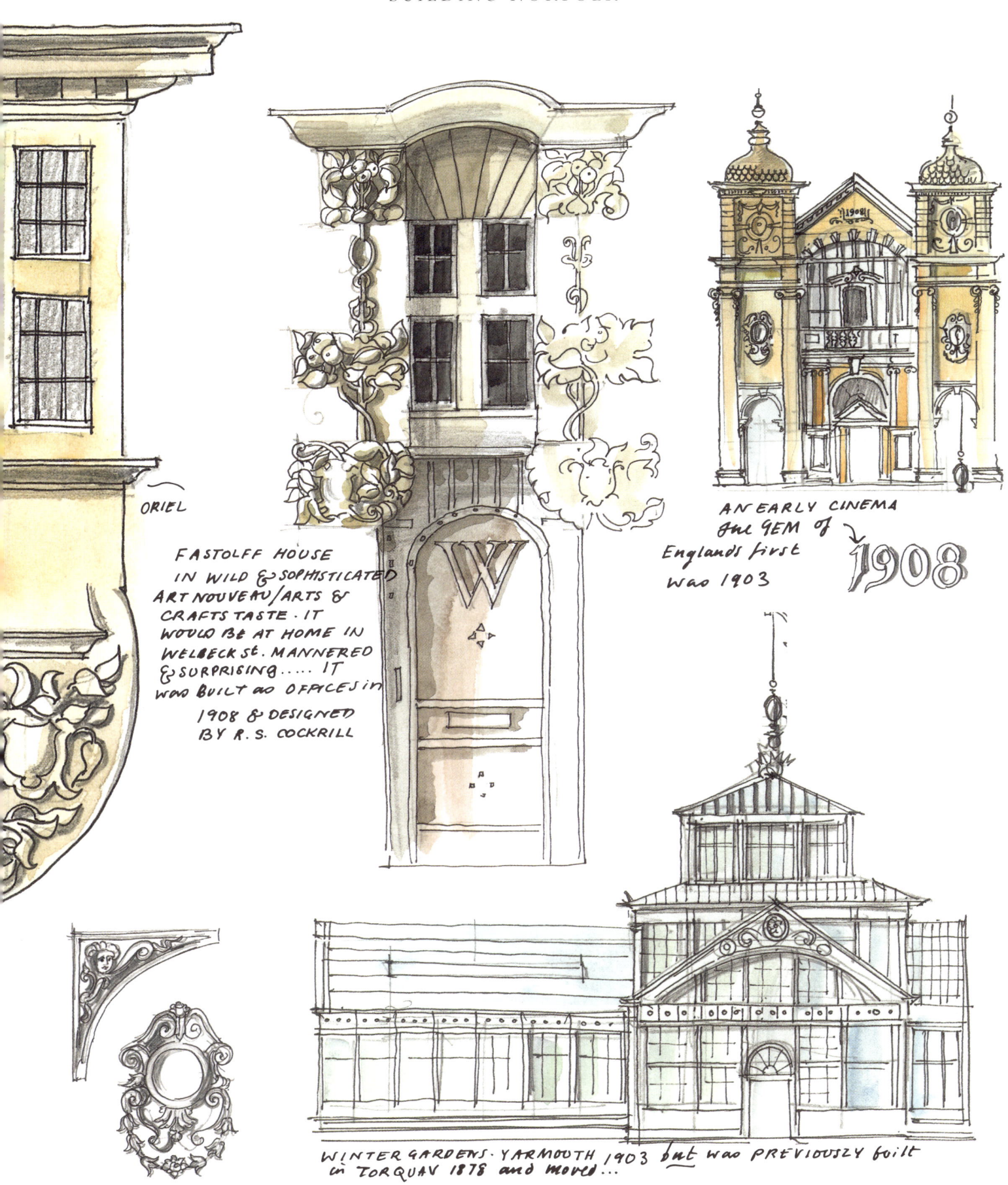

ORIEL

FASTOLFF HOUSE IN WILD & SOPHISTICATED ART NOUVEAU/ARTS & CRAFTS TASTE. IT WOULD BE AT HOME IN WELBECK St. MANNERED & SURPRISING..... IT WAS BUILT AS OFFICES IN 1908 & DESIGNED BY R.S. COCKRILL

AN EARLY CINEMA the GEM of England's first was 1903 1908

WINTER GARDENS. YARMOUTH 1903 but was PREVIOUSLY built in TORQUAY 1878 and moved...

157

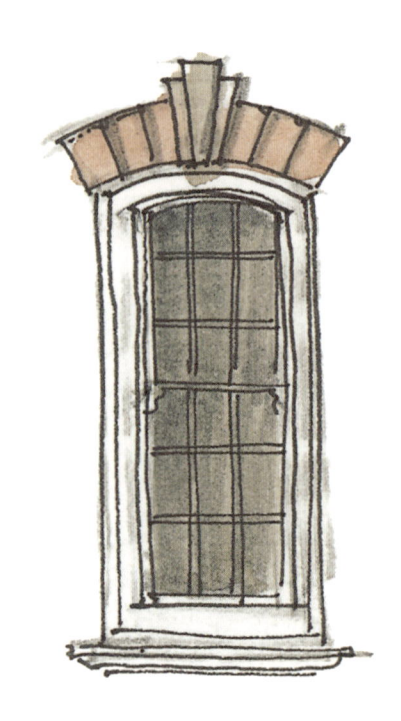

BUILDING NORFOLK

GIBBS SURROUND to DOOR of BANK HOUSE

CUSTOMS HOUSE. KINGS LYNN HENRY BELL 1683 of DUTCH INFLUENCE. IT IS V. WELL SITUATED on the edge of the QUAY & there are good views of every elevation. It houses the TOURIST OFFICE whose garish signs are slightly too visible....

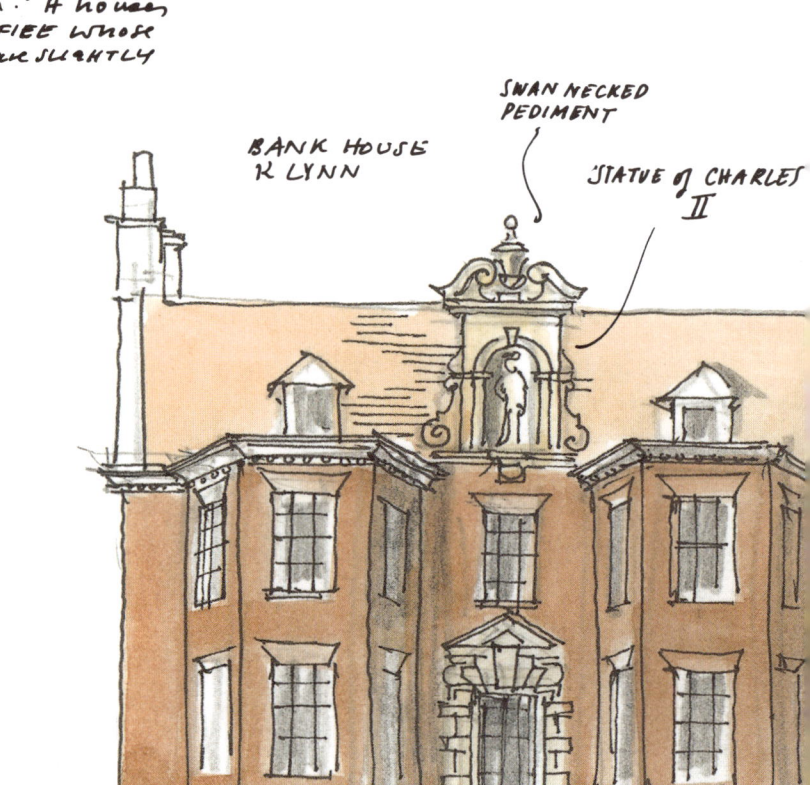

BANK HOUSE K LYNN

SWAN NECKED PEDIMENT

STATUE of CHARLES II

158

BUILDING NORFOLK

St James, Queens Rd, Yarmouth
1878-1908 'HUGE'...

GRANDEUR

18 GRANDEUR IN S. QUAY
GT YARMOUTH but behind are late C16
merchants houses.

Hoist for goods
see page 144

159

17. CROMER – NORFOLK ON HOLIDAY

From the late eighteenth century onwards Cromer became the holiday destination for Norfolk landowning or mercantile families: Astleys, Buxtons, Gurneys, Suffields and Barclays all built themselves summer villas in what was then a small fishing town but with a fine church. By the time the train reached Cromer in 1877 it had assumed its status as pre-eminent seaside town; a season from July to mid-August developed, with sea-bathing and tennis parties, and the hotels, Hotel de Paris, the Marlborough and Westward Ho!, the Belmont and the Grand, and the smaller Cliftonville opened to cater for the London market. Cromer was actively marketed and the term 'Poppyland' was coined by Clement Scott in the early 1880s. The year 1887 was perhaps the beginning of the height of Cromer fashionable history when, for two weeks, the Empress of Austria enjoyed the splendours of the now vanished Tucker's Hotel.

However the Tucker was not alone in attracting crowned or at the very least coroneted heads, the Hotel De Paris' visitors book also records the visits of the Lords Tennyson and Curzon, the Marchioness of Wellesley, Duchess of Marlborough and the Kaiser look-alike Prince Adolf of Schaumburg-Lippe, beginning in the middle of the nineteenth century.

The pier was built rather late, in 1900 and was initially unadorned except for two stylish pavilions. It acquired a theatre in 1902, which remains open, more unusually sustaining a proper seaside show each summer. Older members of the audience remember turning away from a rousing chorus of policemen, gondoliers or pirates and peering through the floorboards of the auditorium to see the North Sea swirling beneath. Sadly it is now close carpeted but the theatre retains some glamour.

All this social activity produced an outbreak of generous and architecturally sophisticated late Victorian and Edwardian buildings: heavily formed wooden balusters and newel posts, balconies and verandas, gothic porches and gables and complex roofscapes, and high quality brickwork and tile hanging occasionally combined with a nod to the vernacular, characterises these buildings.

Seaside glamour has now moved west, houses in the north-west of the county, Brancaster, the Burnhams and Thornham, are a social echo of these Edwardian pleasuredromes.

Large six- or seven-bedroomed houses with very modest gardens located exactly where the holiday will be and used for short periods only, are desirable and quickly sold, perhaps marking a second era of grand Norfolk holiday-making that will leave an interesting architectural legacy reminiscent of the eastern seaboard palaces of Long Island.

The best of surviving Victorian Cromer is on the east and west side of the town. This derives from two significant land sales in 1885. Samuel Hoare, a leading local banker and Benjamin Bond Cabell, whose father, a London lawyer of the same name, had bought the Cromer Hall estate in 1852. These two coastal magnates owned the land on the east and west of Cromer respectively. Bond Cabell was a most businesslike developer and keen to advance the prosperity of a town so much of the surroundings of which were his property. He chartered a special train on Wednesday June 17th 1885 to bring 200 enthusiastic investors from Liverpool Street. After lunching among the then refined Regency splendours of the Hotel de Paris, the potential purchasers descended like locusts on the auction, devouring the plots in a feeding frenzy of acquisition.

Over the next ten years, the plots sold were developed and those remaining are a copybook of late Victorian and Edwardian seaside architecture. Although a lot of the gardens have now been infilled with indifferent modern pale imitations there is still a Dornford Yates atmosphere of leisure and fun about the streets around Cliff Avenue. Ancient wisterias winding around the bulbous columns of loggias, esoteric porches of outlandish sub Arts and Crafts design and cherry trees heavy with blossom in April.

Cromer was not the only town to make this break. Mundesley was subject to valiant efforts to imitate its better established neighbour but somehow, despite the hotels sea views with a smattering of villas and a plucky little seafront, its failure to establish itself is all too clear; and it has become a depressing shadow, home to a drug rehab clinic and providing inexpensive holidays for the unsuspecting stranger.

Cromer continued to be a busy holiday town until the outbreak of cheap foreign holidays in the 1970s. The once glorious Hotel de Paris is now a low cost holiday for pensioners from the Midlands, the bar silent and gloomy and *the dansant* silent. However, ghosts of its heyday remain. The dining room windows' stained glass frame sepia views of Norfolk's nearest country houses, Felbrigg, Barningham, Heydon and Blickling as well as other less elevated local beauty spots. Surely this is a more felicitous advertisement of Norfolk's charms than the threefold A6 leaflet of glossy photographs of go-carting, Broads boat trips and the Wroxham narrow gauge railway in the dispenser by the reception desk.

While many of the hotels and great houses have now fallen on hard times and been subdivided or turned into old peoples' homes, Cromer remains the most likely of Norfolk's seaside towns to capitalize on any future expansion of English holiday-making. Its gracious seafront, dramatic topography and grand architecture must make it potentially attractive to some great developer, hotelier or restaurateur who, like Rick Stein in Padstow can help it to return to its Belle Époque glamour.

HOTEL DE PARIS · SKIPPER 1895

BUILDING NORFOLK

HOUSE BUILT for CROMER HALL.

BUILT as ESTATE HOUSING for CROMER HALL

BANK HOUSE 1896 a fanciful bit of QUEEN ANNE REVIVAL.

very peculiar porch...

G. RICHES JUNIOR · CABBELL Rd

162

BUILDING NORFOLK

JETTIED
ORIEL
(affording
valuable
SEA VIEWS

Two dainty seaside pavilions for the putting greens

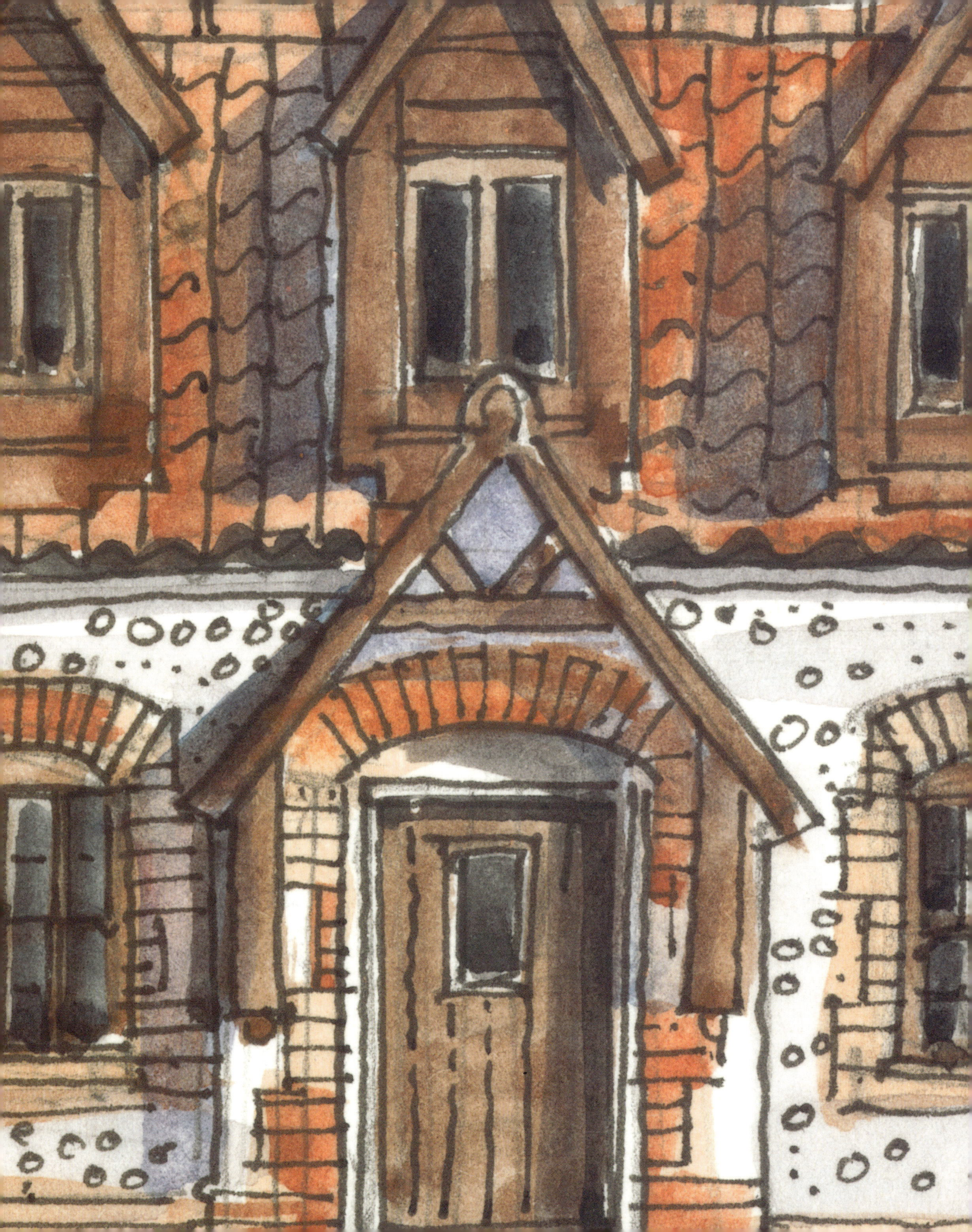

PART TWO
NEW BUILDINGS

18. DESIGNING NEW BUILDINGS

HOUSE IN N. WALSHAM C 1930 Built to a design from a Pattern book. vernacular revival.

The first part of this book has described the building stock of Norfolk, type by type, explaining how the particular features of the county – geological, environmental and economic – have moulded its appearance. It has described a wide-ranging and well-preserved stock of pre-twentieth-century building from the truly vernacular to the hyper-polite. These buildings mirror the history of an economy that has been largely dominated by agriculture and sea trade. The ports of Norfolk have withered, and agriculture, while still significant, has ceased to be the major influence on the county. As the economic base widens, so the buildings have changed. This second part addresses the challenges of adding to those buildings while protecting the existing built environment, thus getting the greatest benefits that can be gained from this well-preserved landscape. It investigates how and why people build as they do in Norfolk and end the book with a fantasy development of my own.

Norfolk is a finite resource. Land defines finite resources; there are 1,327,166 acres (550,000 hectares) in the county, and erosion, flooding and boundary changes apart, that can never change. Every home, shop or factory that is built uses part of that precious acreage, turning it into something of unquestionably greater financial value. It is of particularly high value because people want to live in Norfolk. They want to do this so much that a terraced house in Holt is worth about four times its equivalent in Stoke-on-Trent. That differential is not a reflection of a particularly vibrant economy or of easy connections to a city. It is due to the quality of life in the area. This is the product of a combination of a low density of population, easy access to the coast that borders half of the county, and an unusually unspoilt and beautiful built environment.

Does a county have a duty to maintain and protect this asset as custodians of its countryside, villages and towns? Should it ensure that by conserving that special quality the existing stakeholders are protected and their interests furthered? The county is not only the councils – county, district, town or parish – but extends to a huge and varied body of interested parties. This includes housing associations, property developers, architects, surveyors and, most importantly of all, individual owners. All these people have the ability significantly to affect the built environment both in detail and wholesale.

Norfolk has seen an increase in new building in the last twenty years, and in this it is no different from the rest of Britain. In fact, development pressure in

BUILDING NORFOLK

Norfolk has been less intense than in most of the South; perhaps it is not really a southern county. Cromer and Stoke-on-Trent are very nearly on the same line of latitude, but while Staffordshire is rather a county of the North, Norfolk is considered as southern. This is significant as there has been an inclination towards using a general-purpose non-specific southern style of building in new developments. This blanket adoption of 'anywhere' housing varies from district to district depending on the local council.

'Anywhere' housing is the antithesis to the vernacular. It is, in fact, the language of the commercial developer and is in part a reflection of what house buyers want but governed by maximum financial return alone. Thus, it cannot afford to reflect local styles of building or materials in any but the most cursory way. Despite this lip-service, it means that a house in King's Lynn or Southampton will be virtual twins and all local character will be lost. Detailing, in particular the fenestration of a new house, has a disproportionate effect on the character of the finished building.

The woodwork, windows and doors represent about 10 per cent of the cost of a new house: doubling the expenditure on these things would add £20,000 to the price of a £200,000 house. Perhaps that would not be an unreasonable addition if the consequence of that extra cost was a more pleasing house, genuinely in keeping with its neighbours and enhancing the built environment of its village or town.

This type of poor design is a particular problem in a ring of villages around Norwich, where higher pressure to build is coinciding with a lot of very low density suburban sprawl, often in woodland, leading to a seriously degraded environment. Villages like Poringland or Brisley have very little that is recognisably of Norfolk about them, and what remains of their architectural heritage is swamped in poor quality design and unimaginative planning. This new building is dull and featureless, thought by some to be less offensive than pastiche. But is this really the case?

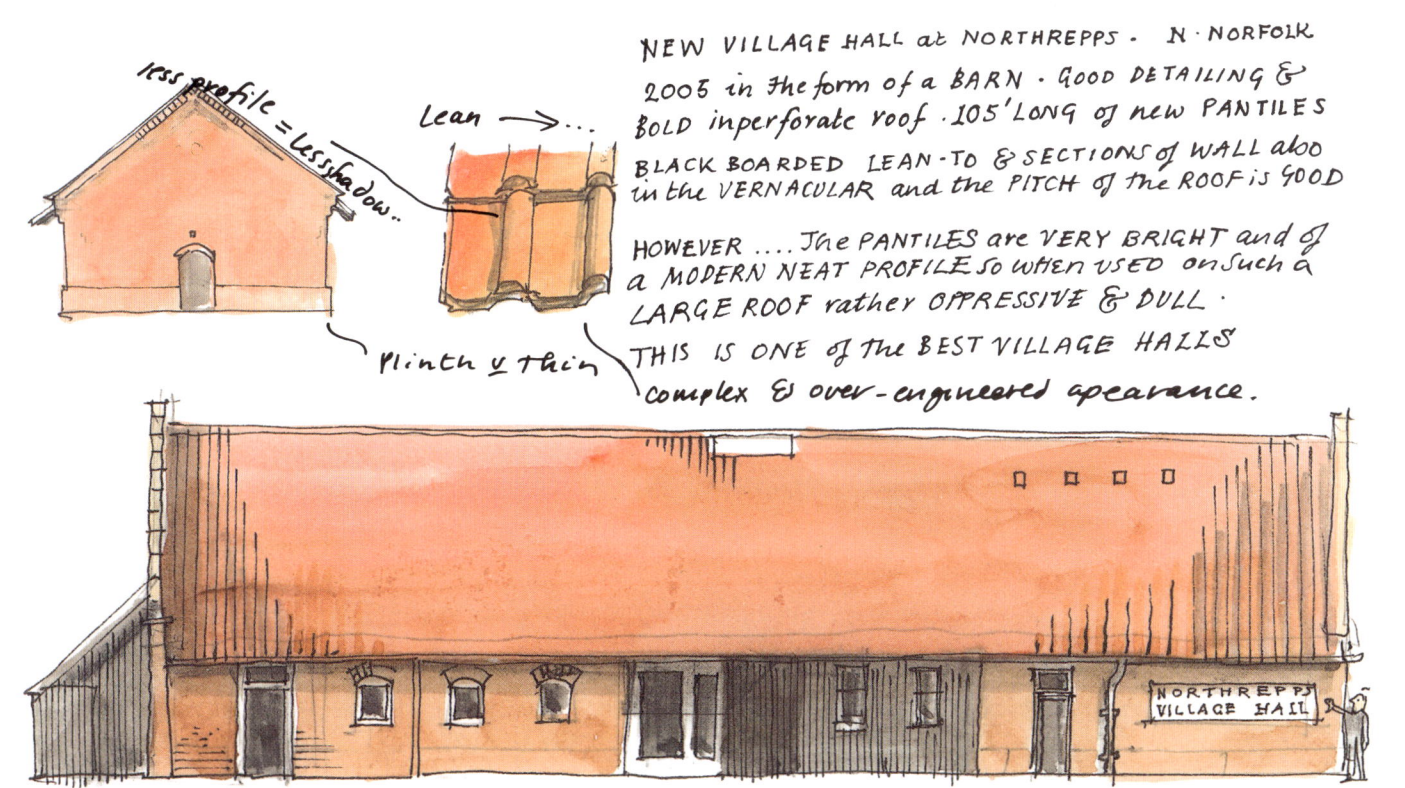

NEW VILLAGE HALL at NORTHREPPS · N · NORFOLK 2005 in the form of a BARN · GOOD DETAILING & BOLD inperforate roof · 105' LONG of new PANTILES BLACK BOARDED LEAN-TO & SECTIONS of WALL also in the VERNACULAR and the PITCH of the ROOF is GOOD

HOWEVER .... The PANTILES are VERY BRIGHT and of a MODERN NEAT PROFILE so when USED on such a LARGE ROOF rather OPPRESSIVE & DULL · THIS IS ONE of the BEST VILLAGE HALLS complex & over-engineered apearance.

less profile = less shadow..
Lean →
Plinth v thin

BUILDING NORFOLK

The term 'pastiche' is too often employed in connection with buildings: almost any building that in any way attempts to imitate or work in the language of a pre-twentieth-century style is currently denigrated as pastiche. The example given is always Poundbury, the Prince of Wales's new village on the edge of Dorchester. 'Poundbury' is a byword for the negation of progress and modernity; its use of local materials and traditional styles and building techniques is seen as a pernicious form of architectural escapism. But Poundbury is *popular* – people want to live there, and prices there have risen far more than in surrounding villages and in the town of Dorchester itself. Likewise, developers have been satisfying a popular demand for the last 100 years by building in the Victorian style or its child, the neo-Tudor. Initially innovative and a natural development of the Arts and Crafts style, it has become increasingly debased and diluted.

Despite its rabid rise, modernism as the intellectually accepted architectural style of the twentieth century has never really caught on in residential building. In his review of the Victoria and Albert Museum's 'Modernism' exhibition for *Apollo* magazine in May 2006, the architectural historian Gavin Stamp states that despite the adoption of the theories of Le Corbusier by the architectural establishment, 'Tudor remained the dominant style in England throughout the twentieth century.' Most suburban building justifies his statement on into the twenty-first.

PORCH of DUBIOUS PARENTAGE dominating This elevation

specious BOARDING

ODD ASYMMETRY

The worst sort of rootless ANYWHERE building – This is the type of house that seriously DILUTES the visual integrity of The built environment...

SEASIDE ART DECO DECORATION

over-engineered plastic barge board

CROMER SCHOOL – IN ART DECO STYLE · 1930s

STYLISH FUTURISTIC CENTRAL BAY

Hmm.... The ARTS + CRAFTS meets MEXICO ... ANOTHER VISUAL DISASTER - INAPPROPRIATE AND CRASS DETAILING WITH NO LOCAL ANCESTRY. AGAIN IT TAKES FEW of these to lose the LOCAL character of a village

There was a spirited sprinkling of Bauhaus-inspired modern houses in the 1930s amongst what the twentieth-century cartoonist and writer Osbert Lancaster described as 'neo-Tudor by-pass variegated' rows of villas, and there was a near-universal adoption of modernist principles in the architecture of tower blocks, factories and public low-rise housing estates during the 1960s and 1970s. But the style has proved to be just that, a style, and not the panacea to all building problems that it purported to be. More specifically, modernism is a style that has been rejected by people for their houses. Le Corbusier's model planned city of Chandrigarh in Madhya Pradesh, once mooted as the new capital of independent India, is now a peeling wreck. Doleful dromedaries plod through the leafy boulevards, and camps of colourful tents, stacks of dung for fuel, and shanty towns bursting with irrepressible real Indian life clutter the architect's intended austere lines and subtle geometrical screens.

If the ascendancy of modernism has passed with the tower blocks, unlamented and unloved, might not the unease with reproduction end as well? There is little or no modernist building in rural Norfolk with the exception of a few seaside rarities and the unlikely Ridlington Manor built by J. Owen Lloyd in 1935. Current developments are less austere, decoration has crept back, and even the standard appearance of a housing association estate is now Enfeebled Victorian. If we are remain culturally backward-looking, would it not be better to work fluently and creatively in the language of tradition than to imitate it superficially and ineptly?

A particularly WELL PRESERVED Inter-war BUNGALOW. Crittall windows with Pantile roof. WHILE THIS IS early ANYWHERE building it is so familiar it is almost an English vernacular of its own, certainly it is TRADITIONAL..

PORCH TROUBLE: an over-specified Pantiled roof and board covers a plastic and dimly GEORGIAN-TYPE door with a base and over glazed panel at the side This is POOR QUALITY DESIGN

No 32 CROMER Rd HOLT

19. PLANNING

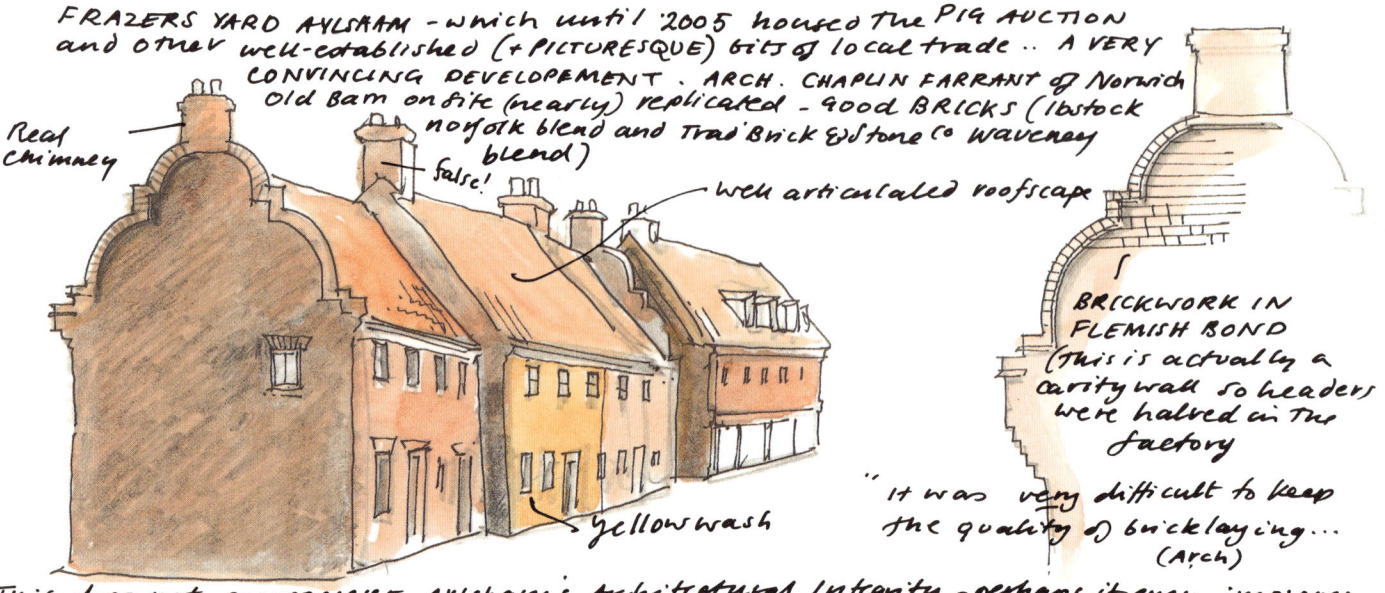

FRAZERS YARD AYLSHAM - which until 2005 housed THE PIG AUCTION and other well-established (+ PICTURESQUE) bits of local trade.. A VERY CONVINCING DEVELOPEMENT. ARCH. CHAPLIN FARRANT of Norwich Old Barn on site (nearly) replicated - good BRICKS (Ibstock Norfolk blend and Trad Brick & stone Co Waveney blend)

Real chimney — false! — well articulated roofscape — yellowwash

BRICKWORK IN FLEMISH BOND (This is actually a cavity wall so headers were halved in the factory

"It was very difficult to keep the quality of bricklaying..." (Arch)

This does not COMPROMISE Aylsham's Architectural Integrity - perhaps it even improves..

The built environment is protected by the planning system. This was established nationally but is controlled locally, currently by the five district councils. North Norfolk is a council that seems particularly concerned about the appearance of new building, a grim irony lost on few who enter its quite extraordinarily ugly offices on the edge of Cromer. It is also probably the area with lowest building pressure and hence the best preserved built environment. It publishes a design guide, currently under revision, that gives a huge amount of help to anyone planning a new building. This is a guide to desirable materials, roof pitches and relationships of one building to another. It also gives examples of best practice, suggesting window and door details, use of brick and flint or chalk, and other architectural features. But this is a guide only: the planning system can oppose and refuse, but is not empowered to insist on what must be done. Indeed, given that a lot of planning officers are relatively untrained in architecture, this may be no bad thing. 'Planning' is much hated and householders understandably resist being told what to do, but the planning authorities have limited powers.

Even in conservation areas, defined parts of each district considered to be of particular importance in terms of landscape and buildings, there are only limited controls available to the local authorities. These areas were established in the 1970s and are often correct in their extent, reflecting a particular estate, village or part of a town with architectural integrity. But they may give a false sense of security. It is hard for the district council to resist the fitting of UPVC double glazing in an unlisted building, even in a conservation area, and anyway opposing the supreme authority of the environmental lobby is perceived as close to treasonable. Most of the available controls concern the dimensions and site of new buildings and, in the case of developments large or small, their density. Elevations and details are outside the planners' control, and making these sensitive to their surroundings is the responsibility of the owner and builder. Planners can refer to the

BUILDING NORFOLK

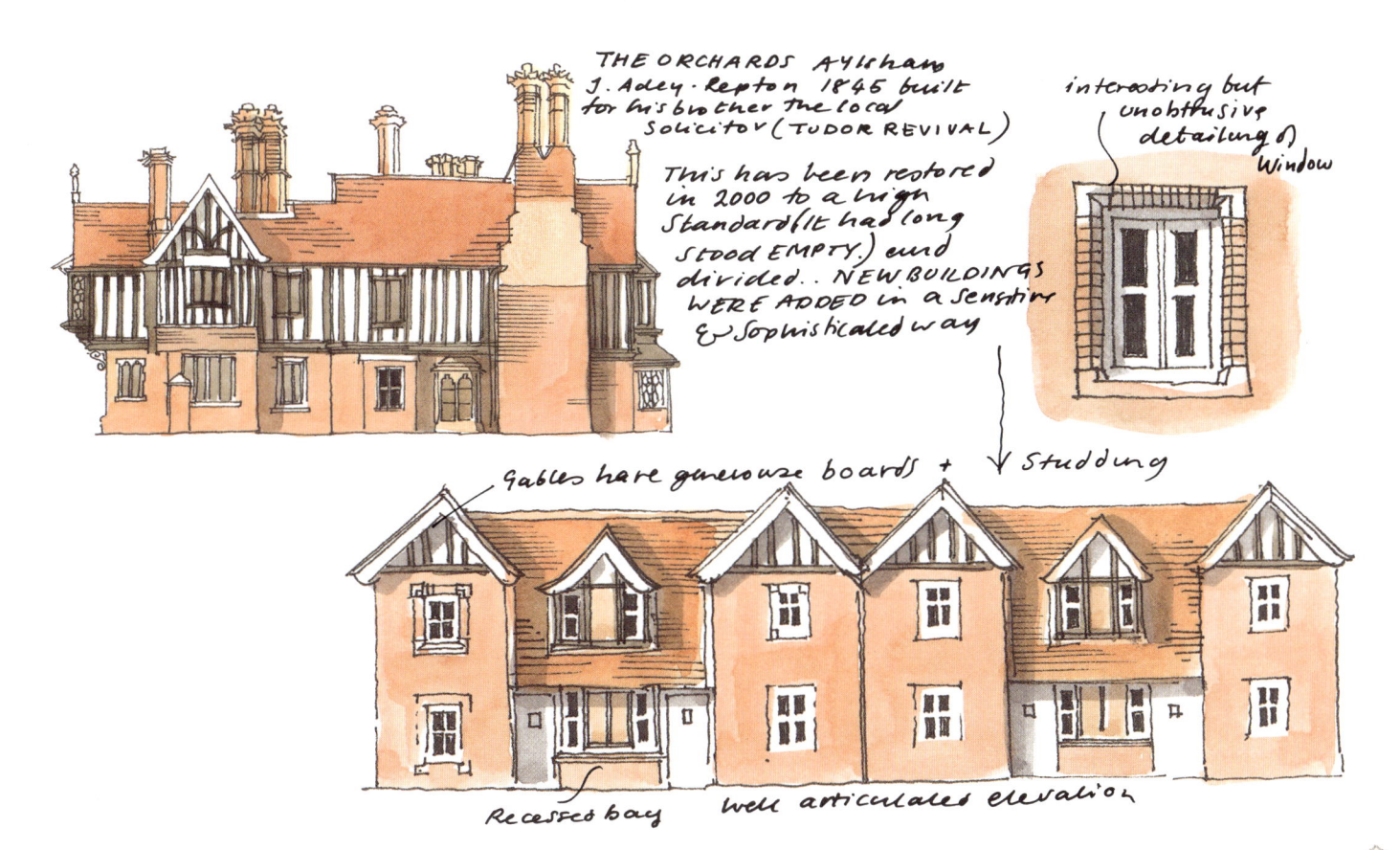

THE ORCHARDS AYLSHAM J. Adey-Repton 1845 built for his brother the local solicitor (TUDOR REVIVAL)

This has been restored in 2000 to a high standard (it had long stood EMPTY) and divided. NEW BUILDINGS WERE ADDED in a sensitive & sophisticated way

interesting but unobtrusive detailing of window

Gables have generous boards + studding

Recessed bay   well articulated elevation

design guide and hope that the builder will take notice, but they are without claws and can only turn down an application for non-aesthetic reasons.

Consequently, a familiarity with the local vernacular, the language of the building in the area, is absolutely essential for builders, owners and architects. The architects prove to be less important than might be imagined, as the majority of smaller buildings are conceived without the involvement of an architect at all. In previous centuries this would have been something of an advantage, or at least no disadvantage, as the restrictions of finance and constraints of availability would have combined with the builder's innate knowledge of local tradition to ensure the production of a satisfactory and truly vernacular building. This unselfconscious correctness is no longer the norm; a complete reliance on alien and industrially produced materials and components means that without the educated eye of an architect, the building will only be an approximation of the local style.

GOOD NEW HOUSE at STANHOE · N. NORFOLK clearly and FIRMLY in the vernacular style but of sophisticated design

171

20. NEW BUILDING TYPES

modest metal chimney

a sensitive barn conversion at BARNEY minimum of new PIERCINGS + roof is inviolate

why the plain boards? is this to maintain honesty or is it economics?

old signal box enlarged

The changes to the economy of Norfolk have brought with them new building types. None is more significant than the barn conversion. These are of great significance in the county both visually and economically because, as a rural and more importantly an arable county, Norfolk is well supplied with large barns. Like churches these are important landscape components, often isolated in open country. Changing agricultural practices and consolidation of small farms onto larger holdings have brought redundancy to many of these buildings, and with that the possibility of conversion to residential use. English Heritage's guide to barn conversion, *The Conversion of Traditional Farm Buildings*, of October 2006 covers a lot of the inherent problems of this change of use but recognises that.

Re-use is inherently sustainable. These buildings represent a historical investment in materials and energy, and contribute to environmentally benign and sustainable rural development. The concept of reuse is not a new one. Farm buildings have often been adapted over a long period to accommodate changing farming practices and technologies. Some have a greater capacity to accommodate change or new use than others, and a small number are such historically or architecturally significant elements of our heritage that they should be conserved with minimal or no intervention.

Local planning regulations are less sensible. There is a general policy of passing applications for multiple units which, while making companionable developments of buildings, increases the number of inhabitants and is likely to lead to even more suburbanisation. More damagingly, the current policies favour holiday accommodation over permanent residences; although superficially good for the local economy, this is not socially beneficial to local rural communities in the way that a family home or even the much despised second home would be. The possibility of building many units in a farmyard drives up the price, thus making it an inevitability.

Ian Johnston runs AVADA, a small developer of barns, and has worked on projects throughout the county. Hall Farm at Sculthorp is visible from the Fakenham to Lynn road. It is now unrecognisable from the rather undistinguished yard it previously was, and yet it retains a strong feeling of being a farmyard and of its component elements being recognisable farm buildings. There is a powerful market for barn conversions. They are popular as second homes, and Johnston sells most of his homes to customers from London. His mantra is 'comfort with character'; to him this means underfloor heating, natural stone floors, Iroko window frames, and exposed beams. These are visible in another development further west at Great Bircham. This was part of the Sandringham estate and has not only been converted to residential use but augmented by two large new houses in the guise of barns. This does rather destroy the argument that conversion conserves the original settlement pattern of a farmyard. While the old barns have been preserved in overall form and little changed in external elevation, the new buildings have little architectural value, and in fact along with the bland walling that divides one plot from another they are probably the weakest link in the project. Internally he has replaced original beams with new trusses made of French oak, and these timber elements are really a little too slight, the trusses being over-simple in that they have no collar, purlins, braces, etc., and feel over-simple in construction because they rely on steel bolts rather than oak pegs in a traditional construction method.

These are the things that Johnston thinks his customers are looking for in a barn conversion: Flint, arched windows, screens, internal exposed beams and old beams in preference to new .

Gardens are not the highest priority for most of these customers, many of whom are holiday homeowners and only really want somewhere to cook and eat outside in the garden. So in the main gardens are small but much walled-about, and in these walls all attention to detail has been abandoned, resorting instead to a completely plain new brick wall with a single line of tiles set transversely and another row of bricks set side-on on top. In some ways these are the dominating feature as you drive through the farm as they are 5 feet (1.5 m) high and are so unarticulated that they become visually intrusive beyond their size; indeed, they are even more dominant when seen from inside the properties. This redundant farmyard has nevertheless been reused, fulfilling English Heritage's ecological requirements, and those buildings that are not completely new are well preserved and will survive.

Another new housing type is the 'outsize cottage'. The cottage is desirable, cosy, manageable and accessible. But it is also small, too small really for many of the people who want to live in them today, as modern domestic requirements are so very different from those of a nineteenth-century farm worker, who lived very simply and without any indoor sanitation or indeed running water. Rather than recognise this problem and instead build a small house, a building type that would more readily accommodate the needs of the owner, there has been a tendency to produce a bastard hybrid that sets out to remedy the difficulties of cramming four large bedrooms, two bathrooms,

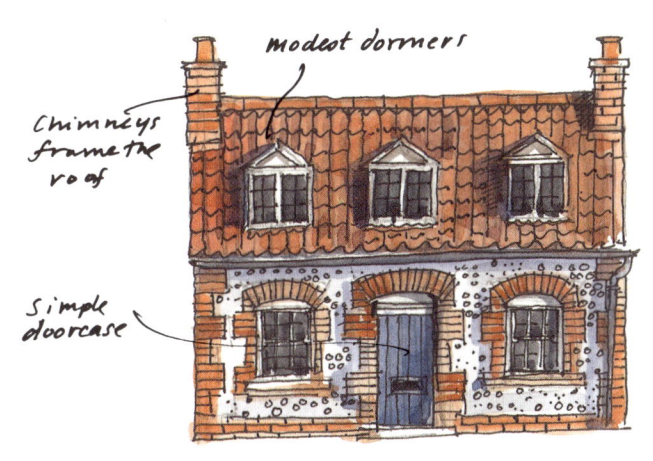

TWO IDENTICAL COTTAGES.. GOOD... and BAD

a sitting room, hall and spacious kitchen and utility room into a format better suited to a kitchen, parlour and two bedrooms above. The result, with giant outsize porch massively overengineered and soaring gable to contain the first-floor rooms, is visually unrestful and sits ill-at-ease, dwarfing its older neighbours. This is important. Destroying the scale of a group of buildings is very compromising to its appearance and takes away from the integrity of the village setting. As with all sensitive development, the design of a new house relies on observation of its neighbours.

What do house buyers want?

Architectural considerations do not seem to rate high in the house buyer's list of priorities, and this is not a problem limited to low-cost buildings or housing estates. Louis de Soissons has run the Norwich office of Savills estate agents for fifteen years and has arranged the sale of many large country houses. He claims that even with properties worth over £1,000,000 priorities are Accommodation, location, setting (garden, drive, etc.) and appearance.

And this order was confirmed by Michael MacNamara, who makes high quality conversions of

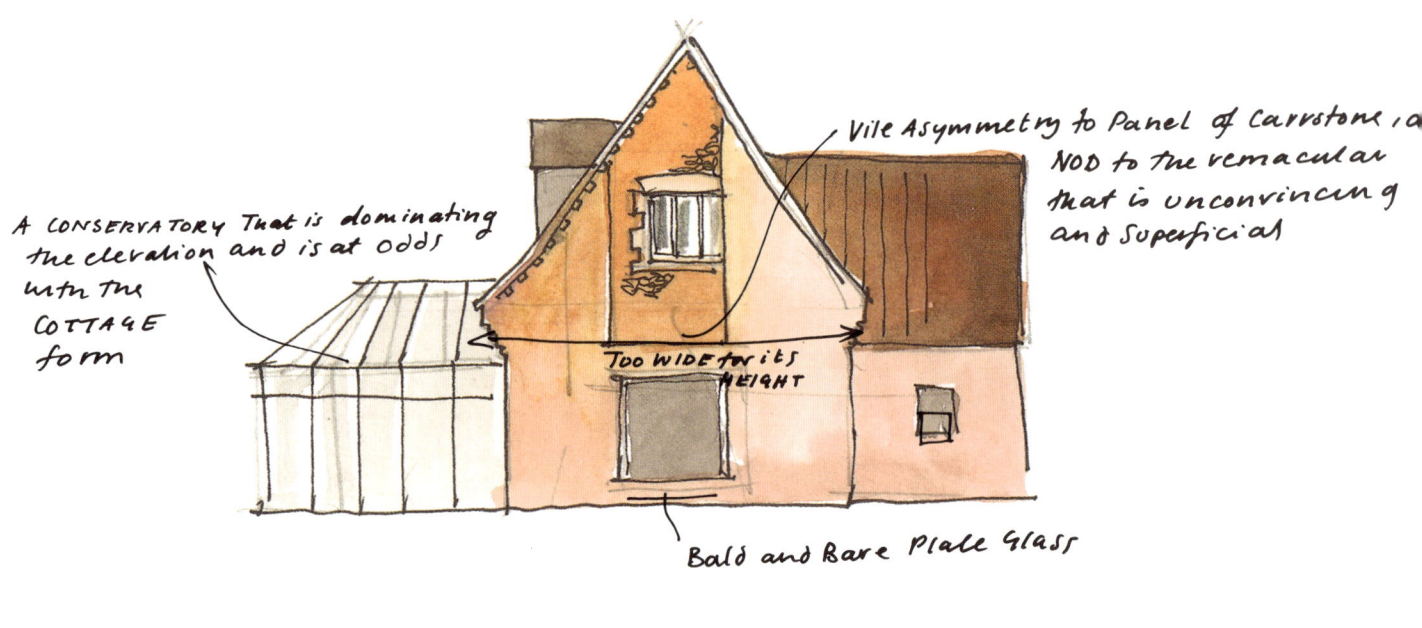

BUILDING NORFOLK

Good end elevation
wasteful garage

Shallow concrete tiled roof
Alien Tile hanging
Pilotti

THESE are three HORRID examples of featureless & bland "ANYWHERE" houses. (all NO DOUBT NICE TO LIVE IN)

THIS TYPE of HOUSING can QUICKLY DOMINATE The BUILT ENVIRONMENT & DESTROY ITS LOCAL INTEGRITY

STALHAM POLICE STATION — VERNACULAR MODERNISM
QUITE JOLLY.. or silly?

a peculiar idea.

insulting panel of flintwork — lip-service to the vernacular

Sturdy chimney stacks
Good hipped roof

FOUR GOOD PAIRS of COUNCIL HOUSES Generous sizes compared to modern SOCIAL HOUSING (or Private)

DULL Rendered elevations DATE 1928.

NICE KICK To the HIP of This ROOF ↳

barns, and by Philip Makepeace, whose company, Norfolk Homes, builds standard properties.

It is the customer, whether house owner embarking on restoration or purchaser of a new or old building, who can set the agenda. A change in priorities, and a consequent willingness to spend more on the visible external detailing and elevations of a house, would imply a recognition of the importance of the visual and architectural integrity of a village, street or piece of countryside and of preserving the very thing that makes it a desirable place to live.

Wells and The Butts

A most irregular bit of planning is The Butts or Buttlands in Wells. Wells has managed to escape the faint miasma of gloom that can hover over Norfolk's seaside towns. It is resolutely jolly. It has none of the Edwardian splendour of Great Yarmouth, Sheringham's Victorian comfort or Cromer's Regency refinement. More than any of these it is a Norfolk town on the sea, its architecture being more vernacular and less affected by the railway, which did in fact reach Wells in 1847.

It is a port and feels ancient. Seventeenth- and even sixteenth-century remnants appear among the colour-washed rendered elevations of the High Street and quay; and in the sadly increasingly built-over or developed yards and courts behind, there is a strong feeling of a medieval plan surviving.

Until the 1970s, when the moving channels and mudbanks finally made Wells Creek unnavigable to all but the smallest fishing vessels, there was a thriving malt trade out of Wells. The jettied warehouses along the quay piped malt and later corn from Norfolk's farms into ships bound in the nineteenth century as far afield as the Guinness brewery in Ireland, returning via South Wales to collect a return cargo of coal. As late as the 1980s smaller Baltic-bound grain ships were loading at the quay.

Ship owners, maltsters and corn dealers needed accommodation, and in the early nineteenth century an elegant and spacious square was developed a quarter of a mile inland from the waterfront. The west side of Buttlands was open land when Queen Victoria acceded to the throne in 1837, but shortly afterwards the land was sold for development. The east side already existed, and by 1825 the Globe Inn had been created from three earlier cottages.

This square was not planned like one of Nash's Regency terraces in Brighton or Eastbourne but was carried out piecemeal. Many of London's earlier Georgian squares had been built like this: that is, sold lot by lot to prospective owners and speculative developers, who then built with the slight variations that so characterise those squares today. Here the plots were built on with little reference to their neighbours, producing a complete mixture of plot or house size and material. Some kind of homogeneity is provided by all the houses being similar in architectural style. Certainly, there are no more than thirty years between them until the prettily named Roman Catholic church of Our Lady of the Sea, which acts as a late Victorian footnote. The houses themselves vary, as do their relationships to one another: some fully detached, some forming an informal terrace, and some divided by visually significant gaps provided by drives and garden walls.

So successful was this refined and elegant square, home to the leading solicitors and merchants of the town, that the whole focus of Wells life migrated to it. The Crown Inn, built on the garden of an old school, replaced The Fleece, once an Aldeburgh-type Moot Hall on stilts, as commercial and social epicentre. When house numbering was introduced to Wells in the 1920s, The Butts was exempt, a testament to its prominence and importance.

This could be an interesting model for modern developers to follow, combining varied sizes of property from three-bedroom cottages to substantial six- or seven-bedroom houses in a well-articulated and visually engaging way without using the self-conscious Brookside style of informal road plans. The large green also provides useful open space both as an extension of private gardens and as somewhere for a travelling boy on his holidays to kick a football about.

This type of varied mix of house sizes could provide a dynamic and socially cohesive neighbourhood as well as an architecturally interesting proposition. By this I do not mean the dogmatic sprinkling of low-cost homes among bonus-belt West Norfolk palaces, but rather a variation in size that might allow a widow to move from her large family home to a much smaller house nearby without the disruption and emotional upheaval of a more distant move. It would also provide an opportunity for those of slender means to move into an area that they most want to live.

OLD BUILDINGS IN CHURCH PLAIN · WELLS

Behind the busy quayside and lower sections of the High Street, Wells quietens down to an area of rendered and colour-washed streets, undramatic and remarkably well preserved. This is in part due to the town's commercial drift quaywards from the 1960s onward, when the port activity began to dry up and those buildings associated with that trade – wharves, malt houses and warehouses – began to be converted to retail use.

A particularly good example of this is on the east side of Church Plain (see illustration): these houses of quite varying sizes, at least one of them a former shop, form an irregular terrace. The right-hand four are under a common roof – they were originally a set of eighteenth-century almshouses – and the left-hand two are individually roofed in pantiles of slightly varying colour. A broad plat band divides the storeys of the largest house, while variations in colour and relative closeness to the road (see plan) articulate the others. Substantial and unrendered chimneys give relief and punctuate the ridge.

Almost facing the terrace is a new development built in 1993 at the convergence of High Street and Marsh Lane (see illustration). This was originally the site of the Thurgars department store built in the 1880s. Great effort has successfully been employed to ensure that the building on this very visible site does not at all compromise the visual integrity of the area. The elevations are in colour-washed brick, the lowest five courses of which are painted black in imitation of the plinth of their neighbours. The houses are identical in scale to their older neighbours and are roofed in pantiles with chimneys. Parking is centralised and is hidden in the centre of the site, and the windows are all of an appropriate size.

However, there are ways in which, with minor and inexpensive changes, this composition could be altered so as actively to enhance the area rather than simply avoid visual compromise. First, in the ground plan: all the houses have exactly the same relationship to the road and pavement, so there is no variation or interest here. Second, in the elevation (A): again every window is the same in detailing and arranged in too schematic a way, alternating double and triple casements. This imposes too self-conscious an order on what is a vernacular-style building. There are also no doors on the street for very practical reasons. Entry is via the central parking area at the rear of the properties, and two doors would be both wasteful of space and would compromise the internal plan. But this does leave a strangely blank or even blind appearance which is visually unrestful.

The gap between the top of the ground-floor window and the sill of the first-floor window is also worrying and at odds with that relationship among its older neighbours. This proportion is significant and is a major component in the elevation. The windows form a smaller part of the overall elevation and contribute to that feeling of blindness in the façade. This is, of course, an outward manifestation of the improved ceiling heights in the rooms inside.

Gable and roof pitch: only one is visible, at the foot of the High Street elevation. It is entirely unrelated and different from its neighbours – being wide and

178

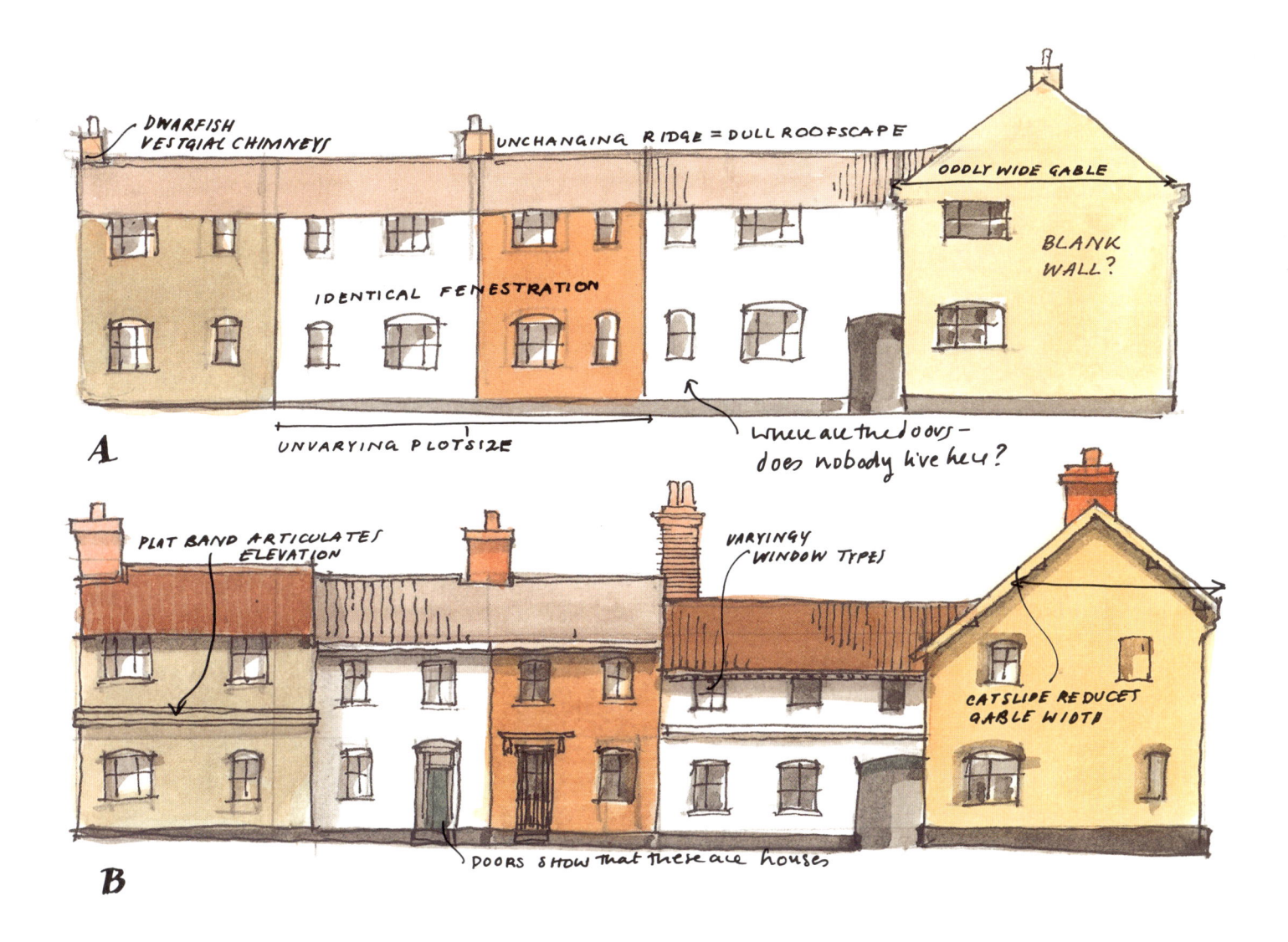

[Figure A annotations: DWARFISH VESTGIAL CHIMNEYS; UNCHANGING RIDGE = DULL ROOFSCAPE; ODDLY WIDE GABLE; IDENTICAL FENESTRATION; BLANK WALL?; UNVARYING PLOTSIZE; where are the doors — does nobody live here?]

[Figure B annotations: PLAT BAND ARTICULATES ELEVATION; VARYINGY WINDOW TYPES; CATSLIDE REDUCES GABLE WIDTH; DOORS SHOW THAT THESE ARE HOUSES]

comparatively featureless — and is completely outside the architectural language of the vernacular, as is the roof, which is dead straight and unvarying and has none of the relief offered by the changing coloured pantiles or varying ridge lines of the Church Plain terrace. Again with the chimney stacks there is too much regularity. Those few that are included in the development have very small and identical bricks layed 3½ x 2 , while neighbouring properties have stacks that are 4 x 3½, 6 x 2½ or 5 x 2½ , i.e. significantly larger.

In Figure B I have adapted A addressing these problems. I have introduced conscious variation in plan fenestration and ridge, while complicating the gable end with a catslide, enlarging the chimney stacks and introducing the plat band between storeys. I have also added some further variation in colour and introduced doors on the High Street elevation.

These changes *articulate* the terrace, making it more visually eventful, and help it to make a positive rather than neutral contribution to the streetscape. They also emulate much more closely the vernacular surroundings. The current development imposes an austere use of the vernacular on the streetscape that adds nothing and has a joyless worthiness about it that is at odds with the pretty jollity of Wells.

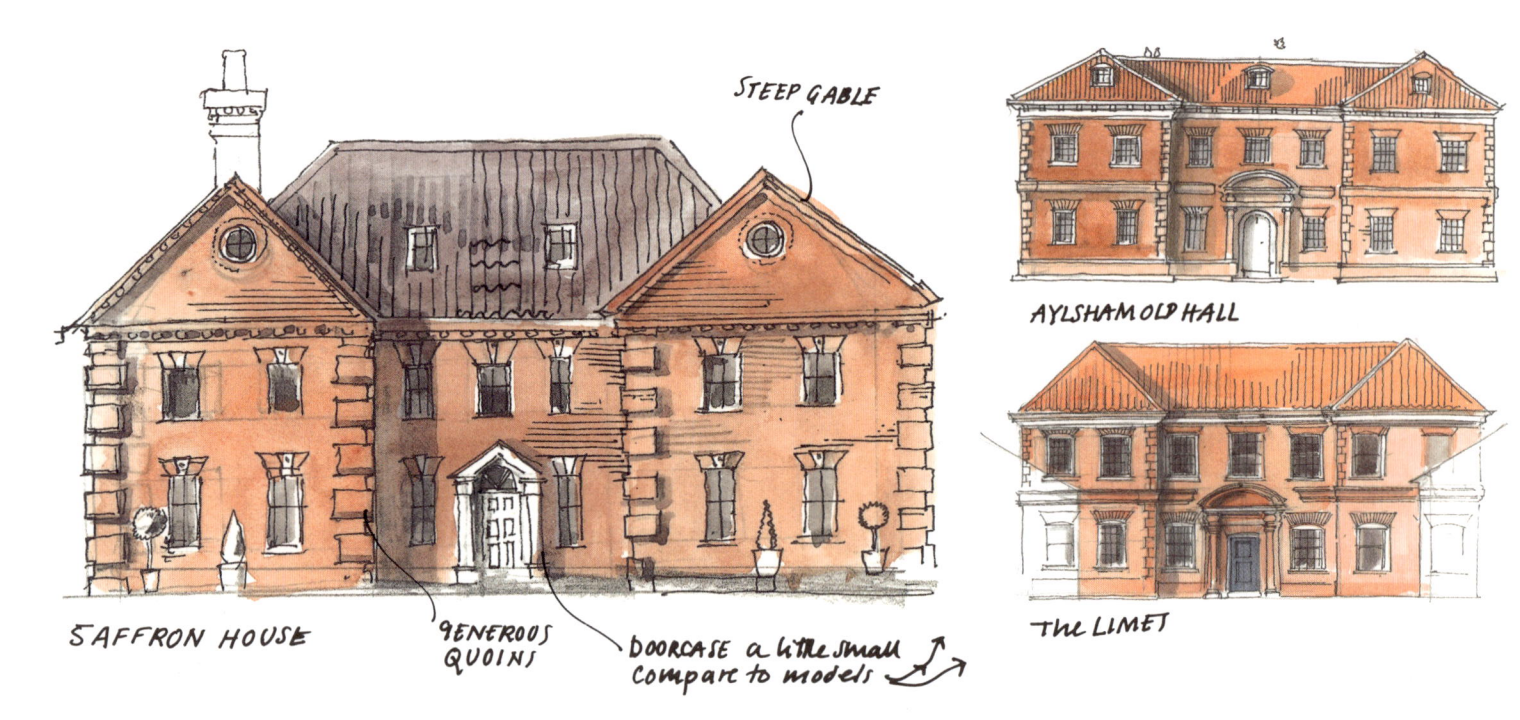

Labels on illustrations:
- SAFFRON HOUSE — STEEP GABLE — GENEROUS QUOINS — DOORCASE a little small compare to models
- AYLSHAM OLD HALL
- THE LIMES

Larger new houses

With cottages and other small buildings it is important to give a feeling of rightness and belonging in the design employed. Architectural statements that are too stridently voiced are out of place in this context, and in some ways the most desirable quality in a new cottage is that it should not seem to be new at all. As commissions get larger so the scope for architectural expression grows, even when the intention is to produce a building in the vernacular or at least referring closely to it. Buildings the size of a large farmhouse are capable of carrying more design and of working in a sophisticated way, either to reproduce or to assimilate building styles of a previous age and turn them into something of value and visual interest. The rest of this chapter looks in a little more detail at some such buildings. All but one are new and look new. The exception is Heath Farm on the Sandringham estate where a genuinely new house has been made out of an old one. The new building is interesting, the old was not, so I think that it can count as new.

One, Saffron House, is in Norwich, but while it is built well within the city limits it is in a style more readily associated with a market town. Another, Heath Farm, is a farmhouse, and although it is an adaptation of an earlier house the design is so new that it merits inclusion here. A third, Eaton Lodge, is to all intents and purposes a new country house, isolated in the landscape with which it connects very closely, while the fourth, St Anthony's Cottage, is on the edge of a coastal village. The last is a group of houses only now being built at Thornham. With the exception of Saffron House this group of buildings is in the north-west of the county, and this is not serendipitous. The high cost of building properties of this size suits them better to an area of high property values. A plot in a less desirable part of the county would make these projects financially unviable.

Saffron House is a striking building, eye-catching from the road and visually surprising. It is in a form with recognisable precedents. It has seven bays and two storeys. Bays one and two, six and seven project. The central bay has a door-case with pediment and the two surrounding bays are smallest. Each projecting wing has a steep pediment and high in the apex a bull's-eye window. A dentilated cornice links the whole elevation and the wings are defined with heavy brick quoins. There is a steep hipped roof and a lone chimney stack. The house is built of a particularly good orange brick, bright but not glaring (strangely it is made for use in Kent), and is laid in Flemish bond throughout. The windows have slightly projecting lintels with good brick voussoirs and a precast cement keystone with a moulded patera in the centre. The roof is of black glazed pantiles. These are the bare bones.

This is a good building. It is reminiscent of the two sibling houses of Blickling Old Hall and The Limes in Coltishall. I have reproduced The Limes again for comparison, which perhaps does not flatter Saffron House. The windows appear a little mean, the doorcase a little underplayed, and the all-important plat band defining the storeys is sorely missed. Are the pediments a little uneasy, their angle too steep, and is the bull's-eye's position at the very apex perplexing? Certainly, the dormers on the older houses add charm and give more relief to the roof than the lights on the newer model.

However, this is nitpicking. The overall effect of this building is as pleasing as its precursors and unusual in its exceptionally high standard of craftsmanship. It is well articulated and complex. It is built by a developer from Beccles called Brian Sabberton and is very similar to one they have built in Beccles. They have sought out the highest quality materials and in doing so significantly increased the costs: the glazed pantiles, for example, are exactly twice the price of their unglazed equivalents. There was no architect, Brian Sabberton saying rather that it was 'designed by committee' but with a clear intention to make a fine house. Initially, there was resistance from the planning department to building such a large house on the site, but an appeal was made to the secretary of state, who overturned the decision. The purchasers came from Essex although with Norfolk connections. They were attracted by a computer-generated impression of the house in the local paper, on the strength of which they bought it as yet unbuilt. Surely this is a justification of such a high specification.

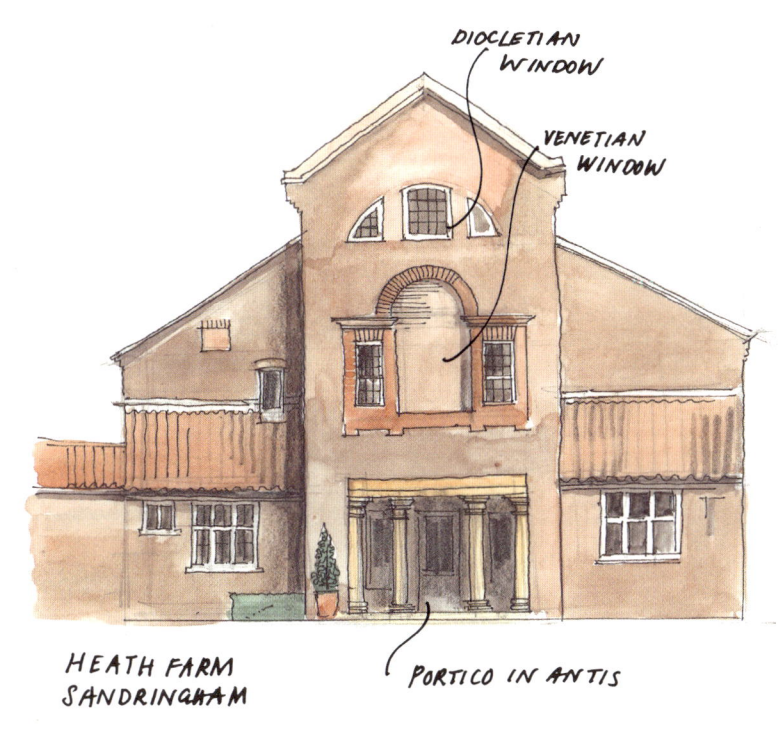

HEATH FARM SANDRINGHAM — *DIOCLETIAN WINDOW*, *VENETIAN WINDOW*, *PORTICO IN ANTIS*

Utterly different is Heath Farm on the Sandringham estate, previously in need of attention. The architect Charles Morris is retained by Sandringham to provide an architectural overview on its many buildings and to do specific work on some of them, and it was to him that the job fell. Morris is an inventive and sensitive architect who works in a style that owes something to Edwin Lutyens. Like Lutyens he combines the aesthetic of the Arts and Crafts movement with classicism and has a particularly good feeling for materials. Morris knew this building well, having driven past it many times admiring its peculiar lines. He saw in the curiously elevated building what he calls a 'raw Palladianism'. It was unlisted, which gave client and architect greater freedoms than are usually available in a building of this date, perhaps 1730. Previously unexceptional fenestration on this south elevation was rearranged to form a Venetian window, the central part of which is blank beneath a bold Diocletian window just below what is nearly, but not, a pediment. On the ground floor a *portico in antis* — that is, one in which all elements are situated behind the flat surface of the façade — in the Tuscan order completes the transformation from the fairly ordinary to the bold and surprising. The rooflines of the two wings form another quasi-pediment at a lower level. This is a great trick of Palladio – used, for example, in his church of San Giorgio Maggiore in Venice.

In Heath Farm, a sophisticated and informed eye has brought out latent qualities in a building that most would have missed, perhaps including the original builder. This has been done using appropriate traditional materials and techniques, and in so doing has made an intriguing and outstanding new building. Unsurprisingly, it was very quickly let.

Eaton Lodge is also the work of Morris. Here he has tackled the project of turning a small and unexceptional double-pile farmhouse built of brick and carrstone into a substantial country house. This he has done in an unexpected way, linking the house to a small cottage with a wing that has become the central bays of a new house. The middle bay rises to a squat tower, lime rendered and with a leaded four-casement window looking over a central courtyard. This is enclosed at the front by a screen in a muscular Tuscan order. The fenestration varies from sash to leaded casements and with some frames of untreated oak and some painted white. This very varied and eclectic elevation is in the language of the neo-Queen Anne style of the 1870s to 1890s. It is in this style that the previous main house on this estate, Ken Hill, was built in 1879 by J. J. Stevenson, a leading figure in that school.

Different again is St Anthony's Cottage, Burnham Norton. This is the work of local architect Nicholas Hills and is again an exercise in eclectisism. Here are varied and direct quotations from assorted sources close at hand: the porch is derived from the great barn at Holkham, the tumbling-in on the steep gable and use of coursed chalk, brick and uncoursed flint are all in the local vernacular. These are combined with more esoteric architectural features like the bull's-eye window at the base of the gable. Again this building draws from the late nineteenth-century 'Queen Anne' and Arts and Crafts tradition, using the vernacular in a creative and familiar way and utilising varying styles without conforming to any past period. J. J. Stevenson said that domestic architecture 'should be homely, like colloquial talk'. This building definitely answers that

EATON LODGE

ST. ANTHONYS COTTAGE — DOOR from HOLKHAM See Page 94

need. Internally a large and sunny kitchen dominates the ground floor, relegating the more formal sitting room to a subsidiary role. A complex staircase with gallery and clever use of internal glazing fills the house with natural light. Importantly, while this is a most sophisticated piece of work, a complex essay in New Norfolk building, it is in no way laboured and sits comfortably with its genuinely vernacular neighbours.

Last of all is a brand new development in Thornham. St George's Court is the brainchild of Charlotte Carter, whose family control R. G. Carter, one of the country's biggest building contractors. This group of houses is on a site overlooking the marshes. Thornham is in the heart of the bonus-belt stretch of coastline that runs from Holkham to Hunstanton, and buildings of the highest specification are bound to find a buyer. Indeed, all of these buildings have been purchased unbuilt.

Rather than adopt the illiterate cul-de-sac masterplan accepted by the planners, these houses are interestingly and dynamically arranged to maximise marsh views and to relate to one another in a visually interesting way. The gable of one house faces the façade of its neighbours, and walls connect the generous gardens in a way that implies an existing settlement pattern. However, it is in the detailing, use of materials and exceptional quality of the building that these houses excell. Each is an essay in the local vernacular; they are in the form of farmhouses, and although rather similar in size, the layout of the site as a whole prevents this from giving any feeling of an estate of executive homes. This can be a problem, for example, in the Hopkins Homes development along the Holt bypass, where relatively creditable but identical eighteenth-century village house reproductions are rendered utterly implausible by being crammed, hugger mugger, in an unimaginative car-centric masterplan of cul-de-sacs and unconvincing sinuous lanes.

At Thornham sensitive use of high quality materials — bricks well pointed with lime mortar and in Flemish bond, pantiles, some black glazed and some terracotta, flint pebbles with the correct depth of pointing, and sophisticated and well-observed woodwork — combine to give an exciting variation of colour and texture. In design there is also diverting variation: a brick and flint gable end with accurate tumbling-in, an unconventional oriel window that steals a sea view by its projection, and throughout the development a series of different garden wall details.

This is a new development and makes no effort to disguise it, but it is an exemplar of how to build new houses in the vernacular, their success proven by their instant sale. It is uncertain if these high quality specifications could be justified in an area of lower house prices like Acle or North Walsham, but here they are appropriate and a model of their type.

THORNHAM

21. CONCLUSION: WHAT HAPPENS NEXT?

This is really a coda to this book. I have described a lot of old houses, but still only a tiny proportion of the extraordinary stock of outstanding buildings in the county. While there is a finite number of great houses to choose from, it would be quite possible to rewrite and illustrate any chapter of this book with a different set of buildings, all equally good examples of their type. There are hundreds of churches and thousands of farmhouses, barns and cottages to choose from, many in good condition and under the sensitive and informed care of their owners.

In Part Two I have covered some of the new building in Norfolk. This has also been done in a far from exhaustive way. Although this county is not badly afflicted with new housing, or at least not beyond the grasping new suburbs of Norwich, there is still plenty going on. During the two years I have been working on this book there have been significant changes, often for the best. There has been a continuing awareness of conservation principles, particularly in the richer parts of the north and north-west of the county, and this has meant that there is a lot of high quality restoration, conversion and addition to observe.

However, bad building is still rife. Poor planning, detailing and quality of building is the norm in commercial developments. The majority of large new estates are unimaginative, mean, and cannot be said to have enhanced the built environment in any way. The very slightest lip-service is paid to the local vernacular in these instances, and the result is a superficial and rather silly *English* style that is really a watered down neo-Tudor of no architectural distinction. Large estates of huge aggregate financial value are often built without the involvement of a creative architect, or indeed sometimes any architect at all, a situation that would be unthinkable in a single building. This is a sorry state of affairs as the visual and environmental effects of a large development on neighbours, and on the wider community, merits greater investment in some kind of vision or masterplan.

The last part of this book is, for me, the most interesting. Travelling around the county I have felt cross and been outspokenly ill-mannered about new developments. Words like 'illiterate' and 'uneducated' or indeed 'insensitive and heavy-handed' are critical and have been used from the safety of the commentator's box. As I am not a property developer I have been safe from counter-attack, so now I shall put my head in the pillory. What follows is a proposal for an entirely imaginary redevelopement of the very picturesque village of Worstead in East Norfolk. It is undetailed and under-resolved, but tackles some of the design issues that the second part of this book has thrown up. These are issues not just of elevation and visual impact, but of planning and social engineering.

Ladies and Gentlemen, soak your sponges …

Supersize Worstead

Settlements change, they migrate across a parish over centuries and grow or shrink, sometimes quickly and sometimes through a slow and inexorable drift. Few villages are totally unchanging and communities are also continuously changing.

Old houses from farmhouses to large country houses have a famous problem today. The kitchen is in the wrong place. Traditionally the domain of the cook or servants, the kitchen is orientated to the north of a building to utilise cool larders and other offices; it is at the back and often rather cut off. But for twenty years we have all wanted to live in our kitchen, a lack of servants and a desire to cook for ourselves surrounded by our family have brought the kitchen to the centre of life, and where this is particularly strongly felt houses have had to be altered.

Similarly, villages have changed. The village of 1907, 1807 or 1507 was built to suit the imperatives of the age, and those have now changed significantly. Until the late twentieth century the village was a self-sufficient unit providing for all its residents' needs. Even the most evolved and functional village no longer does this.

Aldborough, surely a contender for this title with mini-supermarket, butcher, post office and general store, garage, two pubs, a doctor's surgery and most significantly a thriving primary school, is still principally supplied with even everyday needs by supermarkets ten and twenty miles distant. This is undesirable but is currently the case. Cars, a luxury for the richer residents even forty years ago, are both universal and dominating. There are few jobs within the village, and many of these would be unrecognisable to the grandparents of those doing them. It is not unusual to travel hundreds of miles a week to carry out an occupation that will pay for the quality of life that village life can provide.

The village seems to be universally attractive as an environment in which to bring up children and to retire. For many it is the complete ideal. Safety, smallness and most of all *community* are the characteristics that provide this quality of life, as is a proximity to the countryside and access to it both on foot and by eye. Significantly, this is associated with the village being perceived as visually attractive, although of course very many really are not.

The greatest of these strengths is community. The everyday pleasure of recognition and interaction with your neighbours (and, of course, fierce and vile criticism of and by them), and the certain knowledge that others you know are close by, are as valuable to a young mother and sad teenager as to a decrepit granny. It is also a control and check on a wayward teenager, naughty child or low-level criminal. At the risk of straying even further from the subject of a book on vernacular architecture, it is the knowledge that *you are not alone*.

Or is this so far from vernacular architecture? Perhaps the sensible and informed knowledge and use of the local way of building is a statement of community. Maybe a common visual inheritance and its use in all buildings can confirm and strengthen the values that are so desirable in village life; in fact, could it be that it is a visual shorthand for community? Certainly, inappropriate development, cul-de-sacs and dinky closes are antipathetic to the village. They create obscure areas outside the centre of the community. Perhaps actual building styles and quality of work are something that residents can value in common. This does sound a little soggy, but in an atomised and post-nuclear-family-based society actual proactive steps need to be taken to redress the balance and regain a social equilibrium.

In the 2002 film *About a Boy* the issues of the fractured family and relationships are explored in a fairly easy-access kind of a way. After a series of episodes that are either deeply touching or cringe-makingly embarrassing depending on your sensibilities, the unlikely figure of Hugh Grant finds himself the unexpected father figure at a post-Christian, post-marriage but highly functional Christmas lunch. The parentless, husband or wifeless, and otherwise emotionally dispossessed find themselves cuddled up on Grant's expansive leather sofas in the loving embrace of a totally invented wider family supporting them all. This rather schmaltzy message perhaps contains something that needs to be considered in planning a new village. What is its social and emotional centre, what are its practical needs, and how can they be provided and funded? It is not a matter of just building houses, low cost or otherwise, and taking the profits. These and the newer environmental considerations of a climatically challenged world are the background to this proposal for Worstead.

Worstead the village

Worstead is a small settlement four miles south-east of North Walsham. It is really more the relic of a town than a village, although it only contains 200 houses and has a population of 675. In the centre is a long market square, the lower part of which was infilled in the sixteenth century. From this the roads radiate: Withergate, Lyngate, Bengate (-gate is an old suffix meaning road and does not signify a medieval entrance to the town), Honing Row, Station Road and Woodview. In the centre, raised above the street in its yard, is St Mary's church, a towering Perpendicular super-church. Facing it around the square is an exceptionally good group of sixteenth- to eighteenth-century houses. Further from the centre is a fine eighteenth-century pub and a selection of smaller, mainly nineteenth-century cottages. On the edge of the village are some unexceptional twentieth-century houses. There are also several larger houses: the manor house, the Laurels, Holly Grove and the Old Rectory. At the southern edge is Woodview, a local authority estate in two parts, each a cul-de-sac of good houses in a predictably dreary arrangement.

There have been two significant developments in the late twentieth century. St Andrew's Close is a completely indifferent and cramped group of commercial housing, isolated from the village and of no architectural interest. More visually intrusive but built with better intentions is the village hall. This is vast and sensibly is in the form of a great barn with a lean-to on either side of the door. It is made of rather unforgiving materials, glaring orange pantiles and unlovely brick, and sits at a rakish angle below the church overlooking the playing field. Practically it is too large, echoing and unlovely inside, not a magical place for a wedding or party, but still an extraordinary facility; perhaps it would become a better used asset if it were serving a significantly larger village.

Worstead was a weaving town producing the eponymous cloth and at one time was the economic rival to nearby North Walsham. There are still traces of weaving lofts in some buildings, although the industry was fading from the eighteenth century and the last lone weaver dropped his shuttle in 1900. There is little employment in Worstead. There is a farm that completely surrounds the village employing six men, a series of small enterprises near the station, and the pub. There was a market but this had closed by the seventeenth century when the commercial focus had shifted to North Walsham; this was survived by an annual fair held on ground opposite the present school, still named the Fairstead.

Is Worstead good basic material for expansion? I think that it is. It has a centre that is disproportionately grand with the visual focus of square, manor house and church. Surely this would be a convincing and established centre for a larger settlement. There is a railway station with good connections to Norwich which would ideally suit commuting and access to a good road system within two miles. The school has sustained some feeling of community and has been successful in attracting children from outside the village for the last fifteen years.

Does Worstead need to be expanded? Obviously not, in that it is surviving now. Properties sell quickly and it is perceived as a good place to live. But could it be better? A significantly larger population would swell school numbers, make the barely viable pub a busier proposition, and possibly even grow the tiny church congregation. It would also make possible significant and desirable social improvements: a shop, a café, jobs inside the village, better places to walk and play, more friends – in fact, a more active *community*.

The plan

This plan is designed to make some of these changes and is not led by commercial interests, although it would, of course, need to be economically viable. Nor is it led by a desperate need for low- or high-cost housing. It is led by a utopian desire for the perfect village where traditional building techniques and design principles would enhance and to a certain degree define a plan for an inclusive and busy place.

This is my plan for a jolly, happy and sustaining place to live.

There are several key features to the plan. The New Worstead is still centred around the square and church. This visual civic core is both existing and desirable. The fact that it has been there for at least 600 years means that the enlarged settlement immediately has a past and an integrity. Invented civic space is hard to establish as real. This is already a heart to the village although currently with a rather weak beat. I have proposed a café here. Shops are hard to sustain, and one is planned elsewhere, but a place to meet and talk would be good for oldsters, mums walking back from school, perhaps even for older children.

There is a risk of creating alternative centres; doing so could easily lose the benefit of the existing market place, but in this proposal the recreation ground becomes a village green. New housing surrounds it, and instead of being on the edge it becomes part of the village centre. The footballing or cricket playing is watched from all sides. This works very well in Aldborough, where the green is the social centre of the village and where the consequent summer focus of cricket playing is socially cohesive and visually compelling.

Worstead Today

NEW WORSTEAD
112 NEW HOUSES
STATION
GARAGE
STORE
CYCLE PARK
THREE LARGE HOUSES
NEW ROAD
AVENUE OF TREES ON APPROACH TO WORSTEAD
PATH TO MAKE EASY CIRCULAR WALKS
LIGHTLY GRAZED MEADOWS & WILDLIFE RICH WOODLAND. DOG-WALKING & PICNICKING
MEADOWS
OLD VICARAGE
VILLAGE GREEN
CEMETARY
VILLAGE HALL
NEW ROAD LINED WITH TREES
THESE HOUSES have FINE CHURCH VIEWS BEHIND
NEW PLAYING FIELD
CHURCH
MANOR
SURGERY.
VILLAGE FARM 20 ACRES of VEG & SMALL LIVESTOCK EGGS ETC...
STALL IN FARM YARD
PUB
FARM YARD
SQUARE
TEAROOM
CAR PARK
TWO COUNCIL ESTATES ARE UN-CLOSED (LOSS OF 4 HOUSES)
LARGE HOUSE
LARGE HOUSE
LARGE HOUSE
MEADOWS
AVENUE OF TREES ON APPROACH TO WORSTEAD

The railway station is currently isolated from the village. A charmless walk connects the two. This is an obvious area for improvement, and new houses of all sizes would line alternative routes to connect station to village centre that would be visually stimulating and potentially socially interactive.

The station and its surroundings are also subject to a serious rethink. This should be the gateway to Worstead, the desired route to and from Norwich and work. For the station to function fully and securely and for it to feel safe for all passengers on all trains, it needs to be permanently staffed; perhaps finding further uses for the site could make this cost effective. A staffed station would also allow bikes to be left there, a desirable situation both socially and environmentally. So even though it is half a mile from the centre of the village, this is the site for the shop, a place to buy food on the way home from the office, and it is combined with a garage and petrol station. This last function will bring in people from neighbouring villages and ensure the financial viability of the store. The convenience of being able to buy fuel close to home is considerable, and while not attempting to make the village self-sufficient it would prevent many short journeys out.

The village farm — this came about while thinking about what to do with the existing farm buildings. Local food is not just a fad. It is really desirable and for the first time since the intensification of agriculture it is also potentially profitable. Surely a reasonable, and possibly subsidised, lease on 10 or 15 acres (4 or 6 hectares) with a contract to supply the school with eggs, some vegetables and perhaps even meat would be viable, the principal business being selling to village residents through a farm shop. This would be a model for other village farms. As well as food production, the farm would ensure an open space in the centre of the village and an educational resource.

The mix of houses is complete. Large houses, £1 million and more, bring money into the community and importantly employment through the need for skilled tradesmen and domestic labour. Middle-sized houses, £300,000 to £700,000, provide disposable income and professional skills, and smaller houses of £100,000 to £300,000 supply more skills and labour. This mix is really important and needs to be introduced without ghettoisation. Low-cost housing, while vital, does not *make* a village. It is important to engineer a constructive mix through the pricing of houses.

Most, but not all, houses have gardens and all have access to the countryside. While this plan envisages some form of community ownership for the land immediately surrounding the expanded village, it does not promote formless and expensive-to-manage common land. A pattern of footpaths would connect different parts of the village through fields that would continue to be farmed, thus preserving the existing atmosphere of a village surrounded by farmland.

It is most unlikely that any of this will happen, and it is inevitable that many more indifferent or bad buildings will be thrown up in Norfolk — as indeed has always been the case. However, there is a sound economic justification for improving the design of these houses, as the visual integrity of the county, its buildings in the landscape, draws both holiday makers and, more significantly, brings in money made outside.

Homeowners seem to want houses that are traditional in appearance: cottages, farmhouses and rectories for today. Some of these are being built by fine builders, responsible developers and good architects, but many more of the new buildings that are to come would be improved if their designers were to look observantly and intelligently at the old buildings that will surround them. Detailing, roof pitch, materials and most of all scale are all clearly visible, and an understanding of these elements can only improve the resulting buildings.

The future appearance of Norfolk's built environment is governed by the desires of its inhabitants because planners, conservation officers and architects apart, it is the householder whose views will prevail and it is in their hands that this responsibility lies.

Wickmere, 21 February 2008

APPENDIX

Details and materials

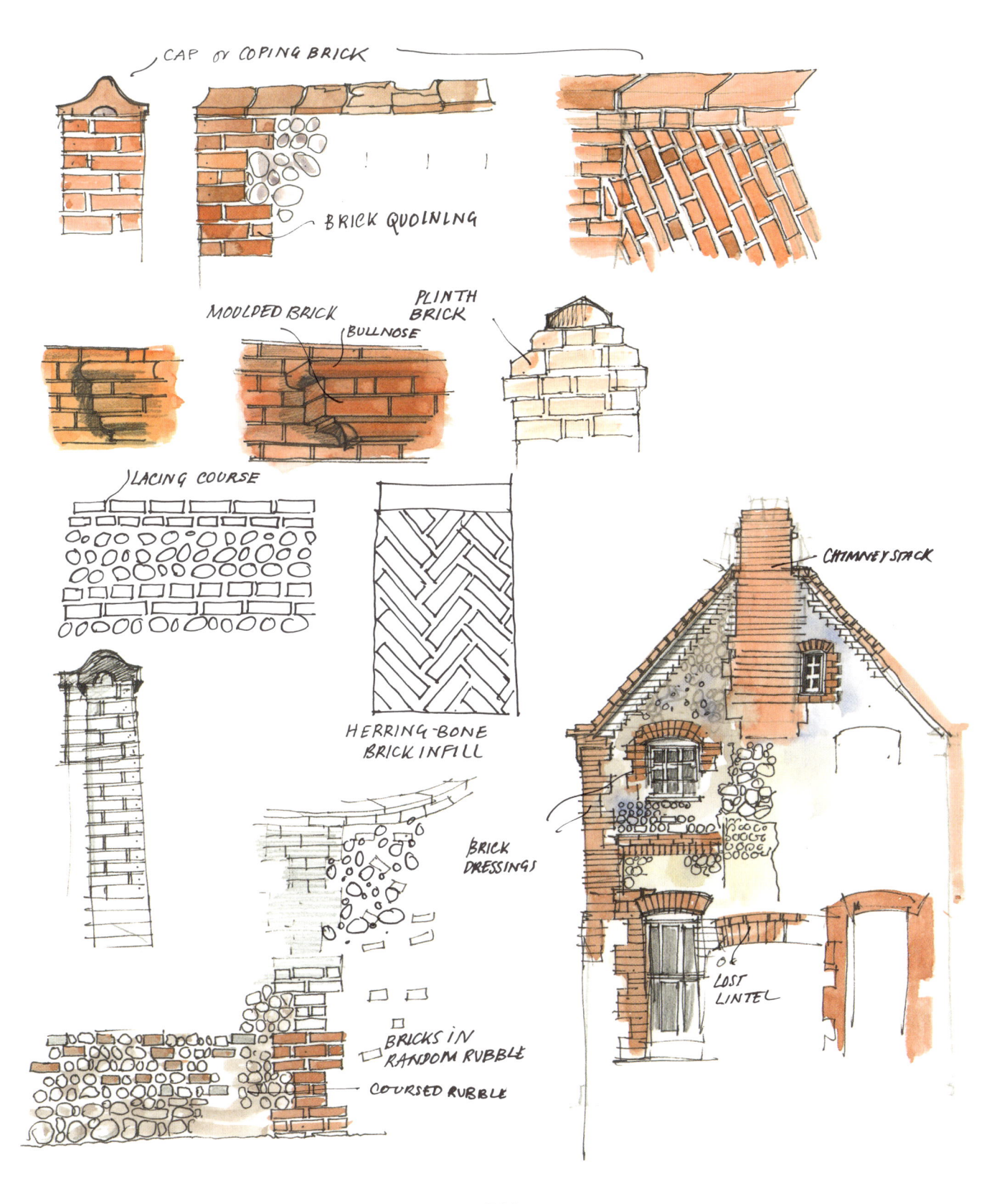

BUILDING NORFOLK

CAP OR COPING BRICK

BRICK QUOINING

MOULDED BRICK   PLINTH BRICK
BULLNOSE

LACING COURSE

HERRING-BONE BRICK INFILL

CHIMNEY STACK

BRICK DRESSINGS

OR LOST LINTEL

BRICKS IN RANDOM RUBBLE
COURSED RUBBLE

193

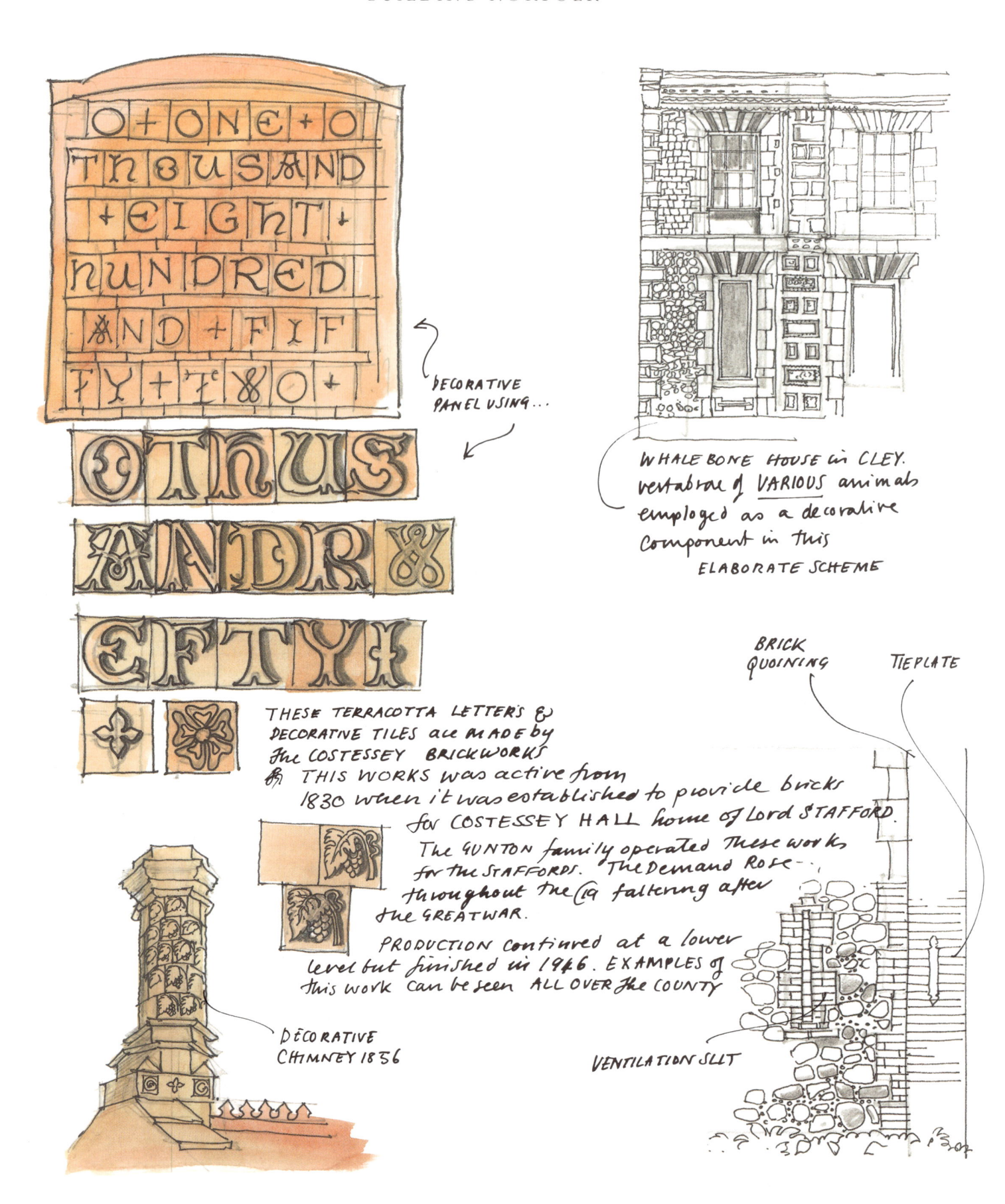

BUILDING NORFOLK

Decorative panel using...

Whalebone House in Cley. Vertabrae of VARIOUS animals employed as a decorative component in this ELABORATE SCHEME

These terracotta letters & decorative tiles are made by the COSTESSEY BRICKWORKS. This works was active from 1830 when it was established to provide bricks for COSTESSEY HALL home of Lord STAFFORD. The GUNTON family operated these works for the STAFFORDS. The demand rose throughout the C19 faltering after the GREAT WAR. Production continued at a lower level but finished in 1946. EXAMPLES of this work can be seen ALL OVER the COUNTY

Decorative chimney 1856

BRICK QUOINING *TIEPLATE*

VENTILATION SLIT

194

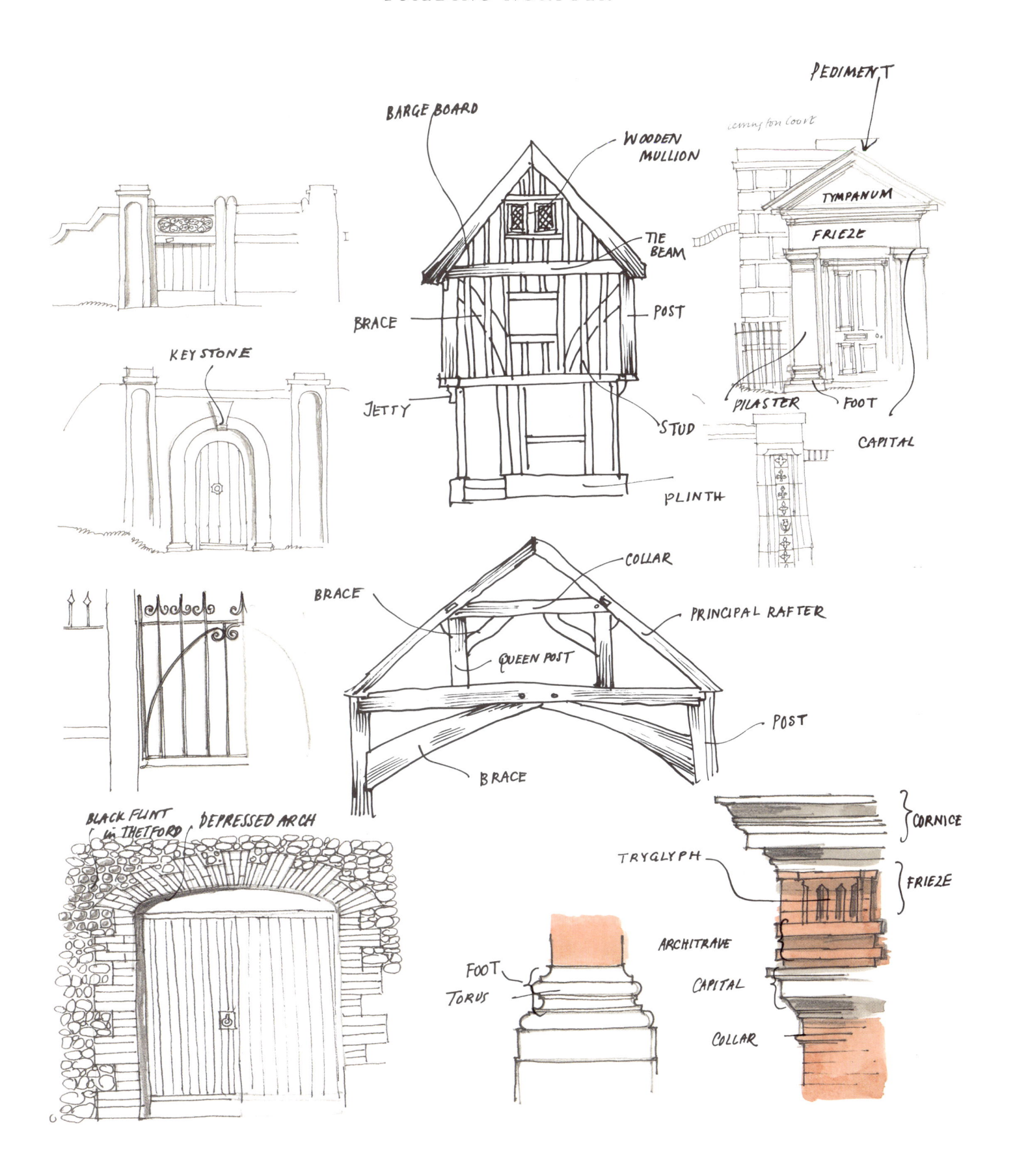

BUILDING NORFOLK

195

BUILDING NORFOLK

196

BUILDING NORFOLK

BAFFLINGLY COMPLEX GLAZING

HOOD MOULD DETAIL

PEDIMENT

PEDIMENTED DORMER

FLASHING

RETICULATED TRACERY

FISH-SCALE GLAZING

N.B. PLENTY of light gets through this DORMER

TREFOIL

GOTHIC ARCH (INTERLOCKING)

Y TRACERY

MULLION

A QUARRY

LEADED GLAZING

SASH

BRICK LINTEL

MUNTIN

ARCHITRAVE

197

FURTHER READING

Aslet, Clive, *The Last Country Houses*, Yale University Press, New Haven and London, 1982.

Batcock, Neil, *The Ruined and Disused Churches of Norfolk*, Norfolk Archaeological Unit, Dereham, 1991.

Bax, B. Anthony, *The English Parsonage*, William Clowes and Sons Ltd, London and Beccles, 1964.

Booth, Bob, *King's Lynn in the 1930s*, Tricky Sam Publishing, King's Lynn, 2006.

Brunskill, R. W., *Brick Building in Britain*, Victor Gollancz, London, 1990.

Cobbett, William, *Rural Rides*, Penguin Books, Harmondsworth, 2001.

Edwards, Derek and Tom Williamson, *Norfolk Country Houses from the Air*, Sutton Publishing, Stroud, 2000.

Harrod, Wilhelmine, *The Norfolk Guide*, 5th edn, The Alastair Press, Bury St Edmunds, 1988.

Hill, Joseph, *Survey of the Houghton Hall Estate*, ed. David Yaxley, Witley Press Ltd, Norwich, 1984.

Kent, Nathaniel, *Hints to Gentlemen of Landed Property*, MICROFI, Royston, 1983 (first published 1775).

Ketton-Cremer, R. W., *Felbrigg: The Story of a House*, Rupert Hart-Davis, London, 1962.

Le Strange, Richard, *Monasteries of Norfolk*, Yates Publications, King's Lynn, 1973.

Pevsner, Nikolaus, *The Buildings of England: North-East Norfolk and Norwich*, Penguin Books, Harmondsworth, 1997.

Pevsner, Nikolaus, *The Buildings of England: North-West and South Norfolk*, , Penguin Books, Harmondsworth, 1997.

Quiney, Anthony, *The Traditional Buildings of England*, Thames & Hudson, London, 1990.

Rawcliffe, Carole and Richard Wilson (eds) *Norwich since 1550*, Hambledon & London, London and New York, 2004.

Robinson, John Martin, *Georgian Model Farms: A Study of Decorative and Model Farm Buildings in the Age of Improvement 1700–1846*, Clarendon Press, Oxford, 1983.

Strong, Roy, *A Little History of the English Country Church*, Jonathan Cape, London, 2007.

Tilbrook, Richard (photography) and C. V. Roberts, *Norfolk's Churches Great and Small*, Jarrold Publishing, Norwich, 1997.

Wade Martins, Susanna, *Norfolk: A Changing Countryside 1780–1914*, Phillimore and Co. Ltd, Chichester, 1988.

Wade Martins, Peter, *An Historical Atlas of Norfolk*, Norfolk Museums Service, Norwich, 1993.

Williamson, Tom, *England's Landscape: East Anglia*, English Heritage, Collins, London, 2006.

Woodforde, John, *The Truth About Cottages*, I. B. Tauris and Co. Ltd, London, 2007.

INDEX

Page numbers in *italic* refer to illustrations and captions

About a Boy (film), 1865
Acle, 114, 183
Adams, Rev. Charles, 121
agriculture
    collapse (1875) and decline, 68, 100-1
    farm buildings and equipment, 98-9
    and overseas imports, 100-1
    revolution and improvement, 8, 44, 55, 98-100, 128
air travel, 147-8
Aldborough, 11, 20, 33, *33*, 112, 185, 187
Aldin, Cecil: *Mrs Tickler's Caravan* (picture), 112
almshouses, 108-9, *110, 111*, 130
Alston family, 101
Anglo-Dutch Farming (company), 101
Antingham, 146
art deco style, 168
Arts and Crafts movement, 14, 21, *64*, 81, 83, 157, 168, 169, 181
Astley family, 160
Astley, Sir Jacob, 72
Aylsham
    Black Boys inn, 113, *115*
    Frazers Yard, *170*
    house prices, 26
    manor house, 58
    market place, 11, 82
    Old Hall, 45, *52, 143,* 180
    The Orchards, 23, *171*
    Stone House, 17

Bacon, Sir Nicholas, 66
Baconsthorpe
    Castle Farm, *107*
    rectory, 121, *123*
Baconsthorpe Castle, 17, 22, 55
Balls, Joseph, 113
Banks, Richardson, 68
Banks, Robert, 78
Banningham: Laurel Farm, 44, *47*
Barclay family, 17, 160
Barnack, Northamptonshire, 10
Barney, 47
Barningham Hall, 25, 55, 66, 71, 80, 161
barns, 92, 98-101, *102, 103, 104, 105, 106, 107*
    conversions, 172-3, *172*
Barry, Charles, Jr, 68, 78
Barton Hall, 89
Barton Turf, 126
Bates, Alan, 72
Battersea, Constance, Lady (née Rothschild), 65
Battersea, Cyril Flower, Baron, 65
Bawdeswell: All Saints church, 129
Bax, Anthony: *The English Parsonage*, 120
beach flint (pebbles), 14
Beauchamp, Rev. T., 121
Beaupre, 69
Beccles, 45
Beeston Priory, 15
Beeston Regis: All Saints church, *134*
Beeston St Lawrence, 68, 77
Beetley: almshouses, 108, *111*
Berney Arms Mill, *148*
Bexwell, near Downham Market, 22
Binham, 9, 28, 29, *34, 143*
    church, 125-6
Birbeck family, 17
Black Death, 32
Blaise Hamlet, near Bristol, 25
Blakeney
    as port, 8
    rectory, 121
Blickling, 45, 113, 141, 161
Blickling Hall, 66, 70, 140, *142*, 181
Blow, Detmar, 64
boat houses, *91*
Booton: St Michael and All Angels church, 128, *136*
Bracciolini, Poggio, 125
Braka, Ivor, 70
Brancaster, 160
Brandon, Suffolk: Barclays Bank, 17
Branthill Farm, *106*
Brecklands, 10, 14
Bredon Water, 146
Brettingham, Matthew, 68, 70, 74, 76
bricks and brickwork, 10, 15, *15*, 25, 28, 29, 56-7, 59, 65, 66, 89, 112-13, 122, 140, 192, 193

Bridge, Rev. W., 129
Brisley: almshouses, *110*
Briston: Congregational church, *138*
Broadland: Lodham Village Hall, *42*
Broads, the, 17, 70
Broomholm Priory, 23, *23*
Brown, Lancelot ('Capability'), 80
Brunskill, R.F., 14
Bure, river, 146
Burgh Castle, Suffolk, 15, 22, 140, 146
Burgh Parva, 147
Burlington, Richard Boyle, 3rd Earl of, 74
Burnham Norton: St Anthony's Cottage, 180, 182-3, *183*
Burnhams, the, 160
Burton, Decimus, 69, 79, 81
Buxton family, 17, 160
Bylaugh: church of St Mary the Virgin, *126*
Bylaugh Hall, 68, 78

Cabell, Benjamin Bond, 160-1
Caistor Castle, 141
Caistor St Edmund (Venta Icenorum), 112, *116*
Camden Society, Cambridge, 128
Campbell, Colen, 67, 74, 113
canals *see* waterways
Cantley sugar beet mill, *149*
Cargill family, 101
carrstone, 16, 65, 81, *84*
Carter, Charlotte, 183
Carter, R.G. (building contractors), 183
Castle Acre Priory, 21, 22, 55
Castle Rising
    church, 125, 130
    Howard almshouses, 109, *110*
Catton: Saffron House, 45
Cawston, 126
    St Agnes church, *134*
chalk
    for building, 16-17
    pits, 10
Chandrigarh, India, 169
Charles II, King, 126
Chatsworth, Derbyshire, 80
chimneys, 16, 28
Cholmondeley, George James, 1st Marquess of, 113
Christie, Julie, 72
Church of England
    administration, 124-6
    clergy incomes, 127
    nineteenth-century revival, 128
    services, 126-7
churches, 124-9, *130, 131, 132-3, 134, 135, 136, 137, 138, 139*
clay lumps, 27, 30
Cley
    beach flint, 14
    as port, 8
Clipsby, *148*
clock towers, 90, *91*
Clun: almshouses, 109
Cobbett, William: *Rural Rides*, 24, 121
Cobham, Kent, 120
Cockerill, Ralph Scott, 152
Coke, Thomas, 8, 44, 74, 99-100, 114
Colegate: Old Meeting House, 129, *138*
Coltishall, 114, *115*, 143
    The Limes, 45, *52,* 180, *181*
concrete, 65
Constable, John, 24
Cook, Thomas, 69, 79, 81
Corbridge, James, 152
Costessey, 28
Costessey Hall (and brickworks), *194*
Coston Rectory, 122
Cotman, John Sell, 21, 24
cottages, 20, 24-6, *27, 28,* 29, *30*, 31, 81-3, *96, 97, 173, 173*
    modernized, 173-4, *173, 174*
country houses, 66-70, 72, *73,* 74-5, 76, 77, 127
Coxford Abbey, 67
Crome, John, 21
Cromer
    Bank House, *162*
    character and development, 160-1, *162-3*
    as holiday resort, 160-1
    Hotel de Paris, *161, 161*

    modern school, *168*
    railway, 9, 160
    Red Lion Hotel, 114
    roads, 147
Cromer Hall, 68, 160, *162*
Crostwight, 125

Dean, G.A., 105
Decorated style, 125
Denver, 36
Denver Hall, 63
Dilham, 146
Diss, 36, 40, 41, *42*
    Dolphin Inn, *40*
    The Shambles, *40*
Donthorne, W.J., 68, 81, 84
doorways, *196*
dower houses, 45
Downham Market
    almshouses, 109, *111*
    clock tower, *40*
    railway station, *150*
    recent development, 10
drainage mills, *148*
Dutch *see* Netherlands

Early English style, 125
East Barsham, 16, 56-7, 80
East Harling
    Church Farm, 62
    rectory, 122
East Wretham, 32
Eaton Lodge, 180, 182
Ebridge Mill, 146
Ederenham, 39
Edge, William, 67
Edgefield, 128
Edward VI, King, 126
Edward VII, King, 82
Egmere, 32
Elmham Hall, 69
Elwin, Rev. Whitwell, 128, *136*
enclosure, 141
English Heritage, 99, 129, 173
    The Conversion of Traditional Farm Buildings, *172*
Enkhuizen, Netherlands, 141
estates
    and agriculture, 98-101
    buildings, 80-3
    see also individual properties

Fakenham, 10, 17, 43, 147
farmhouses, 44-5, *46-7,* 48-9, *53*
Fastolf, Sir John, 141
Felbrigg, 66, 101, 127, 141, 161
Felbrigg estate, 15
fens: drained, 141
flint, 10, 14-17, *16,* 25, *46,* 65, 85, 192
flushwork, 14
Foulsham, 26, 35, 41, 101
    rectory, 122, *123*
Framlingham Earl: Orchard Farm, *141*
Fring, 16

gallets, 16-17, 192
gatehouses *see* lodges
Gibbs, James, 74, 113, 153
Glandford, 128
glebe land, 120
Go-Between, The (film), 72
Gothic Revival (style), 21, 64, 68, 77, 81, 121, 124, 128, *137*
granaries, 104, *105*
Grant, Hugh, 186
Great Bircham, 27, *173*
Great Ouse, river, 146
Great Snoring, 16
    parsonage, 120
Great Witchingham, 66
Great Yarmouth
    character, 152-3
    economic decline, 153
    Fastolff House, 152, *157*
    Fisherman's Hospital, 108, *109*, 111, 152
    Gem cinema, 152, *157*
    industry, 154

    Nelson Monument, 152, *156*
    Northwest Tower, *155*
    as port, 8, 140, 153-4
    railway, 147
    St George's church, 128, 152
    St James''s church, 128, 152, *159*
    St Nicholas church, 152
    South Quay, 152, *159*
    Thoresby College, *155*
    Tollhouse, *155*
    West Prospect (Corbridge engraving, 1726), 152
    Winter Gardens, *157*
Green, Mr (of Kenhill), 69
Greenwich: almshouses, 109
Grimes Grave, 14
Guist, 96
    see also Sennowe Hall
Gunton, 44, 101
    Park Farm, 70
    St Andrew's church, *137*
Gunton Hall (and Park), 68-9, 78-9, 84, 85, 86, 87, 91, 95
Gurney family, 17, 160, 194

Haddiscoe: St Mary church, 130
Hales: church, 125
Halvergate
    Stracey Arms, 45
    Stracey Arms mill, *148*
Halvergate marshes, 141
Hamond, Charles Harbord, 70
Hanseatic League, 140-1
Happisburgh Hall, 64
Harbord family *see* Suffield family
Harbord, Lady Doris, 69
Harbord, Sir William, 76
Harrod, Wilhelmina, Lady, 129
Hastings, Astley, 135
Hastings, Jacob Astley, 17th Baron, 147
Henry III, King, 20, 23
Henry VII, King, 54
Henry VIII, King, 66, 126
Herbert de Losinga, Bishop of Norwich, 125
Heydon (village), 82, 96, 161
Heydon Hall, 66, 72, 81, 90
Hill, Ken, 182
Hillingdon, Charles Henry Mills, 2nd Baron, 64
Hillington
    Ffolkes Arms Inn, 16
    Gothic lodges, 81
Hillington Hall, 68, 84
Hindolveston
    Beck Farm, 44, 50
    Methodist chapel, *138*
Hingham, 38
Historic Churches Preservation Trust, 129
historicism, 23
Hoare, Samuel, 160
Hobart family, 66
Holkham
    agricultural development, 8, 99-101
    almshouses, 108
    farmhouses, 44, 81
    Great Barn, 99-100
    Longlands Farm, 100, *104, 105*
    Model Farm (formerly New Inn), 113-14, *119*
    Reading Room, *83*
    Victoria Hotel, 114
    village, 82
Holkham Hall, 66-7, 69, 74-5, 81, 84, 92-3, 94, 95, 97
Holt
    buildings, 43
    fire, 41
    property values, 166
    rectory, 121
Honing, 67, 73, 81, 83, 94
Hopkins Homes, 183
Horsford, 147
Horsham St Faith, 126, 147
Houghton: New Inn (Hall Farm), 113, *116*
Houghton Hall, 25, 32-3, 66-7, 69, 74-5, 89
    barns, 102, *107*
    estate, 82
Hoveton: St Peter's church, 126
Hundred Years War (1337-1453), 140
Hunstanton: railway, 9

199

ice houses, 95
Industrial Revolution, 8
inns, 112-14, 115, 116, 117, 118, 119
Iteringham, 51
Ivory, Thomas, 113

Johnston, Ian, 172-3

Keble, John, 128
Kelling Hall, near Holt, 14, 64
Kenhill, 69
kennels, 95
Kent, Nathaniel: *Hints to Gentlemen of Landed Property*, 24
Kent, William, 74
Kett, Robert: rebellion (1549), 55
Ketton-Cremer, R.W., 101
Kimberley, 9, 67, 82, 97
Kimberley Hall, 54
King's Lynn
  assembly rooms, 113
  Bank House, 153, 158
  building materials, 17
  character, 152-3
  Clifton House, 140
  Customs House, 140, 141, 158
  Duke's Head, 153-4
  Greenland Fishery, 154
  Greyfriars Tower, 156
  housing, 21
  industry, 154
  neighbouring villages, 32
  as port, 8, 140, 153-4
  railway, 147, 153-4
  tourism, 154
Kip, John, 72
  Britannia Illustrata (with Leonard Knyff), 80
Kirkstead Hall, 71

Lady Cates (manor), 54
Lancaster, Sir Osbert, 169
Langley, 67, 80, 85, 86
larders, 95
Laud, William, Archbishop of Canterbury, 126
Le Corbusier (Charles Édouard Jeanneret), 168-9
Leicester, Edward Douglas Coke, 7th Earl, and Sarah, Countess of, 114
Letchworth Garden City, 83
Letheringsett Hall, 62, 77, 94
Letton, 68
Limes, The *see* Coltishall
Little Melton: rectory, 122
Little Snoring, 125
Little Walsingham, 82
  Abbey House, 76
Little Witchingham, 125
Lloyd, J. Owen, 169
Lloyd, Richard, 68
Loddon (near), 28
lodges and gatehouses, 80-1, 84-5, 86, 87, 97
Lombe, Sir John, 68
London: Mile End Road: Seamen's Hospital, 108
Long Stratton, 35, 99, 102
Lopham, 30, 37
Lowestoft, 147
Ludham, 45, 46
Lutyens, Sir Edwin, 14, 64, 65, 106, 139, 181
Lyminge, Robert, 70, 141
Lyndford Hall, 68
Lynn News, 153

Mackintosh, Charles Rennie, 61
MacNamara, Michael, 174
Makepeace, Philip, 176
Mannington, 66
manor houses
  proprietors and estates, 44-5, 54-5
  small, 44, 48, 49, 50, 51
marl pits, 15
Marsham family, 60
Marsham, 143
  Colenso Cottage, 46
Marsham Givenby, 43
Martin, Kit, 69-70
Matlaske Hall, 80, 98-100
  barn, 103
  estate sale (1923), 120
Melton Constable
  Church Lodge, 85
  country house, 67, 72-3, 80-1, 88
  industrial cottages and housing, 25-6, 150
  railway, 9, 147, 150, 151
Methwold, 120
Metton, 15, 16
Middleton Tower, 66
minsters, 124
Morris, Charles, 181-2

Morris, William, 14, 21
Morston: beach flint, 14
Mundesley, 161

Nar, river, 55
Narborough Hall, 34
Neill family, 101
Nelson, Admiral Horatio, Viscount, 152
Netherlands
  brick making and building, 15
  influence, 140-1, 142, 143, 144, 145, 149, 158
New Houghton, 25
Newman, John Henry, Cardinal, 128
Newton Flotman, 27
Nicklas, Rev. Jack, 121
nonconformists (religious), 128-9
Norfolk
  building materials, 10, 14-17, 19
  degraded and disappearing building, 20-1, 23
  geography and historical development, 8, 166
  geology and soils, 18
  housing, 21
  new buildings and developments, 10, 166-9, 168, 169, 170, 171, 172-83, 175
  planning and regulation, 170-2, 184
  population, 124
  private houses, 40
  public houses, 112
  rivers, 19
  settlement patterns, 32
  trade, 140
  vernacular building, 14-17, 21, 24-5
  wool trade, 8
Norfolk Churches Trust, 129
Norfolk Homes (company), 176
Normans: church building, 124-5, 135
North Barningham, 55, 124
North Lopham, 125
North Walsham
  development, 10, 32, 146
  Dutch immigrants, 141
  modern vernacular building, 166
  waterways, 146
  and Worstead, 186-7
North Walsham and Dilham Canal Company, 146
Northampton, William Compton, 1st Earl of, 109, 110
Northrepps, 167
Norwich
  almshouses, Mousehold Heath, 109
  Assembly House, 113
  Britons Arms, Elmhill, 115
  Hospital of St Giles, 66
  industrial buildings, 146
  railway, 146-7
  river access, 19
  Saffron House, 180-1, 180
  status, 8
Norwich Cathedral
  building, 125
  Ethelburga Gate, 14
  frescoes, 125
Norwich School (artists), 21

Old Beckenham, 37
orangeries, 94
Oulton: Congregationalist chapel, 129, 138
Overstrand, 17
Overstrand Hall, 64
Oxborough, 16, 66
Oxborough Hall, 54
Oxford, Edward Harley, 2nd Earl of, 116
Oxford Movement, 128
Oxnead, 55

Palladianism, 66-7
Palladio, Andrea, 100, 182
pantiles, 25, 31, 34, 141, 167, 169
parsonages, 120-2, 122, 123
Paston family, 55
Paston, Sir Edward, 71
Paterson family, 101
Pembroke, Henry Herbert, 9th Earl of, 67, 89
Perpendicular style, 125
Pevsner, Sir Nikolaus, 63, 67, 82, 108, 152
Pickenham, 69
plague, 55
Pleasance, The (Lutyens building), 14
porches, 97
Poringland, 49, 147, 167
  Church Farmhouse, 45
Poundbery, Dorset, 168
Prior, E.S., 64-5
pubs *see* inns
Pugin, Augustus Welby Northmore, 21, 128
Pulham Market: workhouse, 111
Puritans, 126
Pusey, Edward, 128

Quakers, 17, 129
Queen Anne style, 81
Quidenham, 102
  St Andrew church, 131

Rackheath Hall, 69-70
railways, 8-10, 25, 146-7, 153
Rainthorpe, 66
Ranworth, 17, 126
Raynham, 33
Raynham Hall, 66-7, 72, 141
rectories *see* parsonages
reeds: as thatch, 17
Reformation, 126
Repton, G.S., 75
Repton, Humphry, 67, 79, 80
Repton, John Adey, 80, 171
Riches, G., Jr, 161
Rickman, Thomas, 125
Ridlington Manor, 169
Ringland, 147
Ripley, Thomas, 75, 113
roads, 147
Rollesby, Isle of Flegg, 53
Rowlandson, Thomas, 44
Rushall, 47
Ruskin, John: *Stones of Venice*, 121
Ryston, 67

Sabberton, Brian, 181
St Benets Priory, 22
Salle, 121, 125
Salvin, Anthony, 130
Sandringham, 82, 97, 106
  Heath Farm, 180-2, 181
sawmills, 95
Sco Ruston, 23, 124
Scole, near Diss: White Hart inn, 112, 117
Scott, Clement, 160
Sculthorp: Hall Farm, 172
Sennowe Hall, 69, 78-9, 88, 90, 91, 95
Sharrington: All Saints church, 135
Shaw, Norman, 64
Sheringham
  railway, 9, 147
  St Peter's church, 128, 136
Sheringham Park, 79
shooting (sport), 68-9, 101
Shotesham, 68, 99, 103
Sidestrand, 17
Skipper, George, 69, 79, 81, 88
slate, 34
Smith, John (of Kensington), 114
Soane, Sir John, 68, 80, 85, 86
Society for the Protection of Ancient Buildings, 23
Soissons, Louis de, 174
Somerleyton, 121
South Creake, 66
South Lopham: St Andrew church, 131
South Raynham, 33
Spelman, Sir Henry, 67
Sprowston, 147
stables, 88, 89, 92-3
Stafford family, 194
Stalham: Police Station, 175
Stalham Hall, 59
Stalham Staithe, 149
Stamp, Gavin, 168
Stanhoe, 171
Stannard brothers (painters), 21
Stein, Rick, 161
Stevenson, J.J., 182
Stiffkey, 66
Stratton Strawless Hall, 69
structural features, 195
Strumpshaw Fen, 148
Suffield family (Harbord-Hamonds), 160
Suffield, Anthony Harbord-Hamond, 11th Baron, 70
summerhouses, 81
Summerson, Sir John, 25
Supremacy, Act of (1534), 126
Sutton Bridge, 153
Swaffham
  Assembly Rooms, 40
  Market Cross, 40
  Oakley House, 39
Swanton Abbot: manor farmhouse, 58

Tas, river, 146
Taverham, 147
temples, 81
Terrington Marshland, 29
Terrington St Nicholas, 125
Terrington South Clement, 29
Terringtons, the, 14

Teulon, S.S., 108
thatch, 17, 25, 30, 31, 134
Thatcher, Margaret, Baroness, 26
Thetford
  buildings, 27
  flint industry, 14
Thompson, Flora: *Lark Rise to Candleford*, 24
Thornham, 43, 160
Thorpe Market: St Margaret's church, 137
Thurne, river, 146
Thursford, 69
Thurton: St Ethelburts church, 134-5
tiles, 65
timber and clay lump style, 27
Toleration, Act of (1693), 129
toll house, 151
Townshend, Charles, 2nd Viscount ("Turnip"), 8, 33
Townshend, Sir Roger, 66-7, 141
transport, 146-8
Trimingham, 14
Tunstead: church, 14, 125
Twyford, 126

Upcher family, 128

Vermuyden, Cornelius, 141
Victoria, Queen, 109, 111, 126, 176
villages, 32-3, 185-6, 185
Voewood House, 64-5

Walpole chapel, Suffolk, 129
Walpole, Horace, 1st Baron, 75, 127
Walpole, Sir Horace, 67
Walpole, Sir Robert, 74, 113
Walpole, Robert Horatio, 10th Baron, 54, 122
Walpole St Peter, 34, 125
Walpoles, the, 14
Walsingham, 44
warehouses, 149
waterways, 146
Wells
  The Butts (or Buttlands), 176-7, 176-7
  Church Plain, 178-9, 178
  Crown Hotel, the Buttlands, 119, 177
  development, 176-9, 178, 179
  Globe Inn, the Buttlands, 114, 117, 176
  looks to sea, 146
  Our Lady of the Sea (Catholic church), 177
  as port, 8, 176
  shops, 42
Wensun, river, 146
West Wretham, 32
Westwick Old Hall, 60-1, 87
Weybourne: All Saints church, 132-3
White Friars House, 22
White Horse Farm House, 49
Wickmere, 17, 54, 126-7
  rectory, 121, 123
windmills, 22
windows, 197
Wiveton, 15
Wiveton Hall, 55
Wolterton, 32, 54, 98, 127
  Saracen's Head inn, 113
Wolterton Hall, 67, 75, 127
Woodbastwick, 69, 82, 97
Worstead
  character, 186-7
  church, 14, 125-6, 186
  decline, 32
  Dutch immigrants, 141
  farm, 98
  Manor Farm, 98
  Manor House, 61
  Meeting Hill, 108, 139
  New Inn, 114, 118
  proposals for redevelopment, 184-5, 187, 188-9, 190-1, 190
  railway, 147, 187, 190
Wroxham, 147, 161
Wyatt, James, 68, 70, 76, 105
Wyatt, Samuel, 68, 76, 80-2, 84, 87, 92, 97, 114, 119
Wyatt, William, 80, 87
Wymondham
  Crown Inn, 114, 115, 118
  Greyhound inn, 118
  Market Cross, 40
  shops, 41, 42
  thatched cottages (near), 28

Yare, river, 146, 148
Yarmouth *see* Great Yarmouth

Zelotti, Giambattista, 100

THE WASH

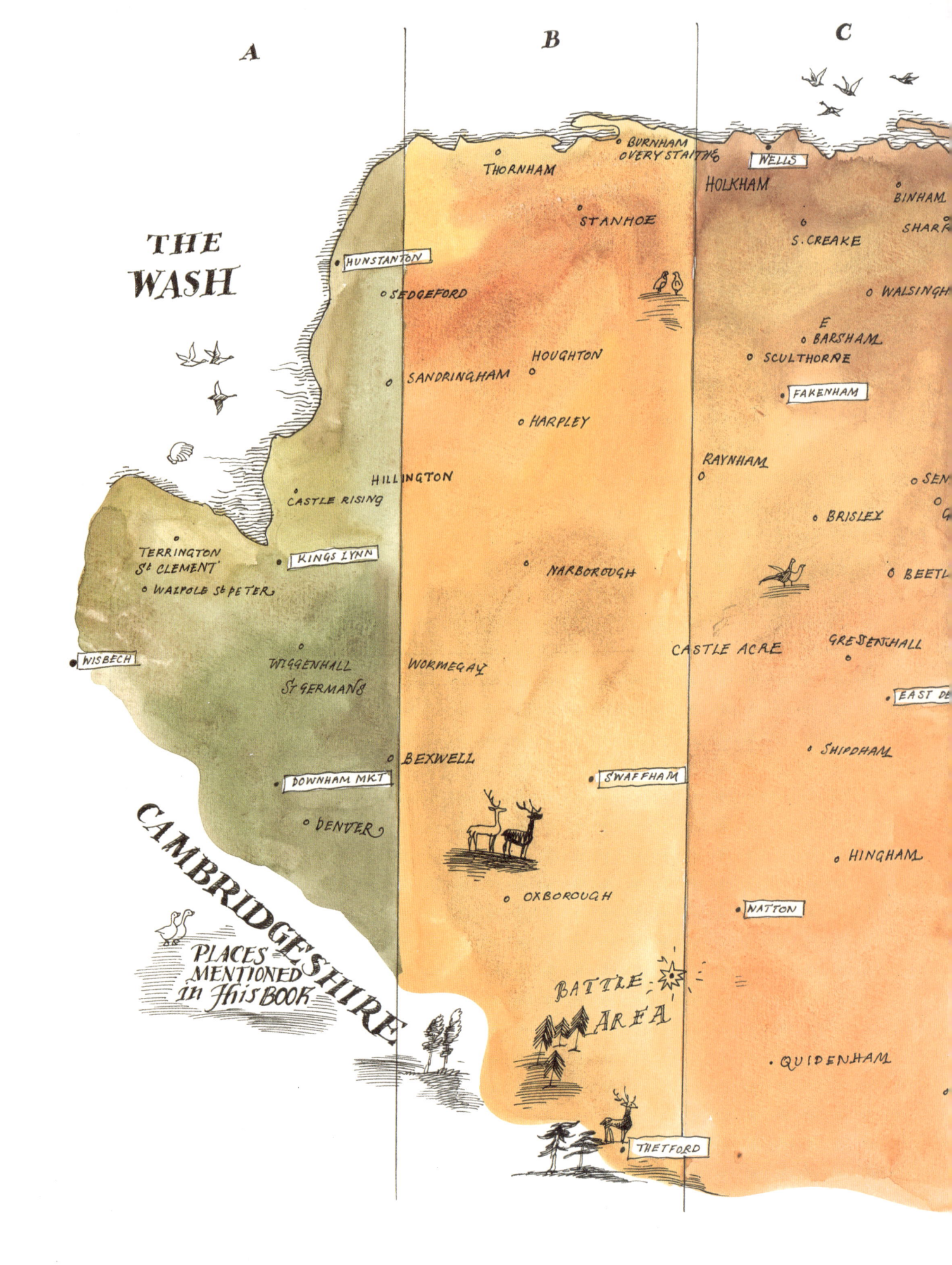

A B C

Burnham Overy Staithe
Thornham
Wells
Holkham
Stanhoe
Binham
Sharr...
S. Creake
Hunstanton
Sedgeford
Walsingh...
E. Barsham
Houghton
Sculthorpe
Sandringham
Fakenham
Harpley
Hillington
Raynham
Sen...
Castle Rising
Brisley
Beetl...
Terrington St Clement
Kings Lynn
Narborough
Walpole St Peter
Castle Acre
Gressenhall
Wisbech
East D...
Wiggenhall St Germans
Wormegay
Shipdham
Bexwell
Swaffham
Downham Mkt
Denver
Hingham
Natton
Oxborough
Battle Area
Quidenham
Thetford

CAMBRIDGESHIRE

Places Mentioned in This Book